LARDNER
ON WAR

LARDNER
ON WAR

RING LARDNER

Edited and with an introduction by
JEFF SILVERMAN

THE LYONS PRESS

Guilford, Connecticut
An imprint of The Globe Pequot Press

The Lyons Press is an imprint of The Globe Pequot Press.

10 9 8 7 6 5 4 3 2 1

Printed in the United States of America

ISBN 1–59228–110–9

Library of Congress Cataloging-in-Publication data is available on file.

For Mud and Tuba . . .
Warriors to be sure . . .

Contents

Contents

II

The Writer Goes to War

Introduction

Those of us condemned to serve at least part of our life sentence on newspapers are united by a common, defective gene. Our twisted strands of DNA propel us off our easy chairs to join the parade—whatever parade; whether or not it's really in our best interests to do so, we are chromosomally incapable of letting the parade just passively pass by. At the first hint of an excitement, we're compelled, at least in our hearts, to set off for where the action is. We need to see it for ourselves. We need to experience it first hand. And we need to describe—if not define—it for those who wade in a less wavy gene pool.

Ring Lardner, an eminently dyspeptic representative of the species, was certainly no different.

If World War I had no plan to come to him on his side of the Atlantic, he had no recourse but to head off to meet it on its own shores. Great newspapermen—and Lardner was among the best ever—can't abide an event so seismic carrying on without them.

Lardner, not surprisingly, had found ways from time to time to weigh in on events in Europe in his Chicago Tribune sports column. He'd dryly suggest that readers avoid German beer and frankfurters at the ballpark, hiss German-named ballplayers, and search for non-Teutonic alternatives to "gesundheit" whenever they found themselves around a sneeze. Still, Lardner's enormously popular column, "In the Wake of the News," wasn't anybody's first stop for any insights into world politics or world wars. The truth is, its proprietor was apolitical, and he didn't much care for this war, or any other war for that matter, unless it happened to be contested on a diamond, a gridiron, in the ring, or over the course of 18 holes.

Yet, Lardner was Lardner. Beyond his own column, he had created one of the most successful fictional franchises of his day in Jack Keefe, his crude rube of a Major League pitcher, and the epistolary Busher stories that the Saturday Evening Post began publishing in 1914. In 1915, the Post presented "Alibi Ike," another remarkable Lardner creation, and over the next several years, Lardner kept short stories hurtling toward the Post, and such other magazines as Metropolitan, McClure's, and Red Book. By 1918, Lardner was an ink-stained force of nature with a built-in readership for whatever happened to scroll through his typewriter.

Colliers, another leading magazine of the day, sensed the marquee potential when it offered Lardner the chance to spend part of August and September of 1917 in Europe and report back on what he found. It was the kind of prestigious, high-profile assignment—eight dispatches to run under the "Reporter's Diary" heading—that Lardner, the professional newsman, couldn't turn down.

It would not be his finest hour.

From the start, nothing went quite the way Lardner had wanted it to. He was denied passage on a troop ship and entrée to real sights and sounds and smells of battle. The closest he could get to the front was a good mile and a half away, and his access to American officers and enlisted men was, at best, limited. Lardner being Lardner, though, did not disappoint his readers, and if he could not always convert the sow's ear he was handed into a silk purse, he was always entertaining.

His dispatches—they make up the second half of this volume—were originally published in Colliers between Sept. 29, 1917 and January 19, 1918, then later that year repackaged into book form as "My Four Weeks in France." What's most notable about them is that they're not really about war at all. They're about American pride and American prejudice, much of it politically incorrect and deliciously so. Of course, his stuff is only P.C. by today's standards; his contemporaries would have considred his take bitingly, caustically and cynically on target.

Writing in diary form, Lardner used his overseas excursion as an opportunity to mock the French; snigger at the customs, food and fashion foreign to him; and sneer at military red tape and its entanglements of frustration and idiocy. Though not all of it is played for laughs—there was, after all, a war going on somewhere, out there, beyond his reach—most of it is still pretty funny stuff, with Lardner the fish out of water at the center of a series of brief adventures played out far enough from war's tragedies to make the war itself seem both oddly at a distance and almost comically unreal. An American's American, he never quite found his traction on French soil.

He was, however, on much more secure footing in the series of stories—featured in the first half of "Lardner on War"—that sent his Busher meal ticket through basic training and then off to France. Lardner wrote 11 war-themed Busher stories in all, all in the familiar form of Jack Keefe's letters home to his friend Al, and all published—between March 9, 1918 ("Call for Mr. Keefe!") and April 19, 1919 ("The Busher Reenlists")—in the Busher's literary incubator, The Saturday Evening Post. Then, still in early 1919, Larder chucked the two bookend stories, which set up and postscript the others, and republished the remaining nine in two slim volumes, "Treat 'Em Rough: Letters from Jack the Kaiser Killer" and "The Real Dope." The first collected the three basic training tales, the second the six that sent Jack overseas.

Between his own trip for Collier's and the continuation of Keefe's in the Post, Lardner had become, in a sense, both a prisoner of war as well and of his own fame and success. As a character, Jack Keefe was now something of an American folk hero, albeit a bumble-headed one to be sure, and heroes fight their country's battles. If Lardner were to bring back Keefe during wartime—and the money encouraged him to do just that—Lardner really had no option but to send him into action.

He had picked up enough local color the year before to paint a credible enough background for Keefe to operate in, and if the stories are a little concocted, Keefe isn't. He's the same stunningly wrought boor in khakis that he was in his baseball flannels. If Lardner could easily serve him up as the butt of his buddies' jokes, he could also use Keefe to represent the characteristics of unhearalded ordinary Joe—or, more precisely, Jack—that writers kept away from in the patriotic nationalism of flag-waving days: as a soldier, Keefe was indifferent at his best, incompetent at his worst, and just plain self-servingly venal when he needs to be. For a writer who viewed the world as skeptically as Lardner did, Keefe was a superb tool; as the first Busher stories comically demystified the ballplayer, these comically deflated the doughboy. Given Lardner's distaste for war, he wasn't about to create a Medal of Honor winner.

This was all perfect preparation for the the next set of war clouds to gather on Lardner's horizon. The 1919 World Series was just a baseball season away. It would be an attack on the national spirit that Lardner would personally prosecute with distinction.

Jeff Silverman
June 2003

LARDNER
ON WAR

I

The Busher Goes to War

Call for Mr. Keefe!

FRIEND AL: Well Al the training trips over and we open up the sesaon here tomorrow and I suppose the boys back home is all anxious to know about our chances and what shape the boys is in. Well old pal you can tell them we are out after that old flag this year and the club that beats us will know they have been in a battle. I'll say they will.

Speaking for myself personly I never felt better in my life and you know what that means Al. It means I will make a monkey out of this league and not only that but the boys will all have more confidence in themself and play better baseball when they know my arms right and that I can give them the best I got and if Rowland handles the club right and don't play no favorites like last season we will be so far out in front by the middle of July that Boston and the rest of them will think we have jumped to some other league.

Well I suppose the old towns all excited about Uncle Sam declairing war on Germany. Personly I am glad we are in it but between you and I Al I figure we ought to of been in it a long time ago right

3

after the Louisiana was sank. I often say alls fair in love and war but that don't mean the Germans or no one else has got a right to murder American citizens but thats about all you can expect from a German and anybody that expects a square deal from them is a sucker. You don't see none of them umpireing in our league but at that they couldn't be no worse than the ones we got. Some of ours is so crooked they can't lay in a birth only when the trains making a curve.

But speaking about the war Al you couldn't keep me out of it only for Florrie and little Al depending on me for sport and of course theys the ball club to and I would feel like a trader if I quit them now when it looks like this is our year. So I might just as well make up my mind to whats got to be and not mop over it but I like to kid the rest of the boys and make them think I'm going to enlist to see their face fall and tonight at supper I told Gleason I thought I would quit the club and join the army. He tried to laugh it off with some of his funny stuff. He says "They wouldn't take you." "No," I said. "I suppose Uncle Sam is turning down men with a perfect physic." So he says "They don't want a man that if a shell would hit him in the head it would explode all over the trench and raise havioc." I forget what I said back to him.

Well Al I don't know if I will pitch in this serious or not but if I do I will give them a touch of high life but maybe Rowland will save me to open up at Detroit where a mans got to have something besides their glove. It takes more than camel flags to beat that bunch. I'll say it does.

Your pal,   Jack.

Chicago, April 15.

FRIEND AL: Well Al here I am home again and Rowland sent some of us home from St. Louis instead of takeing us along to Detroit and I suppose he is figureing on saveing me to open up the home season next Thursday against St. Louis because they always want a big crowd on opening day and St. Louis don't draw very good unless theys some extra attraction to bring the crowd out. But anyway I was glad to get home and see Florrie and little Al and honest Al he is cuter than ever and when he seen me he says "Who are you?" Hows that for a 3 year old?

Well things has been going along pretty good at home while I was away only it will take me all summer to pay the bills Florrie has ran up on me and you ought to be thankfull that Bertha aint 1 of these Apollos thats got to keep everybody looking at them or they can't eat. Honest Al to look at the clothes Florrie has boughten you would think we was planning to spend the summer at Newport News or somewhere. And she went and got herself a hired girl that sticks us for $8.00 per week and all as she does is cook up the meals and take care of little Al and run wild with a carpet sweeper and dust rag every time you set down to read the paper. I says to Florrie "What is the idea? The 3 of us use to get along O. K. without no help from Norway." So she says "I got sick in tired of staying home all the time or dragging the baby along with me when I went out." So I said I remembered when she wouldn't leave no one else take care of the kid only herself and she says "Yes but that was when I didn't know nothing about babys and every time he cried I thought he had lumbago or something but now I know he has got no intentions of dying so I quit worring about him."

So I said "Yes but I can't afford no high price servants to say nothing about dressing you like an actor and if you think I am going to spend all my salary on silks and satans and etc. you will get a big surprise." So she says "You might as well spend your money on me as leave the ball players take it away from you in the poker game and show their own wives a good time with it. But if you don't want me to spend your money I will go out and get some of my own to spend." Then I said "What will you do teach school?" And she says "No and I won't teach school either." So I said "No I guess you won't. But if you think you want to try standing up behind a cigar counter or something all day why go ahead and try it and we'll see how long you will last." So she says "I don't have to stand behind no counter but I can go in business for myself and make more than you do." So I said "Yes you can" and she didn't have no come back.

Imagine Al a girl saying she could make more money then a big league pitcher. Probably theys a few of them that does but they are movie actors or something and I would like to see Florrie try to be a movie actor because they got to look pleasant all the time and Florrie would strain herself.

Well Al the ski jumper has got dinner pretty near ready and after dinner I am going over North and see what the Cubs look like and I wish I pitched in that league Al and the only trouble is that I would feel ashamed when I went after my pay check.

Your old pal,   Jack.

Chicago, May 19.

DEAR FRIEND AL: Well old pal if we wasn't married we would all have to go to war now and I mean all of us thats between 21 and 30. I suppose you seen about the Govt. passing the draft law and a whole lot of the baseball players will have to go but our club won't loose nobody except 1 or 2 bushers that don't count because all as they do any way is take up room on the bench and laugh when Rowland springs a joke.

When I first seen it in the paper this morning I thought it meant everybody that wasn't crippled up or something but Gleason explained it to me that if you got somebody to sport they leave you home and thats fair enough but he also says they won't take no left handers on acct. of the guns all being made for right handed men and thats just like the lucky stiffs to set in a rocking chair and take it easy while the regular fellows has got to go over there and get shot up but anyway the yellow stiffs would make a fine lot of soldiers because the first time a German looked X eyed at them they would wave a flag of truants.

But I can't help from wishing this thing had of come off before I see Florrie or little Al and if I had money enough saved up so as they wouldn't have to worry I would go any way but I wouldn't wait for no draft. Gleason says I will have to register family or no family when the time comes but as soon as I tell them about Florrie they will give me an excuse. I asked him what they would do with the boys that wasn't excused and if they would send them right over to France and he says No they would keep them here till they learned to talk German. He says, "You can't fight nobody without a quarrel and you can't quarrel with a man unless they can understand what you are calling them." So I asked him how about the aviators because their machines would be makeing so much noise that they couldn't tell if the other one was talking German or rag time and he said "Well if you are in an areoplane and you see a German areoplane coming tords you you can pretty near guess that he don't want to spoon with you."

That's what I would like to be Al is an aviator and I think Gleasons afraid I'm going to bust into that end of the game though he pretends like he don't take me in ernest. "Why don't you?" he said "You could make good there all right because the less sense they got the better. But I wish you would quit practiceing till you get away from here." I asked him what he meant quit practiceing. "Well" he said "you was up in the air all last Tuesday afternoon."

He was refering to that game I worked against the Phila. club but honest Al my old souper was so sore I couldn't cut loose. Well Al a mans got a fine chance to save money when they are married to a girl like Florrie. When I got paid Tuesday the first thing when I come home she wanted to borrow $200.00 and that was all I had comeing so I said "What am I going to do the next 2 weeks walk back and forth to the ball park and back?" I said "What and the hell do you want with $200.00?" So then she begin to cry so I split it with her and give her a $100.00 and she wouldn't tell me what she wanted it for but she says she was going to supprise me. Well Al I will be supprised if she don't land us all out to the county farm but you can't do nothing with them when they cry.

Your pal,   Jack.

Chicago, May 24.

FRIEND AL: What do you think Florrie has pulled off now? I told you she was fixing to land us in the poor house and I had the right dope. With the money I give her and some she got somewheres else she has opened up a beauty parlor on 43th St. right off of Michigan. Her and a girl that worked in a place like it down town.

Well Al when she sprung it on me you couldn't of knocked me down with a feather. I always figured girls was kind of crazy but I never seen one loose her mind as quick as that and I don't know if I ought to have them take her to some home or leave her learn her lesson and get over it.

I know you ain't got no beauty parlor in Bedford so I might as well tell you what they are. They are for women only and the women goes to them when they need something done to their hair or their face or their nails before a wedding or a eucher party or something. For inst. you and Bertha was up here and you wanted to take her to a show and she would have to get fixed up so she would go to this place and tell them to give her the whole treatment and first they would wash the grime out of her hair and then comb it up fluffy and then they would clean up her complexion with buttermilk and either get rid of the moles or else paint them white and then they would put some eyebrows on her with a pencil and red up her lips and polish her teeth and pair her finger nails and etc. till she looked as good as she could and it would cost her $5.00 or $10.00 according to what they do to her and if they would give her a bath and a massage I suppose its extra.

8

Well theys plenty of high class beauty parlors down town where women can go and know they will get good service but Florrie thinks she can make it pay out here with women that maybe haven't time to go clear down town because their husband or their friend might loose his mind in the middle of the afternoon and phone home that he had tickets for the Majestic or something and then of course they would have to rush over to some place in the neighborhood for repairs.

I didn't know Florrie was wise to the game but it seems she has been takeing some lessons down town without telling me nothing about it and this Miss Nevins thats in partners with her says Florrie is a darb. Well I wouldn't have no objections if I thought they was a chance for them to make good because she acts like she liked the work and its right close to where we live but it looks to me like their expenses would eat them up. I was in the joint this morning and the different smells alone must of cost them $100.00 to say nothing about all the bottles and cans and tools and brushs and the rent and furniture besides. I told Florrie I said "You got everything here but patients." She says "Don't worry about them. They will come when they find out about us." She says they have sent their cards to all the South Side 400.

"Well" I said "If they don't none of them show up in a couple of months I suppose you will call on the old meal ticket." So she says "You should worry." So I come away and went over to the ball park.

When I seen Kid Gleason I told him about it and he asked me where Florrie got the money to start up so I told him I give it to her. "You" he says "where did you get it?" So just jokeing I said "Where do you suppose I got it? I stole it." So he says "You did if you got it from this ball club." But he was kidding Al because of course he knows I'm no thief. But I got the laugh on him this afternoon when Silk O'Loughlin chased him out of the ball park. Johnson was working against us and they was two out and Collins on second base and Silk called a third strike on Gandil that was down by his corns. So Gleason hollered "All right Silk you won't have to go to war. You couldn't pass the eye test." So Silk told him to get

9

off the field. So then I hollered something at Silk and he hollered back at me "That will be all from you you big busher." So I said "You are a busher yourself you busher." So he said:

"Get off the bench and let one of the ball players set down."

So I and Gleason stalled a while and finely come into the club house and I said "Well Kid I guess we told him something that time." "Yes" says Gleason "you certainly burned him up but the trouble with me is I can't never think of nothing to say till it's too late." So I said "When a man gets past sixty you can't expect their brain to act quick." And he didn't say nothing back.

Well we win the ball game any way because Cicotte shut them out. The way some of the ball players was patting him on the back afterwards you would have thought it was the 1st. time anybody had ever pitched a shut out against the Washington club but I don't see no reason to swell a man up over it. If you shut out Detroit or Cleveland you are doing something but this here Washington club gets a bonus every time they score a run.

But it does look like we was going to cop that old flag and play the Giants for the big dough and it will sure be the Giants we will have to play against though some of the boys seem to think the Cubs have got a chance on acct. of them just winning 10 straight on their eastren trip but as Gleason says how can a club help from winning 10 straight in that league?

Your pal,   Jack.

Chicago, June 6.

FRIEND AL: Well Al the clubs east and Rowland left me home because my old souper is sore again and besides I had to register yesterday for the draft. They was a big crowd down to the place we registered and you ought to seen them when I come in. They was all trying to get up close to me and I was afraid some of them would get hurt in the jam. All of them says "Hello Jack" and I give them a smile and shook hands with about a dozen of them. A man hates to have everybody stareing at you but you got to be pleasant or they will think you are swelled up and besides a man can afford to put themself out a little if its going to give the boys any pleasure.

I don't know how they done with you Al but up here they give us a card to fill out and then they give us another one to carry around with us to show that we been registered and what our number is. I had to put down my name on the first card and my age and where I live and the day I was born and what month and etc. Some of the questions was crazy like "Was I a natural born citizen?" I wonder what they think I am. Maybe they think I fell out of a tree or something. Then I had to tell them I was born in Bedford, Ind. and it asked what I done for a liveing and I put down that I was a pitcher but the man made me change it to ball player and then I had to give Comiskey's name and address and then name the people that was dependent on me so I put down a wife and one child.

And the next question was if I was married or single. I supposed they would know enough to know that a man with a wife dependent on him was probably married. Then it says what race and I had a notion to put down "pennant" for a joke but the man says to put down white. Then it asked what military service had I had and of course I says none and then come the last question Did I claim exemption and what grounds so the man told me to write down married with dependents.

Then the man turned over to the back of the card and wrote down about my looks. Just that I was tall and medium build and brown eyes and brown hair. And the last question was if I had lost an arm or leg or hand or foot or both eyes or was I other wise disabled so I told him about my arm being sore and thats why I wasn't east with the club but he didn't put it down. So that's all they was to it except the card he give me with my number which is 3403.

It looks to me like it was waisting a mans time to make you go down there and wait for your turn when they know you are married and got a kid or if they don't know if they could call up your home or the ball park and find it out but of course if they called up my flat when I or Florrie wasn't there they wouldn't get nothing but a bunch of Swede talk that they couldn't nobody understand and I don't believe the girl knows herself what she is talking about over the phone. She can talk english pretty good when shes just talking to you but she must think all the phone calls is long distance from Norway because the minute she gets that reciever up to her ear you can't hardly tell the difference between she and Hughey Jennings on the coaching line.

I told Florrie I said "This girl could make more than $8.00 per week if she would get a job out to some ball park as announcer and announce the batterys and etc. She has got the voice for it and she would be right in a class with the rest of them because nobody could make heads or tales out of what she was trying to get at."

Speaking about Florrie what do you think Al? They have had enough suckers to pay expenses and also pay up some of the money they borrowed and Florrie says if their business gets much bigger they will have to hire more help. How would you like a job Al white washing some dames nose or leveling off their face with a steam roller? Of course I am just jokeing Al because they won't allow no men around the joint but wouldn't it be some job Al? I'll say so.

Your old pal,   Jack.

Chicago, June 21.

DEAR AL: Well Al I suppose you read in the paper the kind of luck I had yesterday but of course you can't tell nothing from what them dam reporters write and if they know how to play ball why aint they playing it instead of trying to write funny stuff about the ball game but at that some of it is funny Al because its so rotten its good. For inst. one of them had it in the paper this morning that I flied out to

Speaker in the seventh inning. Well listen Al I hit that ball right on the pick and it went past that shortstop so fast that he didn't even have time to wave at it and if Speaker had of been playing where he belongs that ball would of went between he and Graney and bumped against the wall. But no. Speakers laying about ten feet back of second base and over to the left and of course the ball rides right to him and there was the whole ball game because that would of drove in 2 runs and made them play different then they did in the eigth. If a man is supposed to be playing center field why don't he play center field and of course I thought he was where he ought to been or I would of swung different.

Well the eigth opened up with the score 1 to 1 and I get 2 of them out but I got so much stuff I can't stick it just where I want to and I give Chapman a base on balls. At that the last one cut the heart of the plate but Evans called it a ball. Evans lives in Cleveland. Well I said "All right Bill you won't have to go to war. You couldn't pass the eye test." So he says "You must of read that one in a book." "No" I said "I didn't read it in no book either."

So up comes this Speaker and I says "What do you think you are going to do you lucky stiff?" So he says "I'm going to hit one where theys nobody standing in the way of it." I said "Yes you are." But I had to hold Chapman up at first base and Schalk made me waist 2 thinking Chapman was going and then of course I had to ease up and Speaker cracked one down the first base line but Gandil got his glove on it and if he hadn't of messed it all up he could of beat Speaker to the bag himself but instead of that they all started to ball me out for not covering. I told them to shut their mouth. Then Roth come up and I took a half wind up because of course I didn't think Chapman would be enough of a bone head to steal third with 2 out but him and Speaker pulled a double steal and then Rowland and all of them begin to yell at me and they got my mind off of what I was doing and then Schalk asked for a fast one though he said afterwards he didn't but I would of made him let me curve the ball if they hadn't got me all nervous yelling at me. So Roth hit one to left field that Jackson could of caught in his hip pocket if he had been playing right. So 2 runs come in and then Rowland takes me out and I would of busted him only for makeing a seen on the field.

I said to him "How can you expect a man to be at his best when I have not worked for a month?" So he said "Well it will be more than a month before you will work for me again." "Yes" I said "because I am going to work for Uncle Sam and join the army." "Well," he says "you won't need no steel helmet." "No" I said "and you wouldn't either." Then he says "I'm afraid you won't last long over there because the first time they give you a hand grenade to throw you will take your wind up and loose a hand." So I said "If Chapman is a smart ball player why and the hell did he steal third base with 2 out?" He couldn't answer that but he says "What was you doing all alone out in No Mans Land on that ball of Speakers to Gandil?" So I told him to shut up and I went in the club house and when he come in I didn't speak to him or to none of the rest of them either.

Well Al I would quit right now and go up to Fort Sheridan and try for a captain only for Florrie and little Al and of course if it come to a show down Comiskey would ask me to stick on acct. of the club being in the race and it wouldn't be the square thing for me to walk out on him and when he has got his heart set on the pennant.

Your pal,   Jack.

Chicago, July 5.

FRIEND AL: Just a few lines Al to tell you how Florrie is getting along and I bet you will be surprised to hear about it. Well Al she paid me back my $100.00 day before yesterday and she showed me their figures for the month of June and I don't know if you will believe it or not but she and Miss Nevins cleared $400.00 for the month or $200.00 a peace over and above all expenses and she says the business will be even better in the fall and winter time on acct. of more people going to partys and theaters then. How is that for the kind of a wife to have Al and the best part of it is that she is stuck on the work and a whole lot happier then when she wasn't doing nothing. They got 2 girls working besides themself and they are talking about moveing into a bigger store somewheres and she says we will have to find a bigger flat so as we can have a nurse and a hired girl instead of just the one.

Tell Bertha about it Al and tell her that when she comes up to Chi she can get all prettied up and I will see they don't charge her nothing for it.

The clubs over in Detroit but it was only a 5 day trip so Rowland left me home to rest up my arm for the eastren clubs and Phila. is due here the day after tomorrow and all as I ask is a chance at them. My arm don't feel exactly right but I could roll the ball up to the plate and beat that club.

Its a cinch now that the Giants is comeing through in the other league and if we can keep going it will be some worlds serious between the 2 biggest towns in the country and the club that wins ought to grab off about $4500.00 a peace per man. Is that worth going after Al? I'll say so.

Your old pal,   Jack.

Chicago, July 20.

FRIEND AL: Well Al I don't suppose you remember my draft number and I don't remember if I told it to you or not. It was 3403 Al. And it was the 5th number drawed at Washington.

Well old pal they can wipe the town of Washington off of the map and you won't hear no holler from me. The day before yesterday Rowland sends me in against the Washington club and of course it had to be Johnson for them. And I get beat 3 and 2 and I guess its the only time this season that Washington scored 3 runs in 1 day. And the next thing they announce the way the draft come out and I'm No. 5 and its a misery to me why my number wasn't the 1st. they drawed out instead of the 5th.

Well Al of course it don't mean I got to go if I don't want to. I can get out of it easy enough by telling them about Florrie and little Al and besides Gleason says they have promised Ban Johnson that they won't take no baseball stars till the seasons over and maybe not then and besides theys probably some White Sox fans that will go to the front for me and get me off on acct. of the club being in the fight for the pennant and they can't nobody say I'm trying to get excused because I said all season that I would go in a minute if it wasn't for my family and the club being in the race and I give $50.00 last week for a liberty bond that will only bring me in $1.75 per annum which is nothing you might say. You couldn't sport a flee on $1.75 per annum.

Florrie wanted I should go right down to the City Hall or where ever it is you go and get myself excused but Gleason says the only thing to do is just wait till they call me and then claim exemptions. I read somewheres a while ago that President Wilson wanted baseball kept up because the people would need amusement and I asked Gleason if he had read about that and he says "Yes but that won't get you nothing because the rest of the soldiers will need amusement even more than the people."

Well Al I don't know what your number was or how you come out but I hope you had better luck but if you did get drawed you will probably have a hard time getting out of it because you don't make no big salary and you got no children and Bertha could live with your mother and pick up a few dollars sowing. Enough to pay for her board and clothes. Of course they might excuse you for flat feet which they say you can't get in if you have them. But if I was you Al I would be tickled to death to get in because it would give you a chance to see something outside of Bedford and if your feet gets by you ought to be O. K.

I guess they won't find fault with my feet or anything about me as far physical goes. Hey Al?

I will write as soon as I learn anything.

Your pal,   Jack.

Chicago, Aug. 6.

FRIEND AL: Well Al I got notice last Friday that I was to show up right away over to Wendell Phllips high school where No. 5 board of exemptions was setting but when I got over there it was jamed so I went back there today and I have just come home from there now.

The 1st. man I seen was the doctor and he took my name and number and then he asked me if my health was O. K. and I told him it was only I don't feel good after meals. Then he asked me if I was all sound and well right now so I told him my pitching arm was awful lame and that was the reason I hadn't went east with the club. Then he says "Do you understand that if a man don't tell the truth about themself here they are libel to prison?" So I said he didn't have to worry about that.

So then he made me strip bear and I wish you had seen his eyes pop out when he got a look at my shoulders and chest. I stepped on the scales and tipped the bean at 194 and he measured me at 6 ft. 1 and a half. Then he went all over me and poked me with his finger and counted my teeth and finely he made me tell him what different letters was that he held up like I didn't know the alphabet or something. So when he was through he says "Well I guess you ain't going to die right away." He signed the paper and sent me to the room where the rest of the board was setting.

Well 1 of them looked up my number and then asked me did I claim exemptions. I told him yes and he asked me what grounds so I said "I sport a wife and baby and besides I don't feel like it would be a square deal to Comiskey for me to walk out on him now." So he says "Have you got an affidavit from your wife that you sport her?" So I told him no and he says "Go and get one and bring it back here tomorrow but you don't need to bring none from Comiskey." So you see Comiskey must stand pretty good with them.

So he give me a blank for Florrie to fill out and when she gets home we will go to a notary and tend to it and tomorrow they will fix up my excuse and then I won't have nothing to think about only to get the old souper in shape for the big finish.

Your pal,   Jack.

Chicago, Aug. 8.

DEAR OLD PAL: Well old pal it would seem like the best way to get along in this world is to not try and get nowheres because the minute a man gets somewhere they's people that can't hardly wait to bite your back.

The 1st. thing yesterday I went over to No. 5 board and was going to show them Florrie's affidavit but while I was pulling it out of my pocket the man I seen the day before called me over to 1 side and says "Listen Keefe I am a White Sox fan and don't want to see you get none the worst of it and if I was you I would keep a hold of that paper." So I asked him what for and he says "Do you know what the law is about telling the truth and not telling the truth and if you turn in an affidavit thats false and we find it out you and who ever made the affidavit is both libel to prison?" So I said what was he trying to get at and he says "We got informations that your wife is in business for herself and makeing as high as $250.00 per month which is plenty for she and your boy to get along on." "Yes" I said "but who pays for the rent of our flat and the hired girl and what we eat?" So he says "That don't make no difference. Your wife could pay for them and that settles it."

Well Al I didn't know what to say for a minute but finely I asked him where the information come from and he says he was tipped off in a letter that who ever wrote it didn't sign their name the sneaks and I asked him how he knowed that they was telling the truth. So he says "Its our business to look them things up. If I was you I wouldn't make no claim for exemptions but just lay quiet and take a chance."

Then all of a sudden I had an idea Al and I will tell you about it but 1st. as soon as it come to me I asked the man if this here board was all the board they was and he says no that if they would not excuse me I could appeal to the Dist. board but if he was me he wouldn't do it because it wouldn't do no good and might get me in trouble. So I said "I won't get in no trouble" and he says "All right suit yourself." So I said I would take the affadavit and go to the Dist. board but he says no that I would have to get passed on 1st. by his board and then I could appeal if I wanted to.

So I left the affadavit and he says they would notify me how I come out so then I beat it home and called up Florrie and told her they was something important and for her to come up to the flat.

Well Al here was the idea. I had been thinking for a long time that while it was all O. K. for Florrie to earn a little money in the summer when I was tied up with the club it would be a whole lot better if we was both free after the season so as we could take little Al and go on a trip somewheres or maybe spend the winter in the south but of course if she kept a hold of her share in the business she couldn't get away so the best thing would be to sell out to Miss Nevins for a good peace of money and we could maybe buy us a winter home somewheres with what she got and whats comeing to me in the worlds serious.

So when Florrie got home I put it up to her. I said "Florrie I'm sick in tired of haveing you tied up in business because it don't seem right for a married woman to be in business when their husbands in the big league and besides a womans place is home especially when they got a baby so I want you to sell out and when I get my split of the worlds serious we will go south somewheres and buy a home."

Well she asked me how did I come out with the affadavit. So I said "The affadavit is either here nor there. I am talking about something else" and she says "Yes you are." And she says "I been worring all day about that affadavit because if they find out about it what will they do to us." So I said "You should worry because if this board won't excuse me I will go to the Dist. board and mean while you won't be earning nothing because you will be out of business." Well Al she had a better idea then that. She says "No I will hold on to the business till you go to the Dist. board and then if they act like they wouldn't excuse you you can tell them I am going to sell out. And if they say all right I will sell out. But if they say its to late why then I will still have something to live on if you have to go."

So when she said that about me haveing to go we both choked up a little but pretty soon I was O. K. and now Al it looks like a cinch I would get my exemptions from the Dist. board because if Florrie says she wants to sell out they can't stop her.

Your pal,   Jack.

Chicago, Aug. 22.

FRIEND AL: Well Al its all over. The Dist. board won't let me off and between you and I Al I am glad of it and I only hope I won't have to go before I have had a chance at the worlds serious.

My case came up about noon. One of the men asked me my name and then looked over what they had wrote down about me. Then he says "Theys an affadavit here that says your wife and child depends on you. Is that true?" So I said yes it was and he asked me if my wife was in business and I said yes but she was thinking about selling out. So he asked me how much money she made in her business. I said "You can't never tell. Some times its so much and other times different." So he asked me what the average was and I said it was about $250.00 per month. Then he says "Why is she going to sell out?" I said "Because we don't want to live in

Chi all winter" and he said "You needn't to worry." Then he said "If she makes $250.00 per month how do you figure she is dependent on you?" So I said "Because she is because I pay for the rent and everything." And he asked me what she done with the $250.00 and I told him she spent it on clothes.

So he says "$250.00 per month on clothes. How does she keep warm this weather?" I said "I guess they don't nobody have no trouble keeping warm in August." Then he says "Look here Keefe this affadavit mitigates against you. We will have to turn down your appeal and I guess your wife can take care of herself and the boy." I said "She can't when she sells out." "Well" he said "You tell her not to sell out. It may be hard for her at first to sport herself and the boy on $250.00 but if the worst comes to the worst she can wear the same shoes twice and she will find them a whole lot more comfortable the second time." So I said "She don't never have no trouble with her feet and if she did I guess she knows how to fix them."

Florrie was waiting for me when I got home. "Well" I said "now you see what your dam beauty parlor has done for us." And then she seen what had happened and begin to cry and of course I couldn't find no more fault with her and I called up the ball park and told them I was sick and wouldn't show up this P. M. and I and Florrie and little Al stayed home together and talked. That is little Al done all the talking. I and Florrie didn't seem to have nothing to say.

Tomorrow I am going to tell them about it over to the ball park. If they can get me off till after the worlds serious all right. And if they can't all right to.

Your old pal,   Jack.

P.S. Washington comes tomorrow and I am going to ask Rowland to leave me pitch. The worst I can get is a tie. They scored a run in St. Louis yesterday and that means they are through for the week.

Chicago, Aug. 23.

Dear Al: Well Al the one that laughs last gets all the best of it. Wait till you hear what come off today.

When I come in the club house Rowland and Gleason was there all alone. I told them hello and was going to spring the news on them but when Rowland seen me he says "Jack I got some bad news for you." So I said what was it. So he says "The boss sold you to Washington this morning."

Well Al at first I couldn't say nothing and I forgot all about that I wanted to tell them. But then I remembered it again and here is what I pulled. I said "Listen Manager I beat the boss to it." "What do you mean?" he said so I said "I'm signed up with Washington all ready only I ain't signed with Griffith but with Uncle Sam." That's what I pulled on them Al and they both got it right away. Gleason jumped up and shook hands with me and so did Rowland and then Rowland said he would have to hurry up in the office and tell the Old Man. "But wait a minute" I said. "I am going to quit you after this game because I don't know when I will be called and theys lots of things I got to fix up." So I stopped and Rowland asked me what I wanted and I said "Let me pitch this game and I will give them the beating of their life."

So him and Gleason looked at each other and then Rowland says "You know we can't afford to loose no ball games now. But if you think you can beat them I will start you."

So then he blowed and I and Gleason was alone.

"Well kid" he says "you make the rest of us look like a monkey. This game ain't nothing compared to what you are going to do. And when you come back they won't be nothing to good for you and your kid will be proud of you because you went while a whole lot of other kids dads stayed home."

So he patted me on the back and I kind of choked up and then the trainer come in and I had him do a little work on my arm.

Well Al you will see in the paper what I done to them. Before the game the boss had told Griffith about me and called the deal off. So while I was warming up Griffith come over and shook hands. He says "I would of like to had you but I am a good looser." So I says "You ought to be." So he couldn't help from laughing but he says "When you come back I will go after you again." I said "Well if you don't get somebody on the club between now and then that can hit something besides fouls I won't come back." So he kind of laughed again and walked away and then it was time for the game.

Well Al the official scorer give them 3 hits but he must be McMullins brother in law or something because McMullin ought to of throwed Milan out from here to Berlin on that bunt. But any way 3 hits and no runs is pretty good for a finish and between you and I Al I feel like I got the last laugh on Washington and Rowland to.

Your pal,   Jack.

Chicago, Sept. 18.

FRIEND AL: Just time for a few lines while Florrie finishs packing up my stuff. I leave with the bunch tomorrow A.M. for Camp Grant at Rockford. I don't know how long we will stay there but I suppose long enough to learn to talk German and shoot and etc.

We just put little Al to bed and tonight was the first time we told him I was going to war. He says "Can I go to daddy?" Hows that for a 3 year old Al?

Well he will be proud of me when I come back and he will be proud of me if I don't come back and when he gets older he can go up to the kids that belong to some of these left handers and say "Where and the hell was your father when the war come off?"

Good by Al and say good by to Bertha for me.

Your Pal,   Jack.

P.S. I won't be in the serious against New York but how about the real worlds serious Al? Won't I be in that? I'll say so.

Treat 'Em Rough
Letters from Jack the Kaiser Killer

Camp Grant, Sept. 23.

FRIEND AL: Well Al I am writeing this in the recreation room at our barracks and they's about 20 other of the boys writeing letters and I will bet some of the letters is rich because half of the boys can't talk english to say nothing about writeing letters and etc. We got a fine bunch in my Co. Al and its a cinch I won't never die in the trenchs because I will be murdered in my bed before we ever get out of here only they don't call it bed in the army.

They call it bunk and no wonder.

Well Al I have been here since Wed. night and now it is Sunday and this is the first time I have not felt sick since we got here and even at that my left arm is so sore it is pretty near killing me where I got vacinated. Its a good thing I am not a left hander Al or I couldn't get a ball up to the plate but of course I don't have to think of that now because I am out of baseball now and in the big game but at that I guess a left hander could get along just as good with a sore arm because I never seen one of them yet that could break a pain of glass with their fast ball and if they didn't have all the luck in the world they would be rideing around the country in a side door Pullman with all their baggage on.

Speaking about baseball Al I suppose you seen where the White Sox have cinched the penant and they will be splitting the world serious money while I am drawing $30.00 per mo. from the Govmt. but 50 yrs. from now the kids will all stop me on the st. and make me tell them what hotel we stayed at in Berlin and when Cicotte and Faber and Russell begins to talk about what they done to the Giants everybody will have themself paged and walk out.

Well Al a lot of things come off since the last time I wrote to you. We left Chi Wed. noon and you ought to seen the crowd down to the Union station to bid us good by. Everybodys wifes and sisters and mothers was there and they was all crying in 40 different languages and the women wasn't allowed through the gates so farewell kisses was swapped between the iron spokes in the gates and some of the boys was still getting smacked yet when the train started to pull out and it looked like a bunch of them would get left and if they had I'll say their wifes would of been in tough luck.

Of course wife Florrie and little son Al was there and Florrie was all dressed up like a horse and I bet a lot of them other birds wished they was in my shoes when the kissing battle begun. Well Al we both blubbered a little but Florrie says she mustn't cry to hard or she would have to paternize her own beauty parlors because crying makes a girl look like she had pitched a double header in St. Louis or something. But I don't know if you will believe it or not but little Al didn't even wimper. How is that for a game bird and only 3 yrs. old?

Well Al some alderman or somebody had got a lot of arm bandages made for us with the words Kaiser Killers printed on them and they was also signs stuck on the different cars on the train like Berlin or Bust and etc. and the Stars and Strips was flying from the back platforms so we certainly looked like regular soldiers even without no uniforms and I guess if Van Hindburg and them could of seen us you wouldn't of needed a close line no more to take their chest measure.

Well all our bunch come from the south side and of course some of them was fans and the first thing you know they had me spotted and they all wanted to shake hands and I had a smile for all of them because I have got it doped out that we are all fighting for Uncle Sam and a man ought to forget who you are and what you are and be on friendly turns with everybody till after the war.

Well Al they had told us to not bring much baggage and some of the boys come without even their tooth brush but they hadn't some of them forgot to fetch a qt. bottle and by the time we got outside of the city limits the engineer didn't have to blow his whistle to leave people know we were comeing. Somebody had a cornet and another fellow had a trombone and a couple of them had mouth organs and we all sung along with them and we sung patriotic songs like Jonah Vark and Over There and when they started on the Star Spangled Banner the guy I was setting along side of him hollered for them to not play that one and I thought he was a pro German or something and I was going to bust him but somebody asked him why shouldn't they play it and he says because he couldn't stand up and he wasn't the only one either Al.

The train stopped at a burg called Aurora and a bunch of the boys needed air so they got off, some of them head first and one bird layed down on the station platform and says he had changed his mind about going to war and he was going to sleep there a while and catch the first train back to Chi so we picked him up and threwed him back on our train and told him we would have the engineer back up to Chi and drop him off and he says O. K. and of course the train started ahead again but he didn't know if we was going or comeing or looping the loop.

Well the trombone blower finely blowed himself to a nap and while he was asleep a little guy snuck the trombone away from him and says "Look here boys I am willing to give my life for Uncle Sam but I am not going to die to no trombone music." So he threwed the trombone out of the window without opening the window and the guy woke up that owned it and the next thing you know the Kaiser Killers was in their first battle.

Well Al by the time we got to Camp Grant some of the boys looked like they was just comeing from the war instead of just going and I guess I was about the only one that was O. K. because I know how to handle it but I had eat some sandwiches that a wop give me on the train and they must of been poisoned or something because when I got off everything looked kind of blured.

We was met by a bunch of officers in uniform. The guy that had throwed the trombone away had both eyes swelled shut and a officer had to lead him to the head quarters and I heard the officer ask him if he was bringing any liquor into the camp and he says yes all he could carry, but the officer meant did he have a bottle of it and he says No he had one but a big swede stuck his head in front of it and it broke.

Over to the head quarters they give us a couple of blankets a peace and then they split us up into Cos. and showed us our barracks and they said we looked like we needed sleep and we better go to bed right after supper because we would have to get down to hard work the next A.M. and I was willing to go to bed without no supper after eating them dam sandwichs and the next time them wops trys to slip me something to eat or drink I will hang one on their jaw.

Well Al the buggle has blowed for mess which is what they call the meals and you would know why if you eat some of them so I will close for this time and save the rest for the next time and my address is Co. C. 399th. Infantry, Camp Grant, Ill.

Your Pal,   Jack.

Camp Grant, Sept. 24.

FRIEND AL: Well Al they give us some work out today and I am pretty tired but they's no use going to bed till 9 o'clock which is the time they blow the buggle for the men to shut up their noise. They do everything by buggles here. They get you up at a quarter to 6 which is first call and you got to dress in 15 minutes because they blow the assembly buggle at 6 and then comes the revelry buggle and then you eat breakfast and so on till 11 P.M. when they blow the taps buggle and that means everybody has got to put their lights out and go to sleep just as if a man couldn't go to sleep without music and any way a whole lot of the boys go to sleep before 11 because with so many of us here how could the officers tell if we waited for the buggle or didn't wait for it?

Well Al about all we done the first 3 days was try and get the place to looking like something because the men that built the buildings was to lazy to clean up after themself and I wouldn't of minded only for feeling so bad all day Thursday on acct. of that

29

sandwich and Friday I felt rotten because a Dr. vacinated me and fixed me up so as I can't catch small pox or tyford fever and I would rather have the both of them the same day then have that bird work on me again.

Thursday A.M. after breakfast a bunch of us went to the Drs. and they give us a physical examination and before the Dr. examined me he says "Well is they anything the matter with you outside of a headache?" So I said "How do you know I got a headache" and he says because they was a epidemic of them in the camp. Well Al I could of told him why only of course I wouldn't squeel on the rest of the boys so all I told him was about me eating that sandwich and he says all the boys must of eat them and that shows how much them wise Drs. knows.

Well of course he didn't find nothing the matter with me physicly and he says I was a fine specimen and the next place I went was to the head quarters or something where they give us our uniforms and you ought to see me in mine Al only the shoes is 6 sizes to big and I made a holler about it but the man says they wouldn't be so big after I had wore them a while. They must be fine shoes that will srink Al because all the shoes I ever seen the more you wear them they get bigger. They give us each 2 pair shoes one to march in with cleats on the bottom and a hat and a hat cord and 5 pair sox and 2 shirts and a belt and 3 suits under wear and 2 cocky suits.

And we had to tell our family history to a personal officer that writes down all about you on a card and what kind of work you done before so if the General or somebody tears their pants they won't have to chase all over the camp and page a taylor because they can look at the cards and find out who use to be a taylor and send for him to sow them up.

A lot of the boys give this officer a song and dance about how good they can drive a car and etc. so they can get a soft snap like driveing one of the officers cars and I could of got some kind of a snap only I come here to be a soldier and fight Germans and not mend their pants.

The officer asked me my name and age and etc. and what I done in civil life so I said "I guess you don't read the sporting page." So he says "Oh are you a fighter or something?" So I said "I am a fighter now but I use to pitch for the White Sox." So then he asked me what I done before that so I told him I was with Terre Haute in the Central League and Comiskey heard about me and bought me and then he sent me out to Frisco for a while and I stood that league on their head and then he got me back and I been with him about 3 years.

So the officer asked me if I ever done anything besides pitch so I told him about the day I played the outfield in Terre Haute when Burns and Stewart shut their eyes going after a fly ball and their skulls come together and it sounded like a freight wreck and they was both layed out so I and Lefty Danvers took their place and in the 8th. inning I come up with 2 on and hit a curve ball off big Jack Rowan and only for the fence that ball wouldn't of made no stops this side of Indpls.

So then the officer says "Yes but didn't you do something when you wasn't playing ball?" so I told him a pitcher don't have to do nothing only set on the bench or hit fungos once in a while or warm up when it looks like the guy in there is beggining to wobble. So he says "Well I guess I will put you down as a pitcher and when we need one in a hurry we will know where to find one." But I don't know when they would need a pitcher Al unless it was to throw one of them bombs and believe me when it comes to doing that I will make a sucker out of the rest of these birds because if my arm feels O. K. they's nobody got better control and if they tell me to stick one in a German's right eye that is where I will put it and not in their stomach or miss them all together like I was a left hander or something.

Well Al we done a little training Friday and Saturday but today was the first day we realy went to it. First of course we got up and dressed and then they was 10 minutes of what they call upseting exercises and then come breakfast which was oatmeal and steak and bread and coffee. The way it is now you got to get your own dishs and go up to the counter and wait on yourself but of course we will have waiters when things gets more settled. You also got to make your own bed and that won't never kill nobody Al because all as we got is 2 blankets and you don't have to leave the bed open all A.M. like at home because whatever air wanted to get in wouldn't let these blankets stop it.

Then they give us an hour of drilling and that was duck soup for me on acct. of the drilling we done on the ball club last spring and you ought to seen the corporal and sargent open their eyes when they seen me salute and etc. but some of the birds don't know their right from their left and the officers had to put a stick of wood in their right hand so they would know it was their right hand and imagine if some of them was ball players and played left field. They would have to hire a crossing policeman to tell them where to go to get to their position and if they was pitchers they wouldn't know if they was right hand pitchers or left hand pitchers till they begun to pitch and then they would know because if they were hog wild they would be left handers.

The corporals and sargents come from the regular army but after a while Capt. Nash will pick some of us out to take their place and it is a cinch I will be picked out on acct. of knowing all about the drills etc.

The next thing was a lecture on what they could do to us if we got stewed or something and how to treat the officers and we got to sir them and salute them and etc. and it seems kind of funny for a man that every time he walked out to pitch the crowd used to stand up and yell and I never had to sir Rowland or Collins. I'd knock their block off if they tried to make me.

Well every time we wasn't doing something else they sprung some more of them upseting exercises on us and I called the corporal to one side and says if he would excuse me I would pass up some of them because I didn't need to exercise on acct. of playing baseball all summer and besides I was tired and he says these exercises was to fix me so I wouldn't get tired and he made me go through with all of them. How is that for brains Al and I suppose if a man was up all night watching a corpse or something this bird would make you stay awake all the next day so you wouldn't get sleepy.

For dinner we had roast chicken and sweet potatoes and cream corn and biscuits and coffee and for supper they was bake beans with tomato sauce and bread and pudding and cake and coffee and the grub is pretty fair only a man can't enjoy it because you got to eat to fast because if theys anything left on your plate when the rest of them birds gets through you got to fight to keep it from going to the wrong address. Well Al its pretty near time for the tattoo buggle which means the men has got to shut up and keep quiet so I am going to get ready for bed but I don't know if I would rather have them keep quiet or not because when they are keeping quiet you don't know what they are up to and maybe they are snooping a round somewheres waiting for a man to go to sleep so they can cut your throat. Some of them has been use to doing it all their life Al and they are beggining to miss it. But I don't know if I wouldn't just as leave die that way as from them upseting exercises.

Your pal,   Jack.

Camp Grant, Sept. 26.

FRIEND AL: Well Al don't be supprised if you pick up the paper some A.M. and see where I'm gone and you may think I am just jokeing Al but I am telling you the truth and I am glad Florrie is fixed so she can make a liveing for herself and little Al because I wouldn't bet a nickle I will be alive by the time this gets to you.

I guess I all ready told you the kind of birds we got in our Co. Well the worst one in the bunch is a guy named Sebastian and of course he would have to be the one that got the bunk next to mine. Well Al you remember me writeing to you about the little runt that throwed that guy's trombone away, well his name is Lahey but we call him Shorty on acct. of him being so short. Well I hadn't payed much attention to this here Sebastian because he has always got a grouch and don't say nothing only to mumble at the officers when they ask him some question but Shorty knows him and last night he told me all about him and he has been pinched 50 times for stabbing people but he has got some pull or something and they can't never do nothing to him except once he served a turn at Joliet for cutting off a guy's ears because he wouldn't get up and give him a seat on a st. car. He has always got a knife hid on him somewheres and his first name is Nick so they call him Nick the Blade on acct. of always haveing a knife on him.

I don't know if I told you or not but we got a shed outside of the barracks with shower baths and etc. and everybody is supposed to take baths and keep themself clean and of course its a pleasure for a man like I because I got use to takeing them every day after the game and I don't feel right unless I am clean but some of the birds hollered like a Indian the first time the officers made them get under the shower and you would think they never seen water before and I guess some of them hadn't because when they come out afterwards the officers had to ask them their name.

Well Al I was takeing a bath yesterday and this big Nick bird was standing there striped and he couldn't get up the nerve to step under the shower and Corporal Daly come up behind him and give him a shove under the water and he give a bellow that you could hear from here to Rockford and I didn't know who he was then and I couldn't help from laughing and he seen me but he didn't say nothing and I wouldn't of thought no more about it only for what Shorty told me afterwards. Well Shorty was there to and he laughed at him to but Nick didn't see him but he seen me and Shorty says I better keep my eyes pealed because Nick wouldn't think no more of stabbing a man then picking his teeth and if theys one thing he won't stand for its somebody laughing at him.

Well I been keeping my eyes pealed all right and I kept them pealed all night last night but I can't stay awake all night every night and the first time I doze off it will probably be the last time.

Sebastian hasn't spoke to nobody or looked at nobody today and when a man acts like that it means they are makeing plans. Well Al I only wish he was planning to dessert from the army and if I seen him trying to make his get away I wouldn't blow no buggle to wake up the guards. I'll say I wouldn't Al.

I pretty near forgot to tell you that Teddy Roosevelt was here today over looking us and he made a speech but they was about 20 thousand for him to talk to and I was a mile away and couldn't hear nothing but I suppose he told the boys they was fine physical specimens and etc. Well Al that stuff is O. K. but if I wasn't a fine physical specimen I might be somewheres where I could go to sleep without some stabber waiting to carve their initials in my Adams apple.

Your pal,   Jack.

Camp Grant, Sept. 29.

FRIEND AL: Well old pal you see I am still alive and I guess that is because by the time night comes a round Nick the Blade is all wore out with them upseting exercises and etc. and hasn't got enough strenth left to carve nobody or maybe he has figured out the truth which is that I wasn't realy laughing at him Al but when I am takeing a bath I feel so good that I am libel to bust out laughing at nothing you might say.

But Sebastian isn't the only bird I got to watch now Al because last night they sprung a new one on me and he just come into the camp yesterday and the man that was sleeping on the other side of me is sick in the infirmiary so they stuck this new one in his bunk and now I got them on both sides and I don't know which is the worst Nick or him because this one wispers all night and it would be O. K. if he was wispering in his sleep or wispering to himself but he isn't.

I didn't turn in till 11 and Nick was buzzing away like a saw buck and I figured on getting some sleep myself but I hadn't no sooner layed down when the wispering begun on the other side. First I didn't catch what he was trying to get at but I heard him the second time all right and he says "Do you want me to kill?" Well Al for 2 or 3 minutes I couldn't get enough strenth up to turn over and look at him but the next time he repeated it over again I couldn't stand it no more so I said "Are you talking to me?" And what do you think he said Al? He says "I am talking to God."

Well Al the connection couldn't of been very good you might say because he kept asking the same question over and over and not getting no answer but how was I to know when the party at the other end would speak up and maybe say yes and they wasn't no-body closer to him then me for him to work on so you can see what a fine nights rest I got Al and this A.M. I told Shorty Lahey about him and sure enough Al the bird is a gun man named Tom the Trigger and Shorty says he is a nut that thinks he is aces up with the all mighty and some times he imagines that they are telling him to go ahead and shoot and then he takes aim at whoever is handy.

Well Al this was inspections day and everybody was supposed to have a clean shave and their hair brushed and all their buttons sowed on and their beds made up neat and their shoes and mess kits shinned bright and etc. and Capt. Nash and the lieuts. give us all the double O and some of the boys got a nice little baling out for the way they looked but I looked like a soldier ought to look Al and didn't give them no chance to ball me out.

But what difference is it going to make Al for me to look good and have things neat when I am sleeping between a man that if he can ever stay awake till I doze off he will dig a trench system in my chest with a stilleto and on the other side of me they's a bird that the minute the lord says Fire he will make me look like a soup strainer. It don't hardly seem like its worth while to be strick about looks when sooner or later they are bound to muss me and my bed both up.

Your pal,   Jack.

Camp Grant, Oct. 3.

FRIEND AL: Well old pal I just got some good news and this it is Al. Next Saturday they are going to let some of the boys go home on leave and I asked Corporal Daly to fix it up for me to go and he says he didn't know if he could or not because most of the ones that's going is men that has been here a mo. or more but on acct. of me haveing been with the White Sox they fixed it so as I could go and the world serious opens up in Chi Saturday and I won't get away from here till Saturday noon so I can't get there for the first game but I will see the Sunday game and won't Gleason and them pop their eyes out when I go down to the bench with my cocky suit on and shake hands with them and I bet Rowland will wish I was wearing the White Sox uniform instead of Uncle Sam's uniform.

Well Al I can't hardly wait to get home and see Florrie and little Al and of course I will see them Saturday night and I will take them to the game Sunday and leave for back here after the game because a man has got to be back in camp at 11 Sunday night and the funny part is that Florrie was going to bring little Al and come and see me next Sunday but now I am going to see her and I have wrote her to not come.

Well I am feeling to good to go to bed but that is where I ought to be Al because I wasn't never so tired in my life because they hung a new one on us this P.M. Instead of giveing us upseting exercises from a quarter to 4 till a quarter after they made us all run 20 minutes without stopping and they says it was to improve our wind. Well before we was half through I didn't have no wind to improve and I suppose some day they will pull all our teeth so as we can chew better. At that I would of been O. K. only my feet got to hurting and now I can't hardly walk and all because the shoes they give you are about 6 sizes to small and they keep lectureing us about feet hygeine but how is a man going to keep your feet O. K. when they make you wear shoes that Houdini couldn't get in or out of them.

But listen Al the news about going to Chi isn't the only peace of good news I got today because I also found out that this bird that Shorty called Tom the Trigger isn't no gun man at all and this here Nick the Blade won't do nothing to me because he is scared of the officers so I won't have to lay awake no more nights worring but I didn't find it out till today and here is how it come off.

This A.M. I went to sleep right at breakfast and couldn't keep my eyes open so Corporal Daly come up to me afterwards and asked me what was the matter so I told him I was to nervous to sleep nights on acct. of a crazy man bunking next to me and any minute he might take a notion and shoot me full of holes. I didn't say nothing about Nick the Blade on the other side of me because he was standing where he could hear us. So Corporal Daly asked me who I was talking about and I told him and he laughed and says that if I waited for Castle which is this other bird's name to start shooting I would probably die of old age or something because he is one of these objecters that don't beleive in war and he told them about it the first day we got here and says he objected to being a soldier. So Capt. Nash asked him if he would object to unloading a few cars of coal and that is what he has been doing up and till last Friday and then he begun objecting to a shovel and he says he would like to join the rest of us and see what it was like and maybe he would loose his objections. So now they are giveing him a week to make up his mind what he is going to do and he is talking it over all the while with the Lord and if the Lord tells him its O. K. to kill people why well and good but he won't practice on us because in the first place he hasn't no gun and if he had one he wouldn't know if it was to shoot with or stir your coffee.

So afterwards I told Shorty Lahey he had made a mistake about Castle and he says "All right and if he is a objecter it is up to us to talk him out of it." So after supper tonight Castle was seting right near me in the recreation room and Shorty come up to him and says "Well Castle haven't you been able to get that party on the wire yet" so Castle asked him what he meant and he says he heard Castle was waiting for a message from somewheres telling him if he should be a soldier or not so Castle didn't answer and begun to read. So Shorty says "You ain't the only one that objects to war but we got to make the world safe for Democrats and you shouldn't ought to object to getting your head blowed off in a good cause." So Castle spoke up and said he didn't object to getting killed but what he objected to was killing other people. So Shorty says "Well then all you got to do is stick along side of me in the trenches and when you get orders to go over the top you can slip me your gun and bayonet and I will see that they don't nobody sneak off with them dureing your absents." So then Castle got up and walked out on us.

So I says to Shorty I said, "You certainly had the wrong dope on that bird and maybe you got Sebastian wrong to." So he says "No I haven't and I may as well tell you what he told me today. He told me he would of cut you up in slices long ago only if he done it here in the camp he wouldn't have no chance to make his get away and he is waiting till some time he catchs you outside of the camp and then he will go to work on you. And if I was you and a married man I would rather get it here then in France because if you get it here your Mrs. can tend the funeral provide it they find enough of the slices to make it worth while."

Well Al he has got a sweet chance to catch me outside of the camp because when he is outside of the camp I will be inside of the camp and I am glad I found out the truth about both he and Castle and now maybe I can get some sleep.

So all and all I feel a whole lot better then I did only for my feet but feet or no feet I will enjoy myself in Chi and I only wish I was going tomorrow instead of wait till Sat.

Your pal,   Jack.

Camp Grant, Oct. 7.

FRIEND AL: Well Al its Sunday night and I haven't been to Chi or nowheres else and I don't care if I ever go anywheres and the sooner they send me to France to the front line trenches I will be tickled to death.

Well old pal I decided yesterday A.M. to stay here and not go and I made up my mind all of a sudden and it was partly because I wasn't feeling good and my feet pretty near killed me and besides they are going to pick some of us out for corporals and sargents pretty soon and I figured a man would have a better chance of getting a officer job if you didn't ask them for leave all the while. So as soon as I changed my mind about going I found one of the boys that was going and asked him to call Florrie up as soon as he got to Chi and tell her I couldn't get off and for her to come out here today and see me and bring little Al.

Well Al yesterday and today has been the 2 longest days I ever spent and it seems like a yr. since yesterday A.M. and it don't hardly seem possible that I was feeling so good yesterday A.M. and now I don't care if school keeps or not as they say. Yesterday A.M. I was up before the buggle blowed all ready and so excited I couldn't hardly eat breakfast and just before inspections Shorty Lahey seen me smileing to myself and asked me what was the joke and I told him they wasn't no joke only I was going home and he says he hoped I would have a good trip and come back safe in sound so I said I guessed they wasn't no danger of anything happening to me and he says "You will be O. K. if you keep your eyes open." So I said "What do you mean keep my eyes open."

So he says "Your a game bird but they's no use of you takeing reckless chances so you want to be on the look out every minute till you get back."

So then I asked him what and the hell he was talking about and he says "Didn't you know that Nick the Blade was going along with you?"

Well Al it seems like Sebastian got wise that I was going home on leave and he seen a chance to get even with me for laughing at him or that is he thought I was laughing at him but I really wasn't but any way as soon as he found out I was going he told them his brother in law had fell and struck his head on the brass rail and was dying and wanted him to come home and they eat it up and give him leave. So when Shorty tipped me off I said I would wait and go on a later train but Shorty says that wouldn't do me no good because Nick wouldn't be a sucker enough to try and pull anything on the train amidst all them soldiers but would wait till we was in Chi and then he would get his gang and lay for me and the way he generally worked was come right up to your flat and get you and if your wife or kid says 1 yes or no it would be taps for them to. And Nick could come back here to camp and they wouldn't never know he was mixed up in it.

Well Al I guess you know I am not scared of anything in the world as far as myself personly am concerned but Florrie isn't one of the kind that would set there in a rocker and pair her finger nails while their husband was getting massacreed and little Al is a game bird to and a chip of the old block and they would both holler like a Indian and call for the police and you know what would happen to the both of them and I wouldn't care for myself but if anything happened to them I would feel like I was the murder.

So while I just laughed at Sebastian and his gang on my own acct. I would be a fine stiff to in danger my wife and baby and besides as I said I eat something for breakfast that didn't set good on me and I don't know if it was the coffee or the milk or what it was but I eat something that was poisoned and that's a fine way to treat soldiers is to give them poison food and the easiest way to get the

Germans killed off would be to invite them out here and board a while. And in the second place if a man asks for leave when he hasn't only been here 2 wks. it would hurt my chance to get a corporal or a sargent and any way I figured Florrie would rather see something new like the camp then set through a ball game and of course it would be different if I was pitching but I suppose it was Faber's turn today and I see where Cicotte trimmed them yesterday but at that the score would of been 1 and 1 if Felsch hadn't of hit that ball out of the park and Sallee must be his brother in law or something to give him a ball like that to hit. If I was pitching he would be lucky to hit one up in the press box.

So I told Sargent Leslie I wasn't feeling good and would he fix it for me to take my leave some other time and he says I was the only soldier he ever seen that was to sick to go on their leave so then I told him my wife and kid was comeing out here to see me today and he says all right.

So I didn't go Al and the funny part of it is that somebody must of tipped Sebastian off that I wasn't going and what does he do but get his leave called off to and he has been here all yesterday and today and that proves he is laying for me and just wanted to go because I was going and it looks like the only way I can ever get away from here is sneak out without letting nobody know I am going and even then he would probably send word to his gang in Chi to keep their eye on me till he come.

I have caught him looking at me 2 or 3 times and I had a notion to ask him if he seen anything green but what is the use Al of starting something with a man like he and if I was to loose my temper and bust him Capt. Nash might hear about it and shut us both up in the guard house together and one or the other of us wouldn't never come out alive and which ever one it was it would give the camp a black eye.

Well Al about all I done today was look for Florrie and little Al and I didn't give them up till 5 o'clock tonight because I thought maybe they had missed the A.M. trains and would come later and every time I seen a woman and kid toddleing up the road I would think sure it was them this time and I was dissapointed about 30 thousand times because they was at least that many women and kids here today and if they was all somebody's wife Camp Grant must be infected with Mormons.

All the women had baskets and boxs full of pie and jell and fried cakes and what all but they wasn't no package of goodys with my name and address on them Al and they wasn't no little schaefer yelling theres daddy when they seen me and running up to get huged.

Well Al the man that was to call up Florrie come back this P.M. and come in the barracks just before I started this letter and I asked him I said "Well Bishop did you call up my wife like I told you?" His name is Bishop. "Hell" he says "I forgot all about it." And honest Al his size is all that saved him the little srimph and if he was anywheres near a man I would of Bishoped him right in the eye. But I managed to keep my hands off of him and all as I said was for him to get out of my way before it was to late and then he begun to whine and says how sorry he was and he says "I got some excuse because I reached home just in time to be presented with a baby girl."

How is that for an excuse Al and the only wonder is that he didn't forget if it was a boy or a girl before he got back here but of course a man like he wouldn't have nothing but a girl. But isn't it just my luck Al for me to trust somebody to do something and then for them to go and have a baby on me? And I hope every time he gos home she is yelling all night with the collect.

Your pal,   Jack.

Camp Grant, Oct. 10.

FRIEND AL: Well Al I wrote to Florrie Sun. night and told her what had came off and about this fat head forgetting to call her up and I just got a letter back from her and she says her and little Al both of them cried themself to sleep Saturday night because I didn't show up and she had let little Al set up till 9 o'clock so as he could see his daddy in a uniform and when I didn't come then or Sun. A.M. neither they thought I didn't care for them no more so they went to the ball game Sun. P.M., and McGraw started another left hander and you probably read what happened to him and I suppose everybody is saying what a whale Faber is and who wouldn't be a whale if they get 5 runs for you in one inning but even if you are a whale that don't excuse you from trying to steal a base that one of your own men all ready got there ahead of you and hasn't left yet.

But Florrie and little Al are comeing out here next Sunday Al and this time they won't be no mix up because I won't depend on no half wit that the minute they become a father they go all to peaces.

But what I wanted to tell you about was Sebastian. Well Al Shorty Lahey was trying to make me believe this bird was a bad egg and that they called him Nick the Blade because he always went a round with a knife and whittled you if you looked X eyed at him but the next time Shorty wants to kid somebody he better try it on some yapp that hasn't been in the big league and I let him think he was stringing me just to see how far he would go with it but if he thought he had me fooled the shoes was on his feet not mine.

Well Al Sebastian's name is just plain Nick without no Blade on it and the only blade he ever pulled was a blade of grass or something because he use to help take care of the grounds at Washington Pk. before he was drafted and he has been one of my admirers for a long while and that is why he kept looking at me and he says he use to always try and get to the games when it was my turn to pitch and he has been wanting to talk to me ever since we been here but today was the first time he got up the nerve and he never had no intentions of going on leave last Sat. and to prove it he showed me a letter he got from his wife last Friday and she don't spell very good but she spoke in the letter about comeing here to see him this next Sunday and nothing about him comeing there to see her and she is going to bring their 2 kids along and he says he never seen a man

44

with a prettier wind up then I got and all together he is O. K. and when Shorty trys to make you beleive somebody is a murder he ought to pick out a man that looks like the part.

I haven't said nothing to Shorty and I won't but what I will do is play a joke on him right back only I will make it a good one and not no fizzle like some of his.

And oh yes Al they have sent Castle over to the quarter masters dept. and he won't have a chance to kill nobody there except when they come after a pair of shoes.

Your pal,   Jack.

Camp Grant, Oct. 12.

FRIEND AL: Well old pal I am writeing this in the Y. M. C. A. where a man has got some chance to hear yourself think as they say but if you try and write over in the barracks if they don't joggle your arm or tip your seat over for a joke they are all the time jabbering back and forth in foreign languages till you get so balled up that instead of writeing a letter a man is libel to make out his will in Eskimo or something.

Speaking about foreign languages Al the next time I see you I will be talking French like a regular Frenchman and you will have to ask me to translate what I am talking about. Of course I am just jokeing about that because I wouldn't spring a lot of stuff on you that you wouldn't understand and I might just as well go up to a statue and ask them how their father stood his operation or something. But what I am getting at is that I am going to join the French lesson class here and its something that you don't have to belong to it unless you want to but I figure a man is a sucker if they don't take advantage of a chance like this because in the first place it don't cost you nothing and in the second place the men that knows how to talk French will have all the best of it when we get over there because suppose you was in Paris and felt like you wanted a glass of pilsner and if you said it in French they would fetch it to you but if you just said pilsner they wouldn't know if you was asking for something to drink or a nasal dooch or what not.

But besides that Al after we get to France the French officers will want to tip us off on this and that about the Germans and of course they won't talk to the privates but they will only talk to the officers and if I am a officer by that time which it looks like a cinch I will be one by that time at the outside why suppose I was standing by 1 of our genls. and a French genl. wanted to tell him what was what and etc. but couldn't talk nothing but French and our genl. couldn't make head or tales of it then I could act like an interpeter between the both of them and the first thing you know all the high monkey monks when they want to talk back and forth will be pageing Capt. Keefe or Major Keefe or whatever officer I am by that time.

Some of the boys laughed at me tonight when I told them about going to attend the lessons but I will be the one that does the laughing when we get across that old pond and Shorty Lahey the smart alex that I told you about says to me "We won't do all our training with the French army but we will do some of it with the English army so while you are at it you better learn to talk English to." So I said "You better learn to talk English yourself" and he shut his mouth.

Well Al Florrie and little Al will be here to see me Sunday and I can't hardly wait for them to get here and I suppose Florrie will bring along some daintys of some kind that she cooked up herself or maybe got the swede girl to do it but of course I am not worring about whether she brings anything or don't bring anything as long as she brings herself and the kid only most of the wifes that comes out here Sundays brings something along to show they been thinking of you though if I was most of these birds wifes the only time I would think about them would be when I said my prayers at night and then I would thank God they had joined the army.

Your pal,   Jack.

Camp Grant, Oct. 14.

FRIEND AL: Well Al its Sunday night and I been entertaining company. Florrie and little Al got out here just after noon and I was in the barracks reading about the world serious game in Chi yesterday and Florrie says she asked 1 of the boys where I was at and he told her I was polishing the general's shoes and wouldn't he do just as well. How is that for a fresh bum Al and of course I don't have to polish the general's shoes or any shoes and if I could find out who it was that Florrie was talking to I would polish their jaw for them.

Well of course Florrie didn't beleive him and the next man she asked was Nick Sebastian and he come and got me and you ought to seen Florrie stair when she got a look at me in my uniform and little Al didn't know me at first and when Florrie says to him who is it he says it was the capt. Well Al it is to soon to be calling me a capt. but if they are running this game on the square it won't be long and they will be calling me more then that.

Well Florrie handed me a box and she says I was to not open it till she was gone and then I showed them over the camp and the way the boys staired at Florrie I couldn't help from being proud of her but of course if some of them had of got to fresh I would of fixed them so they wouldn't do no stairing for a couple of wks. Sebastian's wife and 2 kids was here to visit him and we run into them and we all went a round together and I made the remark that it would be nice for Mrs. Sebastian and her kids and Florrie and little Al to all go back to Chi on the same train together and it was O. K. with Mrs. Sebastian but when I and Florrie was alone together for a few minutes she started to ball me out for makeing the suggestion and I asked her what was the matter with it and she says she wasn't going to set in the same seat on the train with a woman that looked like she had left home before she got up and little Al would probably catch something from the 2 Sebastian kids so I said that Mrs. Sebastian done real work for a liveing and you couldn't expect her to look like Sarah Bernhart but Florrie is the kind that if she takes a dislike towards somebody its good night to them and it don't do no good to tell her that a person can't help their looks and that is all the more reason you should try and not hurt their feelings. So Mrs. Sebastian had a round trip ticket on the C. B. and Q. and so did Florrie but she pretended like hers was on the I.C. and thats the way her and little Al went back so they wouldn't have to set with the Sebastians and take a chance of little Al catching something though from what I seen of the Sebastian kids they looked as strong as a horse and they wasn't no danger of catching nothing from them unless maybe it was the banana habit.

I suppose I would of been a grass widower long ago if I was ugly and how will it be if I get shot up in the war and Florrie would sew me for a bill of divorce on the grounds that I didn't have no nose to smell the cooking.

Well Al after they had gone Sebastian made the remark that I had a beautiful wife and I couldn't help from feeling kind of sorry for him so I says "Never mind old boy" I said to him "as long as your Mrs. is a good mother and willing to work you should not worry if she is no Eva Tanguay." But I didn't feel so sorry for him when we opened up the boxs they had broughten us and Sebastian's wife had give him dough-nuts and a pie and part of a cake and goodys of all kinds and when I opened up my box it was a lb. of candy like you get in a union station for 60 cts and if it wasn't for the picture of a girl on the cover it would be all profit and a man can't eat the picture which was the only part of it that hadn't ran together like chop sooy and Florrie would of made just as big a hit with me if she had of put in the time bakeing me a mess of cookys that she spent toneing up her ear lobs or something.

Well Al I suppose you read about yesterday's game in Chi. I been saying right along that the White Sox was to lucky to loose and the only way I can figure out yesterday's game is that they must be a rule in the National League where you can't change from 1 pitcher to another pitcher till the other team gives their consent. From what I read in the papers Sallee could of been turned loose with his fast ball in a looking glass factory without damageing the goods and when Jackson and Collins begins to take a toe hold against a left hander its time to summons the Red X. You will notice Rowland

48

didn't waist no time getting Russell out of there and the next time he starts a left hander will be on the training trip next spring in Wichita where if you beat them to bad they won't give you a card to the Elks.

Your pal,   Jack.

Camp Grant, Oct. 16.

MY CHER AMI: I suppose you will think I have gone crazy when you read the way I started this letter out and you will wonder if I have gone crazy. Well Al that is the French word for my dear friend in English so you see I have not gone crazy after all. I took my first lesson last night and it is going to be nuts to learn it because most of the words is just like English only spelled different and you don't say them the same but the man learns us a dozen words and tells us how to say them and we keep saying them over till we get them down and it won't be long when we got enough of them learned so as we can jabber back and forth in front of the boys that didn't have sense enough to learn it and they won't know if we are calling them names or getting ready to murder them.

Well Al we had Gen. Barry out overlooking us yesterday and he said we was a fine looking bunch of soldiers as he even seen and we put in most of the day digging trenchs just like the ones they got over in Germany and when we get them fixed up we will practice fighting for them till we can go through them Dutchmen like they was fly paper and I wouldn't be surprised Al if we got word soon to pack up and start because Red Sampson one of the boys in our Co. has got a brother thats over there all ready and he is Gen. Pershing's right hand bower and so he gets the dope pretty straight and in a letter Red got from him he says Gen. Pershing had asked Secty. Daniels to send over the best looking lot of soldiers from each camp and from what Gen. Barry said about us I suppose we will be the first to go but it may not be for a wk. or so because Red said he heard we wasn't going till each Co. had a rifle.

If we do have to go in a hurry I won't be able to write you about where we are leaveing from and etc. on acct. of the censure because the German spy might get next to it and he could wire across to Germany and the submarine U boats would be on the outlook for us. But between you and I Red says we are libel not to go where the submarines can get a crack at us but we may slip around the other way and light in Japan and make the rest of the trip by R. R. and he says we may even not go to France but stay and help the Russians out. So Shorty Lahey was there and he has always got to say something so people will think he knows it all so he said the Russians didn't need nobody to help them out because they were pretty near out now. So Red said "You will notice they didn't loose much ground yesterday" and Shorty says "No they only loose 2 miles and they must of been a strong east wind blowing but I will bet you that if we do make the trip that way we will bump into them along about Ogden Utah." So Red says "No because if they ever get to Utah they will hide in Salt Lake City where the Germans couldn't tell them by their beards." So then Shorty seen he was getting kidded and shut up.

This A.M. we spent a half hour listening to a speech about the German gas and of course you have read about the gas Al and it isn't like regular gas but its some kind of poison that the Germans lets it loose in the air and it floats across Nobodys land and comes to the other trenchs and if you haven't got no mask its good night but we are all going to have masks to wear so the gas can't hurt us. Red says thats one thing where the Russians have got it on us and they don't have to be scared of dying from gastritis because the Germans haven't no gas fast enough to catch up with them.

Well Al the world serious is over just like I said it would be with the White Sox winner and each one of the boys gets $3600.00 and that would of been my share only I loved my country more than a few dollars and I bet the boys feel kind of ashamed of themself to think I was the only one that passed up all that jack to work for Uncle Sam at $30.00 per mo. but between you and I Al I have got a scheme where I will make twice that amt. and if some of the rest of the boys here thought about it they could do the same thing but why should I tip them off because you can bet they wouldn't tip me off to a good thing if they thought of it first.

Here is the scheme when a man has got a family the govt. keeps out ½ of your pay every month or more if you want them to and then the govt. sticks the same amt. in with it and sends it to your wife or who ever gets it. Say you are a private and getting about $30.00 per mo. and you tell the govt. to keep out $15.00 of it. So the govt. keeps $15.00 and sticks another $15.00 with it and sends it to your family.

Well Al I am going to tell them to keep out my whole $30.00 per mo. and they will have to put another $30.00 with it and send the $60.00 to Florrie and she won't need it so she can either send it to me or salt it away somewheres in my name and it means I will be getting $60.00 while the rest of them are dragging down $30.00 and if it was just luck on my part I wouldn't think it was hardly fair but when a man figures something out in your head you got a right to take advantage of it and a man that give up a big league salary and the world serious dough to do their bit deserves something extra while the only way some of the rest of these birds could earn $30.00 per mo. outside of the army would be to ask for it with a peace of lead pipe.

Well old pal bon sore for this time and that means good night in French and pretty soon I will be writeing you a whole letter in French only of course I wouldn't do that because it would be like waisting that much paper because they couldn't nobody in Bedford make heads or tales out of it and I might just as well save my labor for my pains as they say.

Your pal,   Jack.

Camp Grant, Oct. 18.

FRIEND AL: Well old pal I got a peace of news for you that I bet you will be tickled to death for my sake when I tell it to you. I guess I told you in my last letter about Gen. Barry inspecting us. Well Al I kind of thought I seen him looking at me like he liked the way I carry myself and etc. but I didn't want to say nothing about it till I was sure but after breakfast this A.M. Capt. Nash sent for me and when I went in his office and saluted he says "Good morning Corporal Keefe." Well Al of course that means I have been appointed a corporal and of course I expected it only I wasn't looking for it so soon and while Capt. Nash didn't say nothing it don't take no Bobby Burns to figure out that the orders come from higher up.

The corporals and sargents we had at first was men from the regular army and they been sending them away lately and now some of the boys from the ranks gets their chance. In order to get a corporal or a sargent a man has got to have the drills down perfect besides being a perfect physical specimen and good appearance and a man that the rest of the boys will look up to him and respect him and a man that don't know the meaning of the word fear. Well Al I must of filled the bill and I will show Gen. Barry he didn't make no mistake.

My command is made up of 7 men that I am the boss of them and they contain Sebastian and Red Sampson and Shorty Lahey and a wop named Janinny or something and a big stropper named Hess and 2 boys named Gardner and Bowen and some of them is pretty rough birds but I won't have no trouble handleing them because they know about my record in baseball and they can't help from respecting a man that give up a big salary to help Uncle Sam out and the only 1 that might try and give me trouble is Lahey and I guess he has got better sense then trying some of his funny jokes with a corporal because when a private monkeys with a officer he is libel to wake up the next A.M. with no place to wear his hat.

Well Al a corporal isn't the highest officer in the army but its a step up and everybody has got to start at the bottom and Napoleon started as a corporal and the soldiers was all nuts about him and called him the little Corporal and maybe they will give me a nick name like that only of course it won't be the little corporal because that would be like calling Jess Willard Tiny Jess or something and the salary is $36.00 per mo. instead of $30.00 and with that scheme I got fixed up with the govt. that will give me twice $36.00 per mo. or $66.00 and I'll say thats a whole lot better then a private at $1.00 per day.

I have all ready wrote and told Florrie about it and I bet she will go crazy when she reads my letter and after this when they call her Mrs. Keefe she can shrink up her shoulders and say "Mrs. Corp. Keefe please" and you will have to salute when you see me Al. Of course I mean that for a joke because what ever honors I get I wouldn't leave them make no difference in our friendship and betwen you and I it will always be just plain Jack Keefe.

Well Al we started today learning to throw bombs and of course that won't be no trick for me and you might say it was waisting time for me to practice at it because when my arm feels O. K. I can throw in your vest pocket but today it was raining and I wouldn't cut loose and take chances with my arm because I figure this war won't last long and I guess I won't have no trouble signing up in the big league at my own turns after what I done. But you ought to seen the officer that was trying to learn us how and if they all throw like he its a wonder they hit Europe to say nothing about the Germans. He kept his arm stiff like he didn't have no elbow joint and he was straight over hand all the while like Reulbach and you know what kind of control he had.

We didn't have no regular bombs but only stones and tomato cans but the way he throwed he couldn't of took a baseball and hit the infield from second base and finely I told him and he said yes but if you crooked your arm you would wear it out because the regular bombs weighs almost 2 lbs. and you had to use a easy motion. How is that Al for a fresh bum trying to talk to me about easy motions and I had a notion to tell him to go back to France with his motions but I kept my temper and throwed a few the right way till my arm got to feeling sore.

Well its 10 o'clock and after and I am going to turn in and it isn't that I feel sleepy but when a man is a officer you feel like you ought to set an example to the men.

Your pal,   Corp. Jack Keefe.

Camp Grant, Oct. 22.

FRIEND AL: Well Al we had some lessons in trench takeing today and I feel like I had been in a football game or something. We would climb up out of the trenchs that was supposed to be the U. S. trenchs and run across Nobody's Land and take the trenchs that was supposed to be the German trenchs and clean them out with rifles and bayonets and bombs and of course we didn't have no real rifles and bombs but if we had of and they had been any Germans in the trenchs it would of been good night to them.

We done it over and over till I was pretty near wore out but of course I pretended like I was fresh as a daisy because a good corporal wouldn't never lay down till he was dead and its their business to set up an example for the boys and inspire them so I kept hollering like Hughey Jennings or somebody and every time we started out of our trenchs I would holler "Come on boys give them hell this time" and I guess it made a hit with the instructers because they kept smileing at me and talking about me between themselfs and I could pretty near guess what they said. But of course it made Shorty Lahey sore to see me getting all the attentions and he says to me "Who do you think you are Jonah Vark?" So I said "You tend to your business and show some life or I will Jonah Vark you in the jaw."

So afterwards when we was in the barracks he come up and says "If you are playing Jonah Vark you should ought to quit telling us to come on boys and give them hell because Jonah Vark wouldn't never use a word like that." So I said "I guess he would say a whole lot worse then that if he had a dirty rat like you in his command." So that shut him up.

Tonight they showed us some pictures that was supposed to be the West Pt. cadets drilling and Capt. Nash says if we ever got so as we could drill like that he would quit working us so hard. Well Al its all O. K. to hand that stuff to the boys that don't know no more then to fall for it but I hope they didn't suppose I was a sucker enough to think those was real pictures but of course I wouldn't say

54

nothing because if looking at a lot of fake pictures makes the boys work harder the sooner we will get sent to France.

I was just talking to Red Sampson and he was telling me about a bird named Chambers in Co. A and it shows some people don't know when they have got a good thing and don't appreciate what people trys to do for them. I remember this bird comeing out with us on the train and they wouldn't nobody go near him on acct. of him being such a bum and Red says he heard that for a while after we got here they had to chase this bird under the shower bath with a bayonet and he done most of his drilling in the guard house. So finely his captain told him he wouldn't stand for no more of his monkey business and he would call him up in front of the court marshall if he didn't behave himself.

So then Chambers says all right he would make a new start and sure enough he cut it all out and begin to take a pride in himself and got the drills down pat and kept clean and his captain wanted to show him it payed to be a man and he made a corporal out of him.

Well Al you can't break the rules when you are a corporal no more than a private but this bird went to Chi the day before yesterday on a leave and he was supposed to be back at 11 P.M. last night but he don't show till 2 A.M. and he was all lit up like the City of Benton Harbor and of course the guard nailed him and he got called up before his captain and he busted him and I don't mean he cracked him in the jaw but when a man gets busted in the army it means you get reduced to a private. So I said to Red what a sucker this bird was and Red says maybe he wanted to get busted because a corporal has got such a load on their shoulders that lots of men would rather be a private. So I said it must be a fine kind of a man that would turn down a job in the army because it was a tough job and Red says "Yes but everybody ain't like you and some men don't want no responsibility but you are one of the kind that the more they have the better they like it and everybody could see you was a born leader the way you acted in that trench drill today."

So I suppose after all a man like Chambers has no business in a job like corporal because it is a cinch nobody would ever call him a born leader unless it was in the gin league but still a person would think he would try and behave himself after the captain give him that chance but still I should not worry and it is none of my business and all I got to do is set up the right kind of an example for my own command and leave the rest of them take care of themselfs.

Your pal,   Jack.

Camp Grant, Oct. 23.

FRIEND AL: Well I have quit takeing French class lessons and I quit because I felt it wasn't fair to either myself or Capt. Nash because when a man is a corporal its all head work you might say and a man ought to keep their mind on their job evenings as well as day times and I felt like I couldn't do that and be monking with French at the same time and it would be like as if I was back pitching baseball and trying to learn to play a saxophone or something at the same time and in the evenings when I ought to be figureing out how to pitch to Pipp instead of that I would have my mind on what keys to blow next though of course I just say that for a comparison because I could learn how to play the whole band and still make a sucker out of that bird because all you got to do is to pitch outside. But besides that I figured that the man who was trying to learn us French didn't know what he was talking about and what is the use of learning it wrong and then you got to start all over again when we got over there. For inst. he asked me what was the English word for very in French so I knew it was tres so I said tres and he says no it was tray because you say the letter e like it was the letter a and you don't pay no attention to the letter s. So I asked him what it was there for then and he said that was just the French of it so I had a notion to tell him to go and take a jump in the lake but I decided to just say nothing and quit. I guess the French people are not crazy and they wouldn't nobody but a crazy man stick a letter in a word and then make up their mind to ignore it you might say and it would be just like as if I wanted a beer and I would go up to the bar and say "Give me a bee" and I guess the man would think I thought I was in a bee hive or something or else he would think I had a bee in my bonnet eh Al?

But laying all jokes to one side I have got to much on my mind to be fooling with it and besides I put in a week on it and I figure I have got it down good enough so as I can get by and besides I am one of those kind that don't have much to say but when theys something to be done you don't have to send no blood hounds to find where I am at.

Red Sampson got another letter today from his brother in France and Red says his brother and Pershing was right up close to the front where they could see the fighting and they was a big battle in Sept. that the papers didn't get a hold of it and about 2500 Frenchmen was killed. So Shorty Lahey asked if they was all privates and Red says No that in the French army they have things different and you don't often see a private killed but when theys 25000 men killed you can figure that at least 20000 of them was corporals and sargents because the corporals and sargents has to go out in front of all the charges.

Well Al I am glad its different in the U. S. army but at that I am not the kind of a man that would hang back for the fear of getting a bullet in me and if I was I would resign from my command and tell them to get somebody else.

Your pal,   Jack.

Camp Grant, Oct. 24.

FRIEND AL: Well Al this was Liberty Day and we had a parade in Rockford and they was also some ball games out here and that is the boys thought they was playing ball and everybody was crazy I should pitch for one of the teams but in the first place I didn't feel like it would be fair and besides I figure its bad dope for the officers to mix up with the men and play games with them and etc.

57

and thats not because I think I am any better then anybody else but if you hold yourself off they respect you that much more and I have noticed that Capt. Nash and the lieuts. don't hang a round with nobody only themselfs and when it comes to the majors and colonels I guess they don't even speak to their own wife only when they are danceing maybe and step on each others ft.

Well Al I decided today to not try and work that little scheme I had about alloting my whole salary to Florrie and then the govt. would put the same amt. with it and I would be salting away $66.00 per mo. instead of $36.00 and I was talking to Corp. Haney about it and he says it couldn't be done and I don't know about that but any way I figured it wouldn't be fair to the rest of the boys so I am going to allot $18.00 per mo. to Florrie to keep for me and that leaves me $18 per mo. to spend that is it leaves me that amt. on paper but when you come to figure it out Al I am paying $5.60 for soldiers insurance and $10.00 per mo. for another liberty bond I bought and that leaves me $2.40 per mo. to spend and how is that for a man that was drawing a salary in the big league but at that I have got it on some of the privates that gives up the same amt. for insurance and a liberty bond and they only gets $30.00 per mo. and ½ of that amt. gos to their wife so when it comes to the end of the month they owe $.60 for being a soldier.

Speaking about the soldiers insurance with the kind I got if I was disabled they would have to give me $50.00 to $60.00 per mo. on acct. of me haveing Florrie and little Al and that would come in handy Al if I got my right arm shot off and couldn't pitch but at that I know birds in the big league now thats drawing $400.00 to $500.00 per mo. and as far as their pitchings conserned they might just as well have both their arms shot off and include their head.

Well anyway we won't have to practice fighting no more with broom sticks and cans and etc. because Sargent James told us tonight that the rifles was comeing so I said to my boys that I hoped they was good shots so we could make a sucker out of the other squads and I told them if they was all as good a shot as me I wouldn't have no kick because I figure that anybody thats got as good control when they throw or pitch should certainly ought to shoot straight. So Red Sampson says that if I was in the French army it wouldn't do me no good to be a crack shot and I asked him why not and he says the corporals in the French army are not allowed to carry no guns but all they supposed to do was run ahead of the privates and draw the fire and maybe if the Germans happened to not hit them they could pull out their scissors and cut the bob wire untanglements so as the privates wouldn't have no trouble getting in to the German trenchs where they could use their bayonets.

Red says "Instead of the pollutes trying to get to be a corporal they try not to because when they appoint you a corporal in the French army its a good night kiss and of course its a honor at that because it shows they think you are a game bird and don't care for your own life as long as you help the cause and that is why they picked you out. Because a corporal don't carry no arms of any kind and all he is is a kind of a decoy to kep the Germans shooting at him so as to protect the regular soldiers and that is why over 80% of the casualtys in the French army is corporals."

Well Al as I said before I am not in the French army and I should worry about what they do to corporals in the French army.

I pretty near forgot to tell you that I am going home on leave Saturday and you can bet I am going this time sick or no sick because from all the rumors a round the camp we might be leaveing for across the pond any day now specially with the rifles comeing and that makes it look like we would soon be on our way and if I didn't see Florrie and little Al before I left it would probably be the last time I would see them because something tells me Al that if I go over there I won't never come back.

Your pal,   Jack.

Camp Grant, Oct. 26.

FRIEND AL: Well don't be surprised if you read in the paper any A.M. where our regt. has been ordered to France but of course I don't suppose they would come out in the paper with it because General Pershing don't want it to get out what regts. is over there and probably you won't hear nothing about it when we do go because they won't be no chance for me to write to you and if you don't hear from me for a long while you will know we have gone and the next time you hear from me will be from over there.

I got the dope tonight from Red Sampson and he heard it from one of the men that was on guard yesterday and this man heard the Col. telling Capt. Gould of Co. B that General Pershing had sent for the best looking regt. out here and Gen. Barry had recommended our regt. and from what Red says we will probably go in a week or so and he don't know if we are going by the way of the Atlantic or the Pacific but all as I hope is that we get there before the war is over.

I am certainly glad now that I arranged for leave this wk. end because it will give me a chance to fix my affairs up before I go and if anything should happen to me they wouldn't be no trouble for Florrie about property and etc. I certainly wish I had enough so as I could leave you and Bertha something to help you along old pal and maybe if they had give me more time I could of fixed things up but all as I can leave you now is my friendship and remember that if anything happens I was your old pal and you boys that stays home is the ones we are laying down our life for and if it wasn't for men like we where would you be at Al and your familys?

Well Al I am proud of my squad the way they took the news and we was the only ones that knew about it and yet they wasn't a man in my command that didn't act like he was tickled to death and thats the right kind of a spirit and I spoke about it to Red Sampson. I said "I am proud of all of you because instead of you whineing and putting on a long face you all act like you was going to a picnic or something." So Red says he guessed the rest of the boys and him didn't have no license to cry as long as I kept up my spirits. He says "Maybe it would be different if we was all corporals because then it would seem like we was leaveing home forever. But you are the bird thats takeing the chance and if you can keep smileing we would be a fine bunch if we broke down and begun to whine and I don't suppose theys a man amongst us that has thought about danger to themselfs but its all whats going to happen to you."

Well Al thats the kind of a bunch to have under you and it makes a man think of Napoleon and how his men looked up at him.

Well maybe you won't get no more letters from me that is if the call comes before I leave tomorrow for Chi but if I get there O. K. I will write to you from there because probably by the time I get back here the orders will be to pack up and move and then I won't have no time to write.

Your pal,   Jack.

Chicago, Oct. 28.

FRIEND AL: Well Florrie is still in the hay yet and little Al is playing with himself on the floor and reading the pictures in the Sunday A.M. paper and I thought I would sleep late this A.M. but when a man gets in the habit of wakeing up early you get so as you can't sleep after you wake up once and thats the way it was with me.

Well Al I suppose you will be surprised at me saying it but I pretty near wish I wasn't no officer but just a private like at first and I got a good notion to go back to the camp like Chambers did behind time and ½ stewed and the reason I feel like that is because I have got attached to my boys and I would pretty near rather give up going to France all together then quit them because it seems like it wouldn't be hardly fair to leave them now that they have got so as they look up at me and I figure that even if I wasn't a corporal no more but just 1 of them I could do more good then if I quit them entirely.

I suppose you will wonder what I am getting at Al. Well on the train comeing from Rockford yesterday I was setting with Shorty Lahey and he was on leave to and I know its a mistake sometimes for a officer to pal a round with their men but I set with him on the train because I can't stand it to hurt a man's feelings and Shorty's hearts in the right place with all his jokeing and etc. So we set down together on the train and got to talking things over and he says "Well Keefe you have got to be a corporal and that means you have made good and I wish I was in your shoes."

So I said that if he took care of himself and minded his business they wasn't no reason why he wouldn't be advanced higher up the ladder some time in the future and he says "Yes but now is the time I would like to be in your shoes because I would like to get over to France and get in it." So I asked him what he meant and he says the dope Red Sampson was giving me was part of it right and part of it wrong and the right dope was that General Pershing hadn't sent for our whole regt. but what he had sent for was all the non commission officers out of the regt. and that means all the corporals and sargents and they was the only ones going this time because the French army had ran out of non commission officers and General Pershing was going to lend them the best ones we had over here in training.

So I said "Well it looks like I was elected and its 100 to 1 that I won't never come back." So Shorty says "Oh I don't know about that and I think Red Sampson is wrong about them killing all them corporals because from what I heard they's a few of them they don't try and kill so they can take them prisoner and get information off them."

So I said "They would have a hell of a chance getting information off me because they could kill me before I would spill anything." So Shorty says "You might not spill nothing at first but you would be a game bird if you stuck through all the tortures because when they ask you something and you don't tell them they cut off a couple of toes and see if that won't make you talk and so on till you don't hardly know if you are alive but if you are game enough to stand all they give you why finely they will see what a game bird you are and then they finish you off so you won't suffer no more. But if you tell them all you know right at first they won't do nothing to you only of course you will be a prisoner there in Germany till the war is over and they make you work your head off without no food and they don't even feed the guards because they want to keep them mad at the prisoners so as they will make them work harder and every time you act like you was loafing or something the guards scratchs their initials in you with their bayonet."

So I asked him where he got his dope and he says he didn't know if it was all true or not but his wife's 2 brothers was in the German army and they had wrote home about it and maybe it was all bunk.

Well Al I figured I would take Florrie to a show somewheres last night because maybe it would be the last time but after supper I felt kind of sick on acct. of the change in food and I asked Florrie if she would just as leave stay home so I went to bed early and I thought I would get a good rest but I didn't get no sleep and as I said I couldn't sleep this A.M. and now I am waiting for her to get up for breakfast.

I only wish they was some way for me to get out of this corporal and it isn't that I can't handle it but it seems like a shame to leave the other boys that almost worships me you might say and here is little Al playing on the floor and if his daddy was just a private I might maybe stay at Camp Grant all winter and come in and see Florrie and he every month.

Your pal,   Jack.

Camp Grant, Oct. 30.

FRIEND AL: Well Al I am not going to France at all that is right away and this time I got the dope straight from Capt. Nash and not from no Lahey or Sampson.

Here is the way I come to find out Al. I was supposed to get back in camp Sunday night but I missed the train out of Chi and I took the first train yesterday A.M. and I got reported for being A. W. O. L., and that means I was absent without no leave so I got called up in the orderly room in front of Capt. Nash.

So he says "Well Keefe don't tell me your aunt died." So I asked him what he meant because I haven't no aunt only by marriage that lives down in Texas. So he says "Do you know what we could do to you for being A. W. O. L." So I said "I suppose you could bust me." So he says "Yes and that isn't all. If you was drunk or some excuse like that we could have you out in front of a fireing party or if we wanted to go easy with you we could send you down to Ft. Leavenworth for 10 yrs." So I said "I wasn't drunk sir and all the trouble was that I missed a train out of Chi and I didn't miss it more than 2 minutes." So he says "Well 2 minutes and 2 wks. don't make no difference in this game. But you have been behaving yourself O. K. and we got a fine record in this Co. and I don't want to loose no non commission officers because I haven't got none now thats worth a dam. So you see that you don't miss no more trains because the next time it will go a whole lot different. You are excused only that you won't get no more leave for a month."

So I said thank you sir and told him I was sorry because I was in a hurry to get to France and didn't want nothing to come up to interfere with me going and he says "You don't want to go no more then I do but it looks like we would all be here till we die of old age." So I asked him if the corporals wasn't going ahead of the rest of the bunch and he says the corporals would go with the privates unless they was all shot by that time for being A. W. O. L.

So here I am Al and I have told the boys I was not going to quit them and I never seen nobody so tickled. Well Al I am glad to in a way and on the other hand its a big dissapointment but a man has got to learn to swallow their dissapointments in the army and take what comes.

Your pal,   Jack.

Camp Grant, Nov. 4.

FRIEND AL: Well Al they have begin to bust up our regt. and take men away from it and the men they take will get to France before the rest of us the lucky stiffs but they don't send them right to France from here but they send them down south to the national guards camps and fill up the national guards with them and the national guards are going to get across the pond first because Secty. Daniels wants to save the good regts. for the finish.

Well Al they can't send me to France to soon but it looks like they wasn't a chance for a man like I to get sent with the national guards because the men we are sending down south is the riff and raff you might say who we want to get rid of them so when Secty. Daniels sends word that the national guards at such and such a place wants 7 or 800 men the officers here picks them out from amidst the kitchen policemen and the guard house.

It looks now like the real soldiers that they got here would be here maybe all winter but between you and I Al I got a scheme to beat that game. I found out today that they are going to start a officers training camp here in Jan. and if a man makes good in it they will give him a lieut. or a capt. and they won't be no riff and raff allowed in the camp only men that would make a good officer so I guess I won't have no trouble getting in the camp and once I win my lieut. or capt. bars they will probably send me straight to France to take command.

Things are going along O. K. without much news to write about. Sarah Bernhart the French comedian was in Rockford Friday and come out to give the boys a treat and for some reason another the most of the boys fell all over their self trying to get up close to her and get her to smile at them. Well Al everybody to their own taste but from what I seen of her she would be perfectly safe around me and if she is a day old she is 50 yrs. old and I will bet money on it. Any way I wouldn't trade Florrie for a dozen like she.

Your pal,   Jack.

Camp Grant, Nov. 7.

FRIEND AL: Here is one for you Al and its just between you and I because I wouldn't have no one else hear about it for the world.

Yesterday we was all presented with some sox made out of knitting and they come in a bunch from the Red X and when I was going to bed I thought I would try mine on and see if they fit and if they didn't maybe I could trade with somebody that they did. Well Al I stuck my foot down in 1 of them and my toe run into something funny and I pulled my foot out and stuck my hand down in it and pulled out a note that was folded in side of the sock. Well of course I opened the note up and read it and I will copy down what it said. It says "Dear Soldier Boy, you may never see me but if you can spare time to write me just a few lines it will make me happier than any one in the world for I am oh so lonesome. You won't disappoint me will you Soldier Boy?" And it was signed Lone Star but down below she had wrote her name and address. Her name is Miss Lucy Chase and she lives in Texas.

Well Al I can't help from feeling sorry for her and if it wasn't for Florrie and little Al I would write her a note back and thank her for the sox though between you and I they are to small and try and say something that would cheer her up. But of course Florrie wouldn't like for me to do it and a married man shouldn't ought to be monking around like that and lead a girl on though of course if I did write to her the first thing I would tell her would be that I am married.

But what has been puzzling me is where she seen me. Maybe it was 1 of the times we played in Texas in the spring trip either that or she seen my picture somewheres. Well Al it must of been a picture without my feet in it or she would of made the sox bigger and I wish she had of because I don't feel like tradeing them off to nobody now that I know they was made for me by a admirer. Laying all jokes to 1 side I do feel sorry for the girl and if she had of made herself known to me a few years sooner things might of been different. Don't say nothing about this even to Bertha because I don't want it to get all over Bedford. I am not the kind that brags around about their admirers especially when its a girl.

I thought once or twice today that I would just drop her a card pretending like the sox fit me to a tea and thanking her for them and giving a hint that I was a married man but on second thoughts I guess its better to just let the whole affair drop right here.

They sprung a new one on us last night. Word come from the head quarters that everybody had to learn to sing and last night was the first lesson and they was about 3000 of us and the teacher was a bird named Nevin and he got up in front and started out on Keep the home fires burning and said we was to all join in. Well Al for some reason another everybody but he had the lockjaw and as far as we was concerned the fires would of all died out. Most of our gang is from Chi where they leave takeing care of the furnace to the janitor. He tried 2 or 3 other songs but we was all deaf and dumb mutes and he finely give up and says he would try some other time when the cat didn't have a hold of our tongue so on the way back to quarters everybody cut loose and sung and you could of heard us in Beloit. We got a lot of good singers right in our Co. that can hit the minors to but we are not going to bust out on no teacher's say so like we was in kindergarden or something.

Well Al I am going to break into a new game football. They are getting up a club here in camp to play against the Great Lakes navy and the Camp Custer club up in Mich. and they want all the men thats played football to come out and try for the club here. Well I never played but I told them I did and they won't know the difference when they see me because when a man is a born athelete they can play any game and especially a college Willy boy game like football. I seen one of their college games out to the university in Chi once and a man built like I could of made a sucker out of both clubs.

The capt. of the camp club here is Capt. Whiting and he played with the university of Chi and they got some other would be stars like Shiverick that played with the Ithaca club down east and Schobinger or something from Champlain college here in Ill. and a man from Princeton name Eddy something. Well I will show them something before I get through with them because an athelete has got to be born and you can't make them out of college

Willy boys that stays up all night doing the foxy trot and gets stewed on chocolate and whip cream.

Your pal,   Jack.

Camp Grant, Nov. 10.

FRIEND AL: Well Al I suppose you read in the papers about that troop train that a gang of spys tried to wreck it and it was a train full of burglars from here that we sent down to Camp Logan to fill up the national guards and the papers made out like the people that tried to wreck it was pro German spys but if you had of seen the birds that was on the train you wouldn't believe it because they wouldn't no Germans waist their time on them because they will all kill each other anyway before they get to France. One of the birds on it was Shorty Lahey that I all ready told you about him and when the national guards sees him they will just about declare war against Camp Grant.

Well Al you remember me writeing to you about that little girl down in Texas that sent me the note in the sox. Well I got to thinking it over and the more I thought about it I got to thinking that it wasn't the square thing to not pay no attention to her when she maybe wore her hands to the bone and strained her eyes so as my feet would keep warm so finely I set down and answered her back and I didn't say nothing mushy of course but just a friendly note to let her know I received the sox and I told her they was a perfect fit and I asked her where it was she ever seen me or my picture or how she come to pick me out and I didn't tell her nothing about being married because what would be the use of hurting her and they can't be no harm done because we will never meet and as soon as she writes and tells me where she seen me that will end it. But I just couldn't stand it to think of the poor kid running to the door every time the mail man come and maybe crying when they wasn't nothing for her. I guess

Florrie wouldn't have no objections under the circumstances but if she did find out and start to ball me out I would tell her to take a jump in the lake because she never even mended me a pair of sox to say nothing about knit them. I also asked the girl to send me a picture of herself because it tickles them to be asked for their picture and of course as soon as I get it I will tear it up but she won't know that.

Well Al I decided to not play on the football club here after all. In the 1st. place theys 3 or 4 privates trying for the club and I don't believe in mixing up with them to much and if Whiting and them other officers wants to all right, but that don't make it all right in my mind. And besides I figured it wasn't fair to either myself or Capt. Nash to run the risk of getting hurt in some fool game to say nothing about learning a lot of fool signals that don't mean nothing but just learning them takes up your time that you ought to spend thinking how to improve your command. And another thing the minute they started to practice I seen they didn't know the game and they will get licked every time they play and I can't stand to be with a looser. They talked about what a great kicker this Shiverick is but I watched him trying to kick gools and he missed 3 out of 10 and one of them rolled right along the ground like a baby had kicked it.

Capt. Whiting come up to me when I come out on the field and asked me my name and etc. and what position did I play and I told him center rush or tackle back it didn't make no difference. So he asked me what college I played at and I told him Harvard which was the 1st. thing that come into my head. So he says "All right we need a good tackle back so you can play there now in signal practice" so they lined up and I stood back of the center rush and they called out some numbers and throwed the ball to one of them and 3 or 4 of us bumped into each other and fell down and I got a bad kick in the head but it wasn't bad enough to make me quit but what is the use of takeing chances. They can have their football Al if they want to waist the govt. time but I got enough to think about thinking about winning this war.

Your pal,   Jack.

Camp Grant, Nov. 14.

FRIEND AL: Well this was our day out to the rifle range and I'll say Secty. Daniels better hurry up and send some teachers here that knows their business. But wait till you hear about it.

In the 1st. place it was a rotten day and a bad wind and so dark you couldn't hardly see and they ought not to of made anybody try to shoot. Well they had some targets that they said was 100 yds. from where we was to shoot from but it was more like ¼ of a mile and they said 100 yds. so we would think it was closer. Well the idear was that each guy was to shoot 10 times and if you hit the target it counted 1 pt. and if you hit the bulls eye it counted 5 pts. so if you hit the bulls eye every time you got 50 pts. but nobody in the world could do that the way they made us shoot. What do you think of them makeing a man lay on their stomach to shoot instead of standing up and I suppose if the Germans got 100 yds. from us we would all lay there like we had a stomache and let them come. Somebody said we layed that way so as to give them less mark to shoot at. How is that for fine dope? Because if you was laying on your stomach faceing them and they hit you at all they couldn't hit you nowheres only in the head and kill you where if you was standing up straight they would be more libel to hit you anywheres except in the head and maybe you would get off with a flesh wound or something.

Well 1 of the smart aleck lieuts. started out and hit the bulls eye 8 times and the target the other 2 times and that give him 42 and he swelled up like a poison pup but the way the wind was blowing you could tell it was just a accident because if he had of really shot at the target the wind would of carried his shots to hell and gone away from it but what he done was shoot with his eyes shut and the wind done the rest of it for him. So some of the other boys shot and some of them had a lot of luck and Red Sampson got 38 and finely it come my turn and I was dizzy from something I eat and besides by that time it was so dark you couldn't hardly make out where the target was and I was all cramped up laying there but at that I just missed the bulls eye the 1st. time and finely quit with

8. So afterwards Red Sampson asked me how it come I didn't have a expert rifle shooter's meddle on me trying to kid me. So I said "I never had to shoot for a liveing because I could go out and pitch baseball and make real money where a man like you every time the family wanted meat for dinner they would send you out to shoot a snake or a tom cat or something." So it was him that got kidded.

Well Al I will be shooting with the best of them as soon as I get the nack and when they get a man here to learn us that knows his business and pick out a day when the wind ain't blowing a mile a minute and pitch dark.

I haven't had no answer from that little girl down in Texas and I hope she has got over her infatuation and decided to forget me.

Your pal,   Jack.

Camp Grant, Nov. 17.

FRIEND AL: Well Al what do you think I got a letter from the girlie down in Texas and the poor kid has gone crazy over me and I only wish they was some way to stop her because of course it has got to end right here and I will just have to drop her a line and tell her the truth that I am a married man and the best thing she can do is try and forget. But I am afraid it will be pretty hard for her and I only wish she hadn't never seen or heard about me.

For some reason another she won't tell me where it was she seen me or she won't send me no picture because she says I might show it to the boys and laugh over that little girl down in Texas and of course I wouldn't do nothing like that and she wouldn't think so if she knew me better. Here is what her letter says.

My Soldier Boy, so you are an officer now. Well that is just grand and I feel all the happier and prouder to hear from you. No Soldier Boy I won't tell you where I saw you. You will just have to guess. Don't you remember that day at——? If you don't I won't tell you. And I won't send you my photo because I know what soldier boys are.

You would show it to everybody in camp and you would all have a good laugh over the little f——l woman down in Texas who is fond of you. Well Boy we will probably never see each other unless you should happen to be sent to one of the camps down here. Is there any chance of that Soldier Boy? So you quit a job in the big league to fight for Uncle Sam? That was fine of you and makes me all the prouder to have your friendship. I am glad you like the hose I knitted for you. Do you want some more or can I make you a helmet or a sweater or something? Just say what you need and I will make my needles fly to furnish you with it. And write to me soon. We are so far apart that it takes your letters days and days to reach me. Au revoir for this time Big Boy.

Well Al I can't remember to save my soul where it was I and she could of met. Maybe I could if she had of put the name of the town in her letter but she just left a dash like I copied it. I been trying to think up all the girls I met in different towns while I was with the ball club and I can remember a lot of them but nobody named Chase but of course she might of give me a fake name the time we met.

Well as I say theys only the 1 thing to do and that is drop her a line and say how things stand with me and for her to forget about me. Its mighty nice of her to offer to knit me them other articles but of course I can't ask her to under the circumstances and all I can do is just to call it off or maybe it would be better to not write to her back but just leave her guess the truth only I am afraid she would think I was a bum to not acknollege her letter. I wish they was somebody to advice me what to do but I guess I can't look for no help from you along those lines eh Al? You never had them looseing their heads and makeing garments for you and etc.

I pretty near forgot to tell you that these college Willy boys got cleaned up 9 to 6 in their game with the sailors from the Great Lakes and the sailors made a monkey out of them and they wasn't a kid on the sailors club that is 20 yrs. old. I bet Capt. Whiting would of gave his right eye for a good husky tackle back when them sailors was pushing his Willys around the field.

Your pal,   Jack.

Camp Grant, Nov. 22.

FRIEND AL: Well they have just sent away another train load of the boys to 1 of the national guards and if they keep it up we won't have more then 30 or 40 left to a Co. I wish I was with the boys that went but theys no chance of that because they are keeping the best men here so as we will be all together when they get ready to send us across. And it looks like I won't be able to get into the officers training camp because I heard today that they won't leave nobody in that can't talk all the languages of the ally countrys. Red Sampson heard 2 of the lieuts. talking about it and 1 of them was saying how even the college boys would have to hustle between now and Jan. because while most of them could talk French and Italian they was very few colleges where you can learn Roman and Australian and etc. so it looks like I would be bared out because while I might pick up the French and maybe 1 or 2 others I couldn't possibly master 8 or 9 languages in hardly a month you might say. I don't know what the idear is but it probably come from the same guy that makes you shoot laying on your stomach.

Speaking about a month my month without leave is pretty near up and I am figureing on going to Chi the 1st. of Dec. and see Florrie and little Al though for all as I know they both may be dead because Florrie won't never suffer from writers cramp on my acct. I have asked her 2 or 3 times to come out for Sunday and bring the kid but no its always to cold or she has got company comeing for dinner or 1 thing another.

Sometimes I pretty near wish I had a wife like Sebastian's thats so homely you can't hardly look at her but still and all you get a chance to once in a while.

Well I wrote to that poor kid down in Texas and told her I didn't want to bother her to make me a helmet or a sweater but I all ready got a helmet. I didn't have the heart to tell her about Florrie or tell her to quit writeing to me but I give her a kind of a hint that I was to busy to spend much time writeing letters and I hope she don't try and keep up a correspondence because it can't do neither of us no good and the best way would be for us to both forget it and of course that wouldn't be no trouble for me but I am afraid a girl don't forget so easy.

Well Al this ain't what you might call a happy letter but I don't know no good news to write only they have gave up our choir practice as a bad job and we don't have to worry no more about letting the fires go out.

Your pal,   Jack.

Camp Grant, Dec. 2.

FRIEND AL: Well Al I just got back from Chi and of all the tough luck a man ever had I had it.

You remember me telling you about the last time I come back from my leave and I got in late and Capt. Nash says I couldn't have no more leave for a month. Well the month was up Friday and I had it fixed so as I could go to Chi Saturday A.M. with the gang that was going to the football game between our club and Camp Custer and the only ones that was allowed to go was the ones that had boughten tickets to the game so I bought a ticket though I didn't have no intentions of waisting my time out to no Willy boy football game.

Well we got to Chi about noon and we had to march all over town and everybody stood on the sidewalks and cheered us to the ecco and I couldn't get away from the bunch till the parade was over though I don't enjoy marching and have everybody stare at you but when it was over I beat it for home. Well I hadn't said nothing to Florrie about comeing because I wanted to surprise her and I thought of course little Al and the Swede would be home and I and little Al could walk in on Florrie over to the beauty parlor and surprise her, but when I got to the flat and rung the bell they wasn't no answer and I rung and rung and finely I seen they wasn't nobody home so I went to the beauty parlor and 1 of the girls there told me that Florrie was takeing the P.M. off and wouldn't be back till Monday A.M.

So I went back to the flat and looked for the janitor to let me in and when you don't want janitors they are always snooping around at your coat tails but when you do want them they are hideing in the ash bbl. or something. So it took me about a hour to find this bird and another hour to get him to open the door up for me and of course they wasn't nobody home so the janitor says maybe I could find out where they went from the neighbors so I rung the woman across the hall's bell and she come to the door. So I said "I'm Corp. Keefe and I wanted to know if you knew where is my wife and kid." So she says "They went out." Well Al I suppose I didn't know they had went out and I felt like saying to her "Oh I thought they might maybe of crawled in between the wall paper to take a nap or I thought maybe they might of left the stopper out of the bath tub and got drained off or something." But I just asked her did she know where they went and she said she didn't.

Well I seen she didn't know nothing about them or probably nothing else so I went back in the flat and waited and waited and it come along 5 o'clock and I called up a saloon over on Indiana and asked them to fetch me over a doz. bottles of beer and I had 2 of them and then went out to a restaurant and had supper and come back and nobody home yet. Well to make a short story out of it I finished the beer up and finely went to bed and I didn't know nothing more till 9 A.M. this morning when the Swede come snooping into the room and seen me and let out a screem and beat it and I got up and dressed and went in the kitchen and she said Florrie had took little Al somewheres to stay all night with some friends and give the Swede permission to go to a ski jumpers dance out to Berwyn and Florrie would be home about 11.

Well Florrie come strutting in with the kid about 12 looking like she hadn't done nothing out of the way and when she seen me she squeeled and come romping over for a kiss. Well Al she didn't get it. I kissed little Al all right but I didn't see where she had a right to expect favors. Well she seen how things stood and begin trying to explain something about spending the P.M. down town shopping and then going to a show with some friends of

75

hers on the north side and they left little Al in charge of the nurse at the friends and they both stayed there all night and why didn't I tell her I would be home so as she could have changed her plans and etc. So I said "Yes you are a fine wife and mother running around town with a bunch of bums and leave your kid all alone in charge of a nurse that you don't know nothing about her and for all as you know she might of cut his ears off like a Belgium." Well I was sore and I give her a good balling out and of course it wound up like usual with her busting out crying and then they wasn't nothing for me to do only say I didn't mean what I had been saying and we had dinner and maybe everything would of been O. K. only we hadn't no sooner gotten up from the table when in come ½ of the south side and their wifes to call. Well they wasn't none of them I ever seen before or ever want to see them again and they was all friends of Florrie's and 2 of the ladys was customers of hers so she didn't dare tell them to get the h——ll out of there and a Mrs. Crane and a Mrs. Somebody else picked on me and got me in a pocket on the Davenport and they didn't even have sence enough to call me Corporal but it was Mr. Keefe this and Mr. Keefe that and when did I think the war would end and wasn't the Germans awful and how many men did we have in France and when was I going and so on. And Mrs. Crane said her and all her friends was so jealous of Mrs. Keefe because her husband was a soldier so I said I had heard they was room in some of the camps for a few more husbands and Mrs. Crane said her husband had tried his hardest to get into something but he had bad teeth so I said why didn't he try and get into some good dentist office. But they wasn't no way I could get them mad enough to go home till 5 o'clock then I and Florrie and the kid had just a hour together before I had to beat it for the train.

Well Al I won't get no more leave off till Xmas and maybe not then but what is the use any way when your wife gives you a welcome like that and all together it was a fine trip and I won't never try and take nobody by surprise after this but at that why couldn't she of stayed home where a woman belongs.

My train was jamed comeing back tonight and I don't know where they got it but everybody was oiled up and celebrating about beating Camp Custer in the football game and I'll say Camp Custer must be a home for cripples or something if that's the kind of a football club they turn out any way I bet they ain't no room to dance in the guard house tonight.

Your pal,   Jack.

Camp Grant, Dec. 4.

Friend Al: I guess I was so full of my swell visit home when I wrote you the last time that I forgot about telling you about that little girlie down in Texas. Well Al they isn't much to tell only that I got another letter from her though I as good as told her I wished she wouldn't write me no more but she wrote any way and she says she can't forget me and theys no use asking her to and she wouldn't tell me where it was we seen each other and they was no use me asking her. It looks from her letter like she was getting in deeper every day and I don't know what will be the end of it all and if she done anything to herself on my acct. I would feel like a murder though of course a man can't help how they look or what a girl thinks about them but still and all you can't help from feeling like you was to blame.

I guess the best way to do is just not answer her letter and hope for the best and hope she won't do nothing rash.

Well Al I started out to write you a long letter but I am to wore out and I guess anybody would be after what we went through today. It was the coldest day I ever seen so they picked it out for us to go on a 19 mile hike and if you could see the roads around here you would know what that means and they can talk all they want to about how the men suffers in France but I would rather go out in the middle of Nobody's Land and start a mumblety peg game then take another of these dam hikes with the weather a million below zero and the road full of rutts as big as the grand canion.

77

If it hadn't been for setting a example to my command I believe I would of pretended like I was sick and when you are sick they make somebody else carry your junk and leave you ride in a wagon thats O. K. for a private that don't care what the rest of them think of him but a corporal has got to keep going and try to keep his men going and when you got a bunch of sap heads like mine it keeps a man on the jump to tend to them. Red Sampson was so bad that I had to keep after him all the while and finely I pulled a good one on him I said "Sampson everybody in the whole regt. is out of step but you." So the rest of them give him the laugh but he can't take a joke no matter how good it is so he says "I haven't heard that one since they fought with spears." So I said "You get in step and show a little life or I'll spear you."

Well its all over now any way and I don't suppose they will send us out again till theys a big blizzard or something and then they will march us to Canada or somewheres for a little work out.

Your pal,   Jack.

Camp Grant, Dec. 7.

FRIEND AL: Well Al I got some big news for you. The govt. have changed their plans all around and decided after this to send the best men from the national army to fill up the national guards and that means theys a big bunch of us leaveing soon for Camp Logan down in Texas and the officers say we musent spill nothing about it that is when we are going because if the pro German spys ever found out that our bunch was going down there they would spread the rails and turn switches on us and probably put torpedos on the track or something. So all as I can say is that you won't hear from me here no more and I can't tell you what units we will be in because we haven't got no official notice yet and all as I know is what some of the boys heard that we would be in Col. House's regt. I thought when I 1st. heard the news that it meant we would be starting for France pretty quick and of course I didn't stop to think that they have closed up navigations for the winter.

Well Al I am glad we are going somewheres for the winter where it isn't so dam cold and of course I don't like to be so far away from home but maybe Florrie can get away and come down there and join me for a while and I am going to have a few hours off any way to say good bye to little Al and she and I wish I could see you and Bertha before I go especially you but theys no chance so good bye and good luck to you and I will write when I can.

I just happened to think Al that Camp Logan is in Texas and thats where that little girl lives but you can bet I won't leave her know where I am because in the 1st. place she would probably be just crazy enough to want to see me or something and besides I wrote her a farewell note yesterday and asked her wouldn't she send me her picture because I thought that would make her feel a little happier to think I wanted her picture even if we don't keep on writeing letters and I don't care if she sends it or not any way if she sent it up here I will probably be gone before that time.

Well Al I will be kind of sorry to leave Camp Grant where all and all we have had a pretty good time and I guess Gen. Martin and them will be sorry to see our bunch duck out and they will have a fine bunch left when we go but I am glad we won't freeze to death this winter and besides that they tell me the national guards is shy of officers and maybe I may not stay a corporal long after I get there but will get something bigger though a corporal can't be sneezed at.

Your pal,   Jack.

Camp Logan, Dec. 14.

FRIEND AL: Well old pal here we are in sunny Texas and its been pretty cold so far but nothing like it was up at Camp Grant and of course it don't never get as cold here as up there on acct. of this being further south.

Well nothing happened to us on the way down though of course it would of been good night nurse if it had got out what road we come on and when we left and even at that we seen some bad eggs at several different stations that looked like Germans that might of tried to pull something if they had a chance but we watched them like a hawk and they was scared to make a false move.

Well Al what do you think they have made Shorty Lahey a sargent down here only thank god he isn't in my Co. or I would be up in front of the court's marshall for murder. But him being a sargent shows they must of been pretty hard up and you can bet they was tickled to death to see our bunch roll in. Well Al if he can get a sargent I will be a gen. in a month. He says to me yesterday he says "Well old sport I wish they had of put you in my Co. and you would do the rest of your drilling with a dish towel." So I said "Yes I would."

Well after thinking it over a while I decided I better write to the little girl and tell her where I was at because I asked her in my farewell note for her to send me her picture of herself and if she sent it up to Camp Grant maybe 1 of them rummys might get a hold of it and open it up and then write back to the girl and kid her about it and I figured maybe if I let her know I was down here that maybe she hadn't sent the picture up there yet. But I didn't give her no encouragement to write to me here and all I said was that if she ever happened to be in Houston and I happened to be in town on leave maybe we might run into each other but I just said that jokeingly because her town is about a 100 miles from here and what would she be doing a 100 miles from home and besides even if I seen her on the st. I doubt if I would know her though I generally almost always remember faces though I can't always remember their names. But if she seen me and spoke to me I would pretend like I didn't hear her and duck because it would only make it tougher for her to talk to me because I would have to tell her the truth. But I guess its all over between us now and any way I hope so.

Your pal,   Jack.

Camp Logan, Dec. 16.

FRIEND AL: Well old pal I am up against a funny proposition now and it isn't so dam funny at that. Here is a letter I received this A.M. from that girlie. I will copy it down.

"Soldier Boy, so we are going to meet at last. Yes we are, that is if you want it to happen. My aunt in Houston has been wanting me to come there for months, but not till now have I really wanted to. You know why I do now, don't you Soldier Boy? You say it is easier for you to get off Sundays. All right. Will you meet me in the lobby of the Rice Hotel a week from today at one in the afternoon. I will let you take me to dinner and we can talk things over. We have a lot to say to each other, haven't we Soldier Boy? Write me at once and say you will meet me. I can hardly wait to get your reply and if you disappoint me I will do something to make you sorry. But you won't will you? I am just finishing your sweater and will bring it to you."

Well Al when the letter come I had a notion to write to her back and tell her to not come but in her letter she said she would do something to make me sorry and I am afraid of what she would do and if she done something rash I would feel like it was my fault and besides if she has got a sweater pretty near made for me it would be kind of mean to of made her do all that work for nothing and besides a man needs a sweater a lot of times even down here and I was going to buy one because I didn't have no idear she was makeing one for me. So I figure the best way to do is to tell her I will meet her and I will take her somewheres to dinner and while we are at dinner I can tell her the truth about me being married and it will be much better to tell her to her face then write it in a letter because it would sound pretty hard in black and white but the only thing is we have got to find some quite spot so as if she makes a seen or something they won't be no crowd around to pop their eyes out at us. But I hope she is a game bird and will take it O. K. and I'm sorry now I didn't tell her in the 1st. place and I wish she wasn't comeing and I sometimes wish I was a little scrimp or ugly so as a girl wouldn't look at me twice and between you and I Al it isn't all a bed of roses to be like I am.

81

I will write and tell you how I come out but I am to exited to write any more now and I wish they was some way I could get out of it all without leaveing no scars.

Your pal,   Jack.

Houston, Tex., Dec. 24.

FRIEND AL: I bet you will pop your eyes out when you read this letter and read what I got to tell you. I will begin at the beginning and tell you what come off so as you will know what come off.

Saturday I pretty near made up my mind that it would be better for me to not see Miss Chase so when I asked for leave for yesterday I hoped they wouldn't give it to me but they give it to me O. K. so I had to come or it would look funny. Well I come into the Rice at about 5 min. to 1 and looked around the lobby and they was only one woman that was alone and she was old about 35 and I looked around and couldn't see no girl that looked like they was waiting for somebody, and while I was looking this woman I seen seen me and come over to where I was standing. Well Al I thought sure it was the girl's aunt and she had heard about our date and was going to raise h——ll or something. Well this woman come up and says wasn't I Corporal Keefe. Well I didn't know what to say and I kind of stalled and she says "Was you expecting to meet some one here?" So I said "Yes I was looking for a man." So then she kind of smirked and says "Well I was expecting to meet a man to and I thought you was him." So I said "No I guess you have got the wrong bird."

Well Al everything would of been O. K. and I could of got away O. K. only just when I had her beleiving it wasn't me who should come up but Lefty Kramer that pitchs in the Texas League and lives here and instead of him just saying "Hello Jack" of course he had to say "Well if here ain't old Jack Keefe" and then it was good night. Well I suppose I turned into all the colors of the rainbow and I didn't know what to say and then Lefty asked right out loud if I wasn't going to introduce him to the lady and she spoke up and said her name Miss Chase and then I had to say something so I said "Oh I didn't know you was really Miss Chase or I would of acted different but I thought you was somebody else." So she kind of give a funny smile and says "Yes you did" and then all of a sudden I heard little Al's voice right behind hollering "There's daddy" and I looked around and it was Florrie and little Al.

Well Al Florrie come up and kissed me right in front of the whole hotel and the next thing I know the 3 of us was away from Kramer and the dame and Florrie was telling me how she had came down to give me a Xmas supprise and she is going to stay about 3 wks. and spend some of the time with her sister over in Beaumont.

Well I took a look just as we was going up in the elevator and Miss Chase was still standing there yet with Kramer and she was looking right at me and I couldn't help from feeling sorry for her the way she looked but a woman her age should ought to know more then start writeing letters to a guy she never seen and maybe this will learn her a lesson and I suppose she can give her sweater to somebody else and maybe Kramer has got it by this time but what he ought to have is a wallop in the jaw for butting in but what can you expect from a left hander.

Well Al I have got a leave off for over Xmas and I am writeing this letter while Florrie is out shopping and she asked me what I wanted for Xmas and I told her a sweater so I won't loose out after all.

Your pal,   Jack.

Camp Logan, Jan. 5.

FRIEND AL: Well Al this may be the last time you will ever hear from me or at least for a long time and maybe never. I'm going over there old pal and something tells me I won't never come back.

I can't tell you what I am going with or when we go or where we sail from because they won't leave us give out none of that dope and all as I can say is that about 30 of us has been picked to fill up a unit and we leave here tomorrow and meet them at the place where we sail from. Well Al its a big honor to be 1 of the men picked and it means they have got a lot of confidence in me and you can bet they are not sending no riff and raff over there but just picked men and I will show them they didn't make no mistake in choosing me.

But its mighty tough to leave Florrie and little Al and I thought Florrie would break her heart when I told her and no wonder. But when its a question of duty I am not the kind that would back out and Florrie wouldn't want me to but its hard all the same.

Well Al I can't waist no more time writeing to you and I am going to meet Florrie in Houston in a little while and it may be for the last time so I will say good bye to you now and say good bye to Bertha for me and she ought to be thankful she has got a husband that stayed at home and didn't enlist. And if we have good luck and nothing happens to us I will write you once in a while from the other side.

Your pal,   Jack.

The Real Dope

And Many a Stormy Wind Shall Blow

On the Ship Board, Jan. 15.

FRIEND AL: Well Al I suppose it is kind of foolish to be writeing you a letter now when they won't be no chance to mail it till we get across the old pond but still and all a man has got to do something to keep themself busy and I know you will be glad to hear all about our trip so I might as well write you a letter when ever I get a chance and I can mail them to you all at once when we get across the old pond and you will think I have wrote a book or something.

Jokeing a side Al you are lucky to have an old pal thats going to see all the fun and write to you about it because its a different thing haveing a person write to you about what they see themself then getting the dope out of a newspaper or something because you will know that what I tell you is the real dope that I seen myself where if you read it in a newspaper you know its guest work because in the 1st. place they don't leave the reporters get nowheres near the front and besides that they wouldn't go there if they had a leave because they would be to scared like the baseball reporters that sets a mile from the game because they haven't got the nerve to get down on the field where a man could take a punch at them and even when they are a mile away with a screen in front of them they duck when somebody hits a pop foul.

Well Al it is against the rules to tell you when we left the old U. S. or where we come away from because the pro German spy might get a hold of a man's letter some way and then it would be good night because he would send a telegram to where the submarines is located at and they wouldn't send no 1 or 2 submarines after us but the whole German navy would get after us because they would figure that if they ever got us it would be a rich hall. When I say that Al I don't mean it to sound like I was swell headed

86

or something and I don't mean it would be a rich hall because I am on board or nothing like that but you would know what I am getting at if you seen the bunch we are takeing across.

In the 1st. place Al this is a different kind of a trip then the time I went around the world with the 2 ball clubs because then it was just the 1 boat load and only for two or 3 of the boys on board it wouldn't of made no difference if the boat had of turned a turtle only to pave the whole bottom of the ocean with ivory. But this time Al we have got not only 1 boat load but we got four boat loads of soldiers alone and that is not all we have got. All together Al there is 10 boats in the parade and 6 of them is what they call the convoys and that means war ships that goes along to see that we get there safe on acct. of the submarines and four of them is what they call destroyers and they are little bits of shafers but they say they can go like he——ll when they get started and when a submarine pops up these little birds chases right after them and drops a death bomb on to them and if it ever hits them the capt. of the submarine can pick up what is left of his boat and stick a 2 cent stamp on it and mail it to the kaiser.

Jokeing a side I guess they's no chance of a submarine getting fat off of us as long as these little birds is on watch so I don't see why a man shouldn't come right out and say when we left and from where we come from but if they didn't have some kind of rules they's a lot of guys that wouldn't know no better then write to Van Hinburg or somebody and tell them all they know but I guess at that they could use a post card.

Well Al we been at sea just two days and a lot of the boys has gave up the ghost all ready and pretty near everything else but I haven't felt the least bit sick that is sea sick but I will own up I felt a little home sick just as we come out of the harbor and seen the godess of liberty standing up there maybe for the last time but don't think for a minute Al that I am sorry I come and I only wish we was over there all ready and could get in to it and the only kick I got comeing so far is that we haven't got no further then we are now on acct. that we didn't do nothing the 1st. day only stall around like we was waiting for Connie Mack to waggle his score card or something.

But we will get there some time and when we do you can bet we will show them something and I am tickled to death I am going and if I lay down my life I will feel like it wasn't throwed away for nothing like you would die of tyford fever or something.

Well I would of liked to of had Florrie and little Al come east and see me off but Florrie felt like she couldn't afford to spend the money to make another long trip after making one long trip down to Texas and besides we wasn't even supposed to tell our family where we was going to sail from but I notice they was a lot of women folks right down to the dock to bid us good by and I suppose they just guessed what was comeing off eh Al? Or maybe they was all strangers that just happened to be there but I'll say I never seen so much kissing between strangers. Any way I and my family had our farewells out west and Florrie was got up like a fancy dress ball and I suppose if I die where she can tend the funeral she will come in pink tights or something.

Well Al I better not keep on talking about Florrie and little Al or I will do the baby act and any way its pretty near time for chow but I suppose you will wonder what am I talking about when I say chow. Well Al that's the name we boys got up down to Camp Grant for stuff to eat and when we talk about food instead of saying food we say chow so that's what I am getting at when I say its pretty near time for chow.

Your pal,   Jack.

On the Ship Board, Jan. 17.

FRIEND AL: Well Al here we are out somewheres in the middle of the old pond and I wished the trip was over not because I have been sea sick or anything but I can't hardly wait to get over there and get in to it and besides they got us jammed in like a sardine or something and four of us in 1 state room and I don't mind doubleing up with some good pal but a man can't get no rest when they's four trying to sleep in a room that wouldn't be big enough for Nemo Liebold but I wouldn't make no holler at that if they had of left us pick our own roomys but out of the four of us they's one that looks like he must of bribed the jury or he wouldn't be here and his name is Smith and another one's name is Sam Hall and he has always got a grouch on and the other boy is O. K. only I would like him a whole lot better if he was about ½ his size but no he is as big as me only not put up like I am. His name is Lee and he pulls a lot of funny stuff like this A. M. he says they must of thought us four was a male quartette and they stuck us all in together so as we could get some close harmony. That's what they call it when they hit them minors.

Well Al I always been use to sleeping with my feet in bed with me but you can't do that in the bunk I have got because your knee would crack you in the jaw and knock you out and even if they was room to strech Hall keeps crabbing till you can't rest and he keeps the room filled up with cigarette smoke and no air and you can't open up the port hole or you would freeze to death so about the only chance I get to sleep is up in the parlor in a chair in the day time and you don't no sooner set down when they got a life boat drill or something and for some reason another they have a role call every day and that means everybody has got to answer to their name to see if we are all on board just as if they was any other place to go.

When they give the signal for a life boat drill everybody has got to stick their life belt on and go to the boat where they have been given the number of it and even when everybody knows its a fake you got to show up just the same and yesterday they was one bird thats supposed to go in our life boat and he was sea sick and he didn't show up so they went after him and one of the officers told him that wasn't no excuse and what would he do if he was sea sick and the ship was realy sinking and he says he thought it was realy sinking ever since we started.

Well Al we got some crowd on the boat and they's two French officers along with us that been giveing drills and etc. in one of the camps in the U. S. and navy officers and gunners and a man would almost wish something would happen because I bet we would put up some battle.

Lee just come in and asked me who was I writeing to and I told him and he says I better be careful to not write nothing against anybody on the trip just as if I would. But any way I asked him why not and he says because all the mail would be opened and read by the censor so I said "Yes but he won't see this because I won't mail it till we get across the old pond and then I will mail all my letters at once."

So he said a man can't do it that way because just before we hit land the censor will take all our mail off of us and read it and cut out whatever he don't like and then mail it himself. So I didn't know we had a censor along with us but Lee says we certainly have got one and he is up in the front ship and they call that the censor ship on acct. of him being on there.

Well Al I don't care what he reads and what he don't read because I am not the kind that spill anything about the trip that would hurt anybody or get them in bad. So he is welcome to read anything I write you might say.

This front ship is the slowest one of the whole four and how is that for fine judgment Al to put the slowest one ahead and this ship we are on is the fastest and they keep us behind instead of leaving us go up ahead and set the pace for them and no wonder we never get nowheres. Of course that ain't the censor's fault but if the old U. S. is in such a hurry to get men across the pond I should think they would use some judgment and its just like as if Hughey Jennings would stick Oscar Stanage or somebody ahead of Cobb in the batting order so as Cobb couldn't make to many bases on a hit.

Well Al I will have to cut it out for now because its pretty near time for chow and that's the name we got up out to Camp Grant for meals and now everybody in the army when they talk about food they call it chow.

Your pal,   Jack.

On the Ship Board, Jan. 19.

FRIEND AL: Well Al they have got a new nickname for me and now they call me Jack Tar and Bob Lee got it up and I will tell you how it come off. Last night was one rough bird and I guess pretty near everybody on the boat were sick and Lee says to me how was it that I stood the rough weather so good and it didn't seem to effect me so I says it was probably on acct. of me going around the world that time with the two ball clubs and I was right at home on the water so he says "I guess we better call you Jack Tar."

So that's how they come to call me Jack Tar and its a name they got for old sailors that's been all their life on the water. So on acct. of my name being Jack it fits in pretty good.

Well a man can't help from feeling sorry for the boys that have not been across the old pond before and can't stand a little rough spell but it makes a man kind of proud to think the rough weather don't effect you when pretty near everybody else feels like a churn or something the minute a drop of water splashes vs. the side of the boat but still a man can't hardly help from laughing when they look at them.

Lee says he would of thought I would of enlisted in the navy on acct. of being such a good sailor. Well I would of Al if I had knew they needed men and I told Lee so and he said he thought the U. S. made a big mistake keeping it a secret that they did need men in the navy till all the good ones enlisted in the draft and then of course the navy had to take what they could get.

Well I guess I all ready told you that one of the boys in our room is named Freddie Smith and he don't never say a word and I thought at 1st. it was because he was a kind of a bum like Hall that didn't know nothing and that's why he didn't say it but it seems the reason he don't talk more is because he can't talk English very good but he is a Frenchman and he was a waiter in the big French resturent in Milwaukee and now what do you think Al he is going to learn Lee and I French lessons and Lee fixed it up with him. We want to learn how to talk a little so when we get there we can make ourself understood and you remember I started studing French out to Camp Grant but the man down there didn't know nothing about what he was talking about so I walked out on him but this bird won't try and learn us grammer or how you spell it or nothing like that but just a few words so as we can order drinks and meals and etc. when we get a leave off some time. Tonight we are going to have our 1st. lesson and with a man like he to learn us we ought to pick it up quick.

Well old pal I will wind up for this time as I don't feel very good on acct. of something I eat this noon and its a wonder a man can keep up at all where they got you in a stateroom jammed in like a sardine or something and Hall smokeing all the while like he was a freight engine pulling a freight train up grade or something.

Your pal,   Jack.

On the Ship Board, Jan. 20.

FRIEND AL: Just a line Al because I don't feel like writeing as I was taken sick last night from something I eat and who wouldn't be sick jammed in a room like a sardine.

I had a kind of a run in with Hall because he tried to kid me about being sick with some of his funny stuff but I told him where to head in. He started out by saying to Lee that Jack Tar looked like somebody had knocked the tar out of him and after a while he says "What's the matter with the old salt tonight he don't seem to have no pepper with him." So I told him to shut up.

Well we didn't have no French lesson on acct. of me being taken sick but we are going to have a lesson tonight and pretty soon I am going up and try and eat something and I hope they don't try and hand me no more of that canned beans or whatever it was that effected me and if Uncle Sam wants his boys to go over there and put up a battle he shouldn't try and poison them first.

Your pal,   Jack.

On the Ship Board, Jan. 21.

FRIEND AL: Well Al I was talking to one of the sailors named Doran to-day and he says in a day or 2 more we would be right in the danger zone where all the subs hangs out and then would come the fun and we would probably all have to keep our clothes on all night and keep our life belts on and I asked him if they was much danger with all them convoys guarding us and he says the subs might fire a periscope right between two of the convoys and hit our ship and maybe the convoys might get them afterwards but then it would be to late.

He said the last time he come over with troops they was two subs got after this ship and they shot two periscopes at this ship and just missed it and they seem to be laying for this ship because its one of the biggest and fastest the U. S. has got.

Well I told Doran it wouldn't bother me to keep my clothes on all night because I all ready been keeping them on all night because when you have got a state room like ours they's only one place where they's room for a man's clothes and that's on you.

Well old pal they's a whole lot of difference between learning something from somebody that knows what they are talking about and visa versa. I and Lee and Smith got together in the room last night and we wasn't at it more than an hour but I learned more then all the time I took lessons from that 4 flusher out to Camp Grant because Smith don't waist no time with a lot of junk about grammer but I or Lee would ask him what was the French for so and so and he would tell us and we would write it down and say it over till we had it down pat and I bet we could pretty near order a meal now without no help from some of these smart alex that claims they can talk all the languages in the world.

In the 1st. place they's a whole lot of words in French that they's no difference you might say between them from the way we say it like beef steak and beer because Lee asked him if suppose we went in somewheres and wanted a steak and bread and butter and beer and the French for and is und so we would say beef steak und brot mit butter schmieren und bier and that's all they is to it and I can say that without looking at the paper where we wrote it down and you can see I have got that much learned all ready so I wouldn't starve and when you want to call a waiter you call him kellner so you see I could go in a place in Paris and call a waiter and get everything I wanted. Well Al I bet nobody ever learned that much in 1 hour off that bird out to Camp Grant and I'll say its some speed.

We are going to have another lesson tonight but Lee says we don't want to try and learn to much at once or we will forget what we all ready learned and they's a good deal to that Al.

Well Al its time for chow again so lebe wohl and that's the same like good by in French.

Your pal,   Jack.

On the Ship Board, Jan. 22.

FRIEND AL: Well Al we are in what they call the danger zone and they's some excitement these days and at night to because they don't many of the boys go to sleep nights and they go to their rooms and pretend like they are going to sleep but I bet you wouldn't need no alarm clock to make them jump out of bed.

Most of the boys stays out on deck most of the time and I been staying out there myself most all day today not because I am scared of anything because I always figure if its going to happen its going to happen but I stay out because it ain't near as cold as it was and besides if something is comeing off I don't want to miss it. Besides maybe I could help out some way if something did happen.

Last night we was all out on deck in the dark talking about this and that and one of the boys I was standing along side of him made the remark that we had been out nine days and he didn't see no France yet or no signs of getting there so I said no wonder when we had such a he——ll of a censor ship and some other guy heard me say it so he said I better not talk like that but I didn't mean it like that but only how slow it was.

Well we are getting along O. K. with the French lessons and Bob Lee told me last night that he run across one of the two French officers that's on the ship and he thought he would try some of his French on him so he said something about it being a nice day in French and the Frenchman was tickled to death and smiled and bowed at him and I guess I will try it out on them the next time I see them.

Well Al that shows we been learning something when the Frenchmans themself know what we are talking about and I and Lee will have the laugh on the rest of the boys when we get there that is if we do get there but for some reason another I have got a hunch that we won't never see France and I can't explain why but once in a while a man gets a hunch and a lot of times they are generally always right.

Your pal,   Jack.

On the Ship Board, Jan. 23.

FRIEND AL: Well Al I was just out on deck with Lee and Sargent Bishop and Bishop is a sargent in our Co. and he said he had just came from Capt. Seeley and Capt. Seeley told him to tell all the N. C. O. officers like sargents and corporals that if a sub got us we was to leave the privates get into the boats first before we got in and we wasn't to get into our boats till all the privates was safe in the boats because we would probably be cooler and not get all excited like the privates. So you see Al if something does happen us birds will have to take things in hand you might say and we will have to stick on the job and not think about ourselfs till everybody else is taken care of.

Well Lee said that Doran one of the sailors told him something on the quiet that didn't never get into the newspapers and that was about one of the trips that come off in December and it seems like a whole fleet of subs got on to it that some transports was comeing so they layed for them and they shot a periscope at one of the transports and hit it square in the middle and it begun to sink right away and it looked like they wouldn't nobody get into the boats but the sargents and corporals was as cool as if nothing was comeing off and they quieted the soldiers down and finely got them into the boats and the N. C. O. officers was so cool and done so well that when Gen. Pershing heard about it he made this rule about the N. C. O. officer always waiting till the last so they could kind of handle things. But Doran also told Lee that they was some men sunk with the ship and they was all N. C. O. officers except one sailor and of course the ship sunk so quick that some of the corporals and sargents didn't have no time to get off on acct. of haveing to wait till the last. So you see that when you read the newspapers you don't get all the dope because they don't tell the reporters only what they feel like telling them.

Well Al I guess I told you all ready about me haveing this hunch that I wouldn't never see France and I guess it looks now more then ever like my hunch was right because if we get hit I will have to kind of look out for the boys that's in my boat and not think about myself till everybody else is O. K. and Doran says if this ship ever does get hit it will sink quick because its so big and heavy and of course the heavier a ship is it will sink all the sooner and Doran says he knows they are laying for us because he has made five trips over and back on this ship and he never was on a trip when a sub didn't get after them.

Well I will close for this time because I am not feeling very good Al and it isn't nothing I eat or like that but its just I feel kind of faint like I use to sometimes when I would pitch a tough game in St. Louis when it was hot or something.

Your pal,   Jack.

On the Ship Board, Jan. 23.

Friend Al: Well I all ready wrote you one letter today but I kind of feel like I better write to you again because any minute we are libel to hear a bang against the side of the boat and you know what that means and I have got a hunch that I won't never get off of the ship alive but will go down with her because I wouldn't never leave the ship as long as they was anybody left on her rules or no rules but I would stay and help out till every man was off and then of course it would be to late but any way I would go down feeling like I had done my duty. Well Al when a man has got a hunch like that he would be a sucker to not pay no tension to it and that is why I am writeing to you again because I got some things I want to say before the end.

Now old pal I know that Florrie hasn't never warmed up towards you and Bertha and wouldn't never go down to Bedford with me and pay you a visit and every time I ever give her a hint that I would like to have you and Bertha come up and see us she always

97

had some excuse that she was going to be busy or this and that and of course I knew she was trying to alibi herself and the truth was she always felt like Bertha and her wouldn't have nothing in common you might say because Florrie has always been a swell dresser and cared a whole lot about how she looked and some way she felt like Bertha wouldn't feel comfortable around where she was at and maybe she was right but we can forget all that now Al and I can say one thing Al she never said nothing reflecting on you yourself in any way because I wouldn't of stood for it but instead of that when I showed her that picture of you and Bertha in your wedding suit she made the remark that you looked like one of the honest homely kind of people that their friends could always depend on them. Well Al when she said that she hit the nail on the head and I always knew you was the one pal who I could depend on and I am depending on you now and I know that if I am laying down at the bottom of the ocean tonight you will see that my wishs in this letter is carried out to the letter.

What I want to say is about Florrie and little Al. Now don't think Al that I am going to ask you for financial assistants because I would know better then that and besides we don't need it on acct. of me having $10000 dollars soldier insurence in Florrie's name as the benefitter and the way she is coining money in that beauty parlor she won't need to touch my insurence but save it for little Al for a rainy day only I suppose that the minute she gets her hands on it she will blow it for widows weeds and I bet they will be some weeds Al and everybody will think they are flowers instead of weeds.

But what I am getting at is that she won't need no money because with what I leave her and what she can make she has got enough and more then enough but I often say that money isn't the only thing in this world and they's a whole lot of things pretty near as good and one of them is kindness and what I am asking from you and Bertha is to drop in on her once in a while up in Chi and pay her a visit and I have all ready wrote her a letter telling her to ask you but even if she don't ask you go and see her any way and see how she is getting along and if she is takeing good care of the kid or leaving him with the Swede nurse all the while.

Between you and I Al what I am scared of most is that Florrie's mind will be effected if anything happens to me and without knowing what she was doing she would probably take the first man that asked her and believe me she is not the kind that would have to wait around on no st. corner to catch somebody's eye but they would follow her around and nag at her till she married them and I would feel like he———ll over it because Florrie is the kind of a girl that has got to be handled right and not only that but what would become of little Al with some horse Dr. for a father in law and probably this bird would treat him like a dog and beat him up either that or make a sissy out of him.

Well Al old pal I know you will do like I ask and go and see her and maybe you better go alone but if you do take Bertha along I guess it would be better and not let Bertha say nothing to her because Florrie is the kind that flare up easy and specially when they think they are a little better then somebody. But if you could just drop her a hint and say that she should ought to be proud to be a widow to a husband that died for Uncle Sam and she ought to live for my memory and for little Al and try and make him as much like I as possible I believe it would make her think and any way I want you to do it for me old pal.

Well good by old pal and I wished I could leave some thing to you and Bertha and believe me I would if I had ever known this was comeing off this way though of course I figured right along that I wouldn't last long in France because what chance has a corporal got? But I figured I would make some arrangements for a little present for you and Bertha as soon as I got to France but of course it looks now like I wouldn't never get there and all the money I have got is tied up so its to late to think of that and all as I can say is good luck to you and Bertha and everybody in Bedford and I hope they will be proud of me and remember I done my best and I often say what more can a man do then that?

Well Al I will say good by again and good luck and now have got to quit and go to chow.

Your pal to the last,   Jack Keefe.

On the Ship Board, Jan. 24.

FRIEND AL: Well this has been some day and wait till you hear about it and hear what come off and some of the birds on this ship took me for a sucker and tried to make a rummy out of me but I was wise to their game and I guess the shoe is on the other foot this time.

Well it was early this A. M. and I couldn't sleep and I was up on deck and along come one of them French officers that's been on board all the way over. Well I thought I would try myself out on him like Lee said he done so I give him a salute and I said to him "Schones tag nicht wahr." Like you would say its a beautiful day only I thought I was saying it in French but wait till you hear about it Al.

Well Al they ain't nobody in the world fast enough to of caught what he said back to me and I won't never know what he said but I won't never forget how he looked at me and when I took one look at him I seen we wasn't going to get along very good so I turned around and started up the deck. Well he must of flagged the first man he seen and sent him after me and it was a 2d. lieut. and he come running up to me and stopped me and asked me what was my name and what Co. and etc. and at first I was going to stall and then I thought I better not so I told him who I was and he left me go.

Well I didn't know then what was comeing off so I just layed low and I didn't have to wait around long and all of a sudden a bird from the Colonel's staff found me in the parlor and says I was wanted right away and when I got to this room there was the Col. and the two Frenchmans and my captain Capt. Seeley and a couple others so I saluted and I can't tell you exactly what come off because I can't remember all what the Colonel said but it was something like this.

In the first place he says "Corporal Keefe they's some little matters that you have got to explain and we was going to pass them up first on the grounds that Capt. Seeley said you probably didn't know no better but this thing that come off this A. M. can't be explained by ignorants."

So then he says "It was reported that you was standing on deck the night before last and you made the remark that we had a he——ll of a censor ship." And he says "What did you mean by that?"

So you see Al this smart alex of a Lee had told me they called the first ship the censor ship and I believed him at first because I was thinking about something else or of course I never would of believed him because the censor ship isn't no ship like this kind of a ship but means something else. So I explained about that and I seen Capt. Seeley kind of crack a smile so then I knew I was O. K.

So then he pulled it on me about speaking to Capt. Somebody of the French army in the German language and of course they was only one answer to that and you see the way it was Al all the time Smith was pretending to learn us French he was learning us German and Lee put him up to it but when the Colonel asked me what I meant by doing such a thing as talk German why of course I knew in a minute that they had been trying to kid me but at first I told the Colonel I couldn't of said no German because I don't know no more German than Silk O'Loughlin. Well the Frenchman was pretty sore and I don't know what would of came off only for Capt. Seeley and he spoke up and said to the Colonel that if he could have a few minutes to investigate he thought he could clear things up because he figured I hadn't intended to do nothing wrong and somebody had probably been playing jokes.

So Capt. Seeley went out and it seemed like a couple of yrs. till he came back and he had Smith and Lee and Doran with him. So then them 3 birds was up on the carpet and I'll say they got some panning and when it was all over the Colonel said something about they being a dam site to much kidding back and fourth going on and he hoped that before long we would find out that this war wasn't no practicle joke and he give Lee and Smith a fierce balling out and he said he would leave Capt. Seeley to deal with them and he would report Doran to the proper quarters and then he was back on me again and he said it looked like I had been the innocent victim of a practicle joke but he says "You are so dam innocent that I figure you are temperately unfit to hold on to a corporal's warrant so you can consider yourself reduced to the ranks. We can't have no corporals that if some comedian told them the Germans was now one of our allies they would try and get in the German trenches and shake hands with them."

Well Al when it was all over I couldn't hardly keep from laughing because you see I come out of it O. K. and the laugh was on Smith and Lee and Doran because I got just what I wanted because I never did want to be a corporal because it meant I couldn't pal around with the boys and be their pals and I never felt right when I was giveing them orders because I would rather be just one of them and make them feel like we were all equals.

Of course they wasn't no time on the whole trip when Lee or Doran or Smith either one of them had me fooled because just to look at them you would know they are the kind of smart alex that's always trying to put something over on somebody only I figured two could play at that game as good as one and I would kid them right back and give them as good as they sent because I always figure that the game ain't over till the ninth inning and the man that does the laughing then has got all the best of it. But at that I don't bear no bad will towards neither one of them and I have got a good notion to ask Capt. Seeley to let them off easy.

Well Al this is a long letter but I wanted you to know I wasn't no corporal no more and if a sub hits us now Al I can hop into a boat as quick as I feel like it but jokeing a side if something like that happened it wouldn't make no difference to me if I was a corporal or not a corporal because I am a man and I would do my best and help the rest of the boys get into the boats before I thought about myself.

Your pal,   Jack.

On the Ship Board, Jan. 25.

FRIEND AL: Well old pal just a line to let you know we are out of the danger zone and pretty near in port and I can't tell you where we land at but everybody is hollering and the band's playing and I guess the boys feels a whole lot better then when we was out there where the subs could get at us but between you and I Al I never thought about the subs all the way over only when I heard somebody else talk about them because I always figure that if they's some danger of that kind the best way to do is just forget it and if its going to happen all right but what's the use of worrying about it? But I suppose lots of people is built different and they have just got to worry all the while and they get scared stiff just thinking about what might happen but I always say nobody ever got fat worrying so why not just forget it and take things as they come.

Well old pal they's to many sights to see so I will quit for this time.

Your pal,   Jack.

Somewheres in France, Jan. 26.

FRIEND AL: Well old pal here we are and its against the rules to tell you where we are at but of course it don't take no Shylock to find out because all you would have to do is look at the post mark that they will put on this letter.

Any way you couldn't pronounce what the town's name is if you seen it spelled out because it isn't nothing like how its spelled out and you won't catch me trying to pronounce none of these names or talk French because I am off of languages for a while and good old American is good enough for me eh Al?

Well Al now that its all over I guess we was pretty lucky to get across the old pond without no trouble because between you and I Al I heard just a little while ago from one of the boys that three nights ago we was attacked and our ship just missed getting hit by a periscope and the destroyers went after the subs and they was a whole flock of them and the reason we didn't hear nothing is that the death bombs don't go off till they are way under water so you can't hear them but between you and I Al the navy men say they was nine subs sank.

Well I didn't say nothing about it to the man who tipped me off but I had a hunch that night that something was going on and I don't remember now if it was something I heard or what it was but I knew they was something in the air and I was expecting every minute that the signal would come for us to take to the boats but they wasn't no necessity of that because the destroyers worked so fast and besides they say they don't never give no alarm till the last minute because they don't want to get everybody up at night for nothing.

Well any way its all over now and here we are and you ought to of heard the people in the town here cheer us when we come in and you ought to see how the girls look at us and believe me Al they are some girls. Its a good thing I am an old married man or I believe I would pretty near be tempted to flirt back with some of the ones that's been trying to get my eye but the way it is I just give them a smile and pass on and they's no harm in that and I figure a man always ought to give other people as much pleasure as you can as long as it don't harm nobody.

Well Al everybody's busier then a chicken with their head off and I haven't got no more time to write. But when we get to where we are going I will have time maybe and tell you how we are getting along and if you want drop me a line and I wish you would send me the Chi papers once in a while especially when the baseball training trips starts but maybe they won't be no Jack Keefe to send them to by that time but if they do get me I will die fighting. You know me Al.

Your pal,   Jack.

Private Valentine

Somewheres in France, Feb. 2.

FRIEND AL: Well Al here I am only I can't tell you where its at because the censor rubs it out when you put down the name of a town and besides that even if I was to write out where we are at you wouldn't have no idear where its at because how you spell them hasn't nothing to do with their name if you tried to say it.

For inst. they's a town a little ways from us that when you say it its Lucy like a gal or something but when you come to spell it out its Loucey like something else.

Well Al any way this is where they have got us staying till we get called up to the front and I can't hardly wait till that comes off and some say it may be tomorrow and others say we are libel to be here a yr. Well I hope they are wrong because I would rather live in the trenches then one of these billets where they got us and between you and I Al its nothing more then a barn. Just think of a man like I Al thats been use to nothing only the best hotels in the big league and now they got me staying in a barn like I was a horse or something and I use to think I was cold when they had us sleeping with imaginery blankets out to Camp Grant but I would prespire if I was there now after this and when we get through here they can send us up to the north pole in our undershirt and we would half to keep moping the sweat off of our forehead and set under a electric fan to keep from sweltering.

Well they have got us pegged as horses all right not only because they give us a barn to live in but also from the way they sent us here from where we landed at in France and we made the trip in cattle cars and 1 of the boys says they must of got us mixed up with the calvary or something. It certainly was some experience to be rideing on one of these French trains for a man that went back and fourth to the different towns in the big league and back in a special Pullman and sometimes 2 of them so as we could all have lower births. Well we didn't have no births on the French R. R. and it wouldn't of done us no good to of had them because you wouldn't no sooner dose off when the engine would let off a screem that sounded like a woman that seen a snake and 1 of the boys says that on acct. of all the men being in the army they had women doing the men's work and judgeing by the noise they even had them whistleing for the crossings.

Well we finely got here any way and they signed us to our different billets and they's 20 of us in this one not counting a couple of pigs and god knows how many rats and a cow that mews all night. We haven't done nothing yet only look around but Monday we go to work out to the training grounds and they say we won't only half to march 12 miles through the mud and snow to get there. Mean time we set and look out the cracks onto Main St. and every little wile they's a Co. of pollutes marchs through or a train of motor Lauras takeing stuff up to the front or bringing guys back that didn't duck quick enough and to see these Frenchmens march you would think it was fun but when they have been at it a wile they will loose some of their pep.

Well its warmer in bed then setting here writeing so I will close for this time.

Your pal,   Jack.

Somewheres in France, Feb. 4.

FRIEND AL: Well Al I am writeing this in the Y. M. C. A. hut where they try and keep it warm and all the boys that can crowd in spends most of their spare time here but we don't have much spare time at that because its always one thing another and I guess its just as well they keep us busy because every time they find out you are not doing nothing they begin vaxinating everybody.

They's enough noise in here so as a man can't hear yourself think let alone writeing a letter so if I make mistakes in spelling and etc. in this letter you will know why it is. They are singing the song now about the baby's prayer at twilight where the little girl is supposed to be praying for her daddy that's a soldier to take care of himself but if she was here now she would be praying for him to shut up his noise.

Well we was in the trenchs all day not the regular ones but the ones they got for us to train in them and they was a bunch of French officers trying to learn us how to do this in that and etc. and some of the time you could all most understand what they was trying to tell you and then it was stuff we learnt the first wk. out to Camp Grant and I suppose when they get so as they can speak a few words of English they will tell us we ought to stand up when we hear the Star spangle Banner. Well we was a pretty sight when we got back with the mud and slush and everything and by the time they get ready to call us into action they will half to page us in the morgue.

About every 2 or 3 miles today we would pass through a town where some of the rest of the boys has got their billets only they don't call it miles in France because that's to easy to say but instead of miles they call them kilometts. But any way from the number of jerk water burgs we went through you would think we was on the Monon and the towns all looks so much like the other that when one of the French soldiers gets a few days leave off they half to spend most of it looking for land marks so as they will know if they are where they live. And they couldn't even be sure if it was warm weather and their folks was standing out in front of the house because all the familys is just alike with the old Mr. and the Mrs. and pigs and a cow and a dog.

Well Al they say its pretty quite these days up to the front and the boys that's been around here a wile says you can hear the guns when they's something doing and the wind blows this way but we haven't heard no guns yet only our own out to where we have riffle practice but everybody says as soon as spring comes and the weather warms up the Germans is sure to start something. Well I don't care if they start anything or not just so the weather warms up and besides they won't never finish what they start unless they start going back home and they won't even finish that unless they show a whole lot more speed then they did comeing. They are just trying to throw a scare into somebody with a lot of junk about a big drive they are going to make but I have seen birds come up to hit in baseball Al that was going to drive it out of the park but their drive turned out to be a hump back liner to the pitcher. I remember once when Speaker come up with a couple men on and we was 2 runs ahead in the 9th. inning and he says to me "Well busher here is where I hit one a mile." Well Al he hit one a mile all right but it was ½ a mile up and the other ½ a mile down and that's the way it goes with them gabby guys and its the same way with the Germans and they talk all the time so as they will get thirsty and that's how they like to be.

Speaking about thirsty Al its different over here then at home because when a man in uniform wants a drink over here you don't half to hire no room in a hotel and put on your nightgown but you can get it here in your uniform only what they call beer here we would pore it on our wheat cakes at home and they got 2 kinds of wine red and white that you could climb outside of a bbl. of it without asking the head waiter to have them play the Rosery. But they say the champagne is O. K. and I am going to tackle it when I get a chance and you may think from that that I have got jack to throw away but over here Al is where they make the champagne and you can get a qt. of it for about a buck or ½ what you would pay for it in the U. S. and besides that the money they got here is a frank instead of a dollar and a frank isn't only worth about $.19 cents so a man can have a whole lot better time here and not cost him near as much.

And another place where the people in France has got it on the Americans and that is that when they write a letter here they don't half to pay nothing to mail it but when you write to me you have got to stick a 5 cent stamp on it but judgeing by the way you answer my letters the war will be all over before you half to break a dime. Of course I am just jokeing Al and I know why you don't write much because you haven't got nothing to write staying there in Bedford and you could take a post card and tell me all the news that happened in 10 yrs. and still have room enough yet to say Bertha sends kind regards.

But of course its different with a man like I because I am always where they is something big going on and first it was baseball and now its a bigger game yet you might say but whatever is going on big you can always count on me being in the mist of it and not buried alive in no Indiana X roads where they still think the first bounce is out. But of course I know it is not your fault that you haven't been around and seen more and it ain't every man that can get away from a small town and make a name for themself and I suppose I ought to consider myself lucky.

Well Al enough for this time and I will write soon again and I would like to hear from you even if you haven't nothing to say and don't forget to send me a Chi paper when you get a hold of one and I asked Florrie to send me one every day but asking her for favors is like rolling off a duck's back you might say and its first in one ear and then the other.

Your pal,   Jack.

Somewheres in France, Feb. 7.

FRIEND AL: I suppose you have read articles in the papers about the war that's wrote over here by reporters and the way they do it is they find out something and then write it up and send it by cablegrams to their papers and then they print it and that's what you read in the papers.

Well Al they's a whole flock of these here reporters over here and I guess they's one for every big paper in the U. S. and they all wear bands around their sleeves with a C on them for civilian or something so as you can spot them comeing and keep your mouth shut. Well they have got their head quarters in one of the towns along the line but they ride all over the camp in automobiles and this evening I was outside of our billet and one of them come along and seen me and got out of his car and come up to me and asked if I wasn't Jack Keefe the White Sox pitcher. Well Al he writes for one of the Chi papers and of course he knows all about me and has seen me work. Well he asked me a lot of questions about this in that and I didn't give him no military secrets but he asked me how did I like the army game and etc.

I asked him if he was going to mention about me being here in the paper and he says the censors wouldn't stand for mentioning no names until you get killed because if they mentioned your name the Germans would know who all was here but after you are dead the Germans don't care if you had been here or not.

But he says he would put it in the paper that he was talking to a man that use to be a star pitcher on the White Sox and he says everybody would know who it was he was talking about because they wasn't such a slue of star pitchers in the army that it would take a civil service detective to find out who he meant.

So we talked along and finely he asked me was I going to write a book about the war and I said no and he says all right he would tell the paper that he had ran across a soldier that not only use to be a ball player but wasn't going to write a book and they would make a big story out of it.

So I said I wouldn't know how to go about it to write a book but when I went around the world with the 2 ball clubs that time I use to write some poultry once in a wile just for different occasions like where the boys was called on for a speech or something and they didn't know what to say so I would make up one of my poems and the people would go nuts over them.

So he said why didn't I tear off a few patriotic poems now and slip them to him and he would send them to his paper and they would print them and maybe if some of them was good enough somebody would set down and write a song to them and probably everybody would want to buy it and sing it like Over There and I would clean up a good peace of jack.

Well Al I told him I would see if I could think up something to write and of course I was just stalling him because a soldier has got something better to do than write songs and I will leave that to the birds that was gun shy and stayed home. But if you see in the Chi papers where one of the reporters was talking to a soldier that use to be a star pitcher in the American League or something you will know who they mean. He said he would drop by in a few days again and see if I had something wrote up for him but I will half to tell him I have been to busy to monkey with it.

As far as I can see they's enough songs all ready wrote up about the war so as everybody in the army and navy could have 1 a peace and still have a few left over for the boshs and that's a name we got up for the Germans Al and instead of calling them Germans we call them boshs on acct. of them being so full of bunk.

Well Al one of the burgs along the line is where Jonah Vark was born when she was alive. It seems like France was mixed up in another war along about a 100 yrs. ago and they was getting licked and Jonah was just a young gal but she dressed up in men's coat and pants and went up to the front and led the charges with a horse and she carried a white flag and the Dutchmens or whoever they was fighting against must of thought it was a flag of truants and any way they didn't fire at them and the French captured New Orleans and win the war. The Germans is trying to pull the same stuff on our boys now and lots of times they run up and holler Conrad like they was going to give up and when your back is turned they whang away at you but they won't pull none of that stuff on me and when one of them trys to Conrad me I will percu-late them with a bayonet.

Well Al the boys is starting their choir practice and its good night and some times I wished I was a deef and dumb mute and couldn't hear nothing.

Your pal,   Jack.

Somewheres in France, Feb. 9.

FRIEND AL: Well Al I didn't have nothing to do last night and I happened to think about that reporter and how he would be come-ing along in a few days asking for that poultry.

I figured I might as well set down and write him up a couple verses because them fellows is hard up for articles to send their paper because in the first place we don't tell them nothing so they could write it up and when they write it the censors smeers out everything but the question marks and dots but of course they would leave them send poems because the Germans couldn't make head or tale out of them. So any way I set down and tore off 3 verses and he says they ought to be something about a gal in it so here is what I wrote:

Near a year ago today
Pres. Wilson of the U. S. A.
had something to say,
"Germany you better keep away
This is no time for play."
When it come time to go
America was not slow
Each one said good by to their girl so dear
And some of them has been over here
since last year.

I will come home when the war is over
Back to the U. S. A.
So don't worry little girlie
And now we are going to Berlin
And when we the Kaiser skin
and the war we will win
And make the Kaiser jump out of his skin.

The ones that stays at home
Can subscribe to the liberty loan

And some day we will come home
to the girles that's left alone
Old Kaiser Bill is up against it
For all are doing their bit.
Pres. Wilson says the stars and stripes
Will always fight for their rights.

That's what I tore off and when he comes around again I will have it for him and if you see it in the Chi papers you will know who wrote it up and maybe somebody will write a song to it but of course they can't sign my name to it unless I get killed or something but I guess at that they ain't so many soldiers over here that can turn out stuff like that but what my friends won't be pretty sure who wrote it.

But if something does happen to me I wished you would kind of keep your eyes pealed and if the song comes out try and see that Florrie gets some jack out of it and I haven't wrote nothing to her about it because she is like all other wifes and when somebodys else husband pulls something its O. K. but if their own husband does it he must of had a snoot full.

Well today was so rotten that they didn't make us go nowheres and I'll say its got to be pretty rotten when they do that and the meal they give us tonight wouldn't of bulged out a grandaddy long legs and I and my buddy Frank Carson was both hungry after we eat and I suppose you will wonder what do I mean by buddy. Well Al that's a name I got up for who ever you pal around with or bunk next to them and now everybody calls their pal their buddy. Well any way he says why didn't we go over to the Red X canteen resturent and buy ourself a feed so we went over and its a little shack where the Red X serves you a pretty good meal for 1 frank and that's about $.19 cents and they don't try and make no profits on it but just run them so as a man don't half to go along all the wile on what the army hands out to you.

Well they was 3 janes on the job over there and 2 of them would be safe anywheres you put them but the other one is Class A and her old woman must of been pie eyed when she left her come over here. Well Carson said she belonged to him because he had seen her before and besides I was a married man so I says all right go ahead and get her. Well Al it would be like Terre Haute going after George Sisler or somebody and the minute we blowed in she didn't have eyes for only me but I wasn't going to give her no encouragement because we were here to kill Germans and not ladys but I wished you could of seen the smile she give me. Well she's just as much a American as I or you but of course Carson had to be cute and try to pull some of his French on her so he says Bon soir Madam Moselle and that is the same like we would say good evening but when Carson pulled it I spoke up and said "If your bones is soir why don't you go and take the baths somewhere?" Pretending like I thought he meant his bones were wore. Well the little lady got it O. K. and pretty near laughed outright. You see Al when a person has got rhuematism they go and take the baths like down to Mudlavia so I meant if his bones was sore he better go somewheres like that. So the little lady tried to not laugh on acct. of me being a stranger but she couldn't hardly help from busting out and then I smiled at her back and after that Carson might as well of been mowing the lawn out in Nobody's Land. I felt kind of sorry the way things broke because here he is a man without no home ties and of course I have all ready got a wife but Miss Moselle didn't have no eyes for him and that's the way it goes but what can a man do and Carson seen how it was going and says to me right in front of her "Have you heard from your Mrs. since we been over?" And I didn't dast look up and see how she took it.

Well they set us up a pretty good feed and the little lady kept asking us questions like how long had we been here and what part of the U. S. we come from and etc. and finely Carson told her who I was and she popped her eyes out and says she use to go to the ball games once in a wile in N. Y. city with her old man and she didn't never think she would meet a big league pitcher and talk to them and she says she wondered if she ever seen me pitch. Well I guess if she had she would remember it specially in N. Y. because there was one club I always made them look like a fool and they wasn't the only club at that and I guess they's about 6 other clubs in the American League that if they had seen my name in the dead they wouldn't shed off enough tears to gum up the infield.

Well when we come out she asked us would we come again and we said yes but I guess its best for both she and I if I stay away but I said we would come again to be polite so she said au revoir and that's like you would say so long so I said au reservoir pretending like I didn't know the right way to say it but she seen I was just kidding and laughed and she is the kind of a gal that gets everything you pull and bright as a whip and her and I would make a good team but of course they's no use talking about it the way I am tied up so even when I'm sick in tired of the regular rations I won't dast go over there for a feed because it couldn't do nothing only harm to the both of us and the best way to do with those kind of affairs is to cut it out before somebody gets hurt.

Well its time to hop into the feathers and I only wished it was feathers but feathers comes off a chicken or something and I guess these matteresses we got is made out to Gary or Indiana Harbor or somewheres.

Your pal,   Jack.

Somewheres in France, Feb. 11.

FRIEND AL: Well Al they's several of the boys that won't need no motor Laura to carry their pay for the next couple mos. and if you was to mention champagne to them they would ask for a barrage. I was over to the Y. M. C. A. hut last night and when I come back I wished you could of seen my buddys and they was 2 of them that was still able to talk yet and they was haveing a argument because one of them wanted to pore some champagne in a dish so as the rats would get stewed and the other bird was trying to not let him because he said it always made them mean and they would go home and beat up their Mrs.

It seems like one of the boys had a birthday and his folks is well off and they had sent him some jack from the states to buy blankets and etc. with it and he thought it would be a sucker play to load up with bed close when spring was comeing so he loaded up with something else and some of the boys with him and for 50 or 60 franks over here you can get enough champagne to keep the dust layed all summer and of course some of the boys hadn't never tasted it before and they thought you could bathe in it like beer. They didn't pay no more tension to revelry this A. M. then if they was a corps and most of them was at that and out of the whole bunch of us they was only 7 that didn't get reported and the others got soaked 2 thirds of their pay and confined to their quarters and Capt. Seeley says if they was any more birthdays in his Co. we wouldn't wind the celebration up till sunrise and then it would be in front of a fireing squad. Well Al if the boys can't handle it no better then that they better leave it alone and just because its cheap that's no reason to try and get it all at once because the grapes will still be growing over here yet when all us birds takes our teeth off at night with our other close.

Well Al the reporter that asked me to write up the verses ain't been around since and probably he has went up to the front or somewheres and I am glad of it and I hope he forgets all about it because in the first place I am not one of the kind that is crazy to get in the papers and besides I am to busy to be monking with stuff like that. Yes they keep us on the jump all the wile and we are pretty well wore out when night comes around but a man wouldn't mind it if we was learning something but the way it is now its like as if we had graduated from college and then they sent us to kindegarden and outside of maybe a few skulls the whole regt. is ready right now to get up there in the trenches and show them something and I only wished we was going tomorrow but I guess some of the boys would like it to never go up there but would rather stay here in this burg and think they was haveing a good time kidding with the French gals and etc. but that's no business for a married man and even if I didn't have no family the French gals I seen so far wouldn't half to shew me away and I been hearing all my life what swell dressers they was but a scout for the Follys wouldn't waist no time in this burg.

But I'm sick in tired of the same thing day in and day out and here we been in France 2 wks. and all we done is a little riffle practice and stuff we had back home and get soping wet every day and no mail and I wouldn't wonder if Florrie and little Al had forgot all about me and if Secty. Daniels wired them that Jack Keefe had been killed they would say who and the hell is he.

So all and all they can't send us up to the front to quick and it seems like a shame that men like I should be held back just because they's a few birds in the regt. that can't put on a gas mask yet without triping themself up.

Your pal,   Jack.

Somewheres in France, Feb. 13.

FRIEND AL: Well Al wait till you hear this and I bet you will pop your eyes out. I guess I all ready told you about Miss Moselle the little lady over to the Red X canteen. Well I was over there the day before yesterday and she wasn't around nowheres and I was glad of it because I didn't want to see her and just dropped in there to get something to eat and today I was in there again and this time she was there and she smiled when she seen me and come up and begin talking and she asked me how I liked it and I said I would like it a whole lot better if we was in the fighting and she asked me if I didn't like this town and I said well no I wasn't nuts about it and she said she didn't think I was very complementary so then I seen she wanted to get personal.

Well Al she knows I am a married man because Carson just as good as told her so I didn't see no harm in kidding her along a wile so I give her a smile and said well you know the whole town ain't like you and she blushed up and says "Well I didn't expect nothing like that from a great baseball pitcher" so you see Al she had been makeing inquirys about me. So I said "Well they was only one pitcher I ever heard of that couldn't talk and that was Dummy Taylor but at that they's a whole lot of them that if they couldn't say my arm's sore they might as well be tongue tied." But I told her I wasn't one of those kind and I guest when it came to talking I could give as good as I sent and she asked me was I a college man and I kidded her along and said yes I went to Harvard and she said what year so I told her I was there 2 different yrs. and we talked along about this in that and I happened to have them verses in my pocket that I wrote up and they dropped out when I was after my pocket book and she acted like she wanted to know what the writeing was so I showed them to her.

Well Al I wished you could of seen how supprised she was when she read them and she says "So you are a poet." So I said "Yes I am a poet and don't know it" so that made her laugh and I told her about the reporter asking me to write some poems and then she asked me if she could keep a hold of those ones till she made out a copy of them to keep for herself and I said "You can keep that copy and pretend like I was thinking of you when I wrote them." Well Al I wished you could of seen her then and she couldn't say nothing at first but finely she says tomorrow was valentine day and the verses would do for a valentine so just jokeing I asked her if she wouldn't rather have a comical valentine and she says those ones would do O. K. so then I told her I would write her a real valentine for herself but I might maybe not get it ready in time to give her tomorrow and she says she realized it took time and any time would do.

Well of course I am not going to write up nothing for her and after this I will keep away from the canteen because it isn't right to leave her see to much of me even if she does know I am married but if I do write her something I will make it comical and no mushy stuff in it. But it does seem like fate or something that the harder I try and not get mixed up in a flirtation I can't turn around you might say but what they's some gal poping up on my trail and if it was anybody else only Miss Moselle I wouldn't mind but she is a darb and I wouldn't do nothing to hurt her for the world but they can't nobody say this is my fault.

Well Al I pretty near forgot to tell you that the boys is putting on a entertainment over to the Y. M. C. A. Saturday night and they will be singing and gags and etc. and they asked me would I give them a little talk on baseball and I said no at first but they begged me and finely I give my consent but you know how I hate makeing speeches and etc. but a man don't hardly feel like refuseing when they want me so bad so I am going to give them a little talk on my experiences and make it comical and I will tell you about the entertainment when its over.

Your pal,   Jack.

Somewheres in France, Feb. 15.

FRIEND AL: Well Al I just been over to the canteen and I give the little lady the valentine I promised to write up for her and I wasn't going to write it up only I happened to remember that I promised so I wrote something up and I was going to make it comical but I figured that would disappoint her on acct. of the way she feels towards me so here is what I wrote up.

To Miss Moselle
(Private)

A soldier don't have much time
To set down and write up a valentine

but please bear in mind
That I think about you many a time
And I wished I could call you mine
And I hope they will come a time
When I will have more time
And then everything will be fine
And if you will be my valentine
I will try and show you a good time.

Well after I had wrote it I thought I better have it fixed up like a valentine and they's one of the boys in our Co. named Stoops that use to be a artist so I had him draw me a couple of hearts with a bow and arrow sticking through them and a few flowers on a peace of card board and I coppied off the valentine on the card in printing and stuck it in a envelope and took it over to her and I didn't wait for her to open it up and look at it and I just says here is that valentine I promised you and its 1 day late and she blushed up and couldn't say nothing and I come away. Well Al she has read it by this time and I hope she don't take nothing I said serious but of course she knows I am a married man and she can read between the lines and see where I am trying to let her down easy and telling her to not expect no more tensions from me and its just like saying good by to her in a way only not as rough as comeing right out and saying it. But I won't see her no more and its all over before it begun you might say.

Well we passed some German prisoners today and believe me we give them a ride. Everybody called them Heinie and Fritz and I seen one of them giveing me a look like he was wondring if all the U. S. soldiers was big stroppers like I but I stuck out my tongue at him and said "What do you think you are looking at you big pretzel" and he didn't dast say nothing back. Well they was a fine looking gang and they's been a lot of storys going the rounds about no soap in Germany. Well Al its all true.

Well I finely got a letter from Florrie that is if you could call it a letter and to read it you wouldn't never guess that she had a husband over here in France and maybe never see him again but you would think I had went across the st. to get a bottle of ketchup and all as she said about little Al was that he needed a new pair of shoes and they's about as much news in that as if she said he woke up in the night. And the rest of the letter was about how good she was doing in the beauty parlor and for me not to worry about her because she was O. K. only for a callous on her heel and I suppose she will go to the hospital with it and here I am with so many of them that if they was worth a frank a peace I could pay the Kaiser's gas bill. And she never asked me did I need anything or how was I getting along. And she enclosed a snapshot of herself in one of these here war bride outfits and she looks so good in it that I bet she goes to church every Sunday and asks god to prolongate the war.

Your pal,　　Jack.

Somewheres in France, Feb. 16.

FRIEND AL: Well Al they's a certain bird in this camp that if I ever find out who he is they won't need no tonnages to carry him back when the war's over. Let me tell you what come off tonight and what was pulled off on the little lady and I and if you read about me getting in front of the court marshall for murder you will know how it come off.

I guess I all ready told you about the show that was comeing off tonight and they asked me to make a little talk on baseball. Well they was as many there as could crowd in and the band played and they was singing and gags and storys and etc. and they didn't call on me till pretty near the last. Well Al you ought to of heard the crowd when I got up there and it sounded like old times to have them all cheering and clapping and I stepped to the front of the platform and give them a bow and it was the first time I was ever on the stage but I wasn't scared only at first.

Well I had wrote out what I was going to say and learnt the most of it by heart and here is what I give them only I won't give you only part of it because it run pretty long.

"Gentlemen and friends. I am no speech maker and I guess if I had to make speeches for a liveing I am afraid I couldn't do it but the boys is anxious I should say a few words about baseball and I didn't want to disappoint them. They may be some of you boys that has not followed the great American game very close and maybe don't know who Jack Keefe is. Well gentlemen I was boughten from Terre Haute in the Central League by that grand old Roman Charley Comiskey owner of the Chicago White Sox in 1913 and I been in the big league ever since except one year I was with Frisco and I stood that league on their head and Mr. Comiskey called me back and I was still starring with the Chicago White Sox when Uncle Sam sent out the call for men and I quit the great American game to enlist in the greatest game of all the game we are playing against the Kaiser and we will win this game like I have win many a game of baseball because I was to fast for them and used my brains and it will be the same with the Kaiser and America will fight to the drop of the hat and make the world safe for democracy."

Well Al I had to stop 2 or 3 minutes while they give me a hand and they clapped and hollered at pretty near everything I said. So I said "This war reminds me a good deal like a incident that happened once when I was pitching against the Detroit club. No doubt you gentlemen and officers has heard of the famous Hughey Jennings and his eeyah and on the Detroit club is also the famous Tyrus Cobb the Georgia Peach as he is called and I want to pay him a tribute right here and say he is one of the best ball players in the American League and a great hitter if you don't pitch just right to him. One time we was in Detroit for a serious of games and we had loose the first two games do to bad pitching and the first game Eddie Cicotte didn't have nothing and the second game Faber was in the same boat so on this morning I refer to Manager Rowland come up to me in the lobby of the Tuller hotel and said how do you feel Jack and I said O. K. Clarence why do you ask? And he said well we have loose 2 games here and we have got to grab this one this P. M. and if you feel O. K. I will work you because I know you have got them licked as soon as you walk out there. So I said all right Clarence you can rely on me. And that P. M. I give them 3 hits and shut them out and Cobb come up in the ninth innings with two men on bases and two men out and Ray Schalk our catcher signed me for a curve ball but I shook my head and give him my floater and the mighty Cobb hit that ball on a line to our right fielder Eddie Murphy and the game was over.

"This war is a good deal like baseball gentlemen because it is stratejy that wins and no matter how many soldiers a gen. has got he won't get nowheres without he uses his brains and its the same in baseball and the boys that stays in the big league is the boys that can think and when this war is over I hope to go back and begin where I left off and win a pennant for Charley Comiskey the old Roman in the American League."

Well Al they was a regular storm when I got through and I bowed and give them a smile and started off of the platform but a sargent named Avery from our Co. stopped me and set me down in a chair and says I was to wait a minute and I thought of course they was going to give me a cup or something though I didn't expect nothing of the kind but I hadn't no sooner set down when Sargent Avery stepped up to the front of the platform and says "Gentlemen I want to say to you that Private Jack Keefe the great stratejest is not only a great pitcher and a great speech maker but he is also a great poet and if you don't believe me I will read you this beautiful valentine that he wrote to a certain lady that we all admire and who was in the Red X canteen up till today when she went back to Paris to resume other dutys."

Well before I could make a move he read that crazy valentine and of course they wasn't a word in it that I was serious when I wrote it and it was all a joke with me only not exactly a joke neither because I was really trying to let the little lady down easy and tell her good by between the lines without being rough with it. But of course these boobs pretended like they thought I meant it all and was love sick or something and they hollered like a bunch of Indians and clapped and razed he———ll.

Well Al I didn't get a chance to see Sargent Avery after it was over because he blowed right out but I will see him tomorrow and I will find out from him who stole that poem from Miss Moselle and I wouldn't be supprised if the reason she blowed to Paris was on acct. of missing the poem and figureing some big bum had stole it off her and they would find out her secret and make things misable for her and the chances is that's why she blowed. Well wait till I find out who done it and they will be one less snake in this regt. and the sooner you weed those kind of birds out of the army you will get somewheres and if you don't you won't.

But the poor little lady Al I can't help from feeling sorry for her and I only wished I could go to Paris and find her and tell her to not worry though of course its best if she don't see me again but I'm sorry it had to come off this way.

Your pal,   Jack.

Somewheres in France, Feb. 18.

FRIEND AL: Well Al this may be the last letter you will ever get from me because I am waiting now to find out what they are going to do with me and I will explain what I mean.

Yesterday A. M. I seen Sargent Avery and I asked him if I could talk to him a minute and he says yes and I said I wanted to find out from him who stole that valentine from Miss Moselle. So he says "Who is Miss Moselle?" So I said "Why that little lady in the canteen that's blowed to Paris." So he says "Well that little lady's name isn't Miss Moselle but her name is Ruth Palmer and she is the daughter of one of the richest birds in N. Y. city and they wasn't nobody stole no valentine from her because she give the valentine to me before she left." So I said "What do you mean she give it to you?" So he says "I mean she give it to me and when she give it to me she said us birds was in the same Co. with a poet and didn't know it and she thought it was about time we was finding it out. So she laughed and give me the valentine and that's the whole story."

Well Al I had a 20 frank note on me and I asked Sargent Avery if he wouldn't like some champagne and he said no he wouldn't. But that didn't stop me Al and I got all I could hold onto and then some and I snuck in last night after lights out and I don't know if anybody was wise or not but if they are its libel to go hard with me and Capt. Seeley said something about the fireing squad for the next bird that cut loose.

Well I reported sick this A. M. and they could tell to look at me that it wasn't no stall so I'm here and the rest of the boys is gone and I am waiting for them to summons me before the court marshall. But listen Al if they do like Capt. Seeley said you can bet that before they get me I will get some of these birds that's been calling me Private Valentine ever since Saturday night.

Your pal,   Jack.

Stragety and Tragedy

Somewheres in France, March 2.

FRIEND AL: Well Al if it rains a couple more days like its been they will half to page the navy and at that its about time they give them something to do and I don't mean the chasers and destroyers and etc. that acts like convoys for our troop ships and throws them death bombs at the U boats but I mean the big battle ships and I bet you haven't heard of a supper dread 0 doing nothing since we been in the war and they say they can't do nothing till the German navy comes out and that's what they're waiting for. Well Al that's a good deal like waiting for the 30nd. of Feb. or for Jennings to send his self up to hit for Cobb and they can say all they want about the Germans being bullet proof from the neck up but they got some brains and you can bet their navy ain't comeing out no more then my hair. So as far as I can see a man being on a supper dread 0 is just like you owned a private yatch without haveing to pay for the keep up and when they talk about a man on a big U. S. battle ship in danger they mean he might maybe die because he eat to much and no exercise.

So if I was them I would send the big ships here so as we could use them for motor Lauras and I guess they's no place in our whole camp where you couldn't float them and I don't know how it is all over France but if they was a baseball league between the towns where they have got us billeted the fans would get blear eyed look-ing at the no game sign and if a mgr. worked their pitchers in turn say it was my turn tomorrow and the next time my turn come around some of little Al's kids would half to help me out of the easy chair and say "Come on granpa you pitch this afternoon."

Jokeing a side Al if I was running the training camps like Camp Grant back home instead of starting the men off with the regular

126

drills and hikes like they give them now I would stand them under a shower bath with their close on about ½ the time and when it come time for a hike I would send them back and fourth across Rock River and back where they wasn't no bridge. And then maybe when they got over here France wouldn't be such a big supprise.

One of the boys has put a sign up on our billet and it says Noahs Ark on it and maybe you have heard that old gag Al about the big flood that everybody was drownded only Noah and his folks and a married couple of every kind of animals in the world and they wasn't drownded because Noah had a Ark for them to get in out of the wet. Well Noahs Ark is a good name for our dump and believe me they haven't none of the animals been overlooked and we are also going Noah one better and sheltering all the bugs and some of them is dressed in cocky.

Well I am in this war to the finish and you couldn't hire me to quit till we have ran them ragged but I wished they had of gave us steel helmets wide enough so as they would make a bumber shoot and I hope the next war they have they will pick out Arizona to have it there.

Your pal,   Jack.

Somewheres in France, March 6.

FRIEND AL: Well Al I suppose you have read in the communicates that comes out in the paper where the Americans that's all ready in the trenchs has pulled off some great stuff and a whole lot of them has been sighted and give meddles and etc. by the Frenchmens for what they have pulled off and the way they work it Al when one of the soldiers wrists his life or something and pulls off something big like taking a mess of prisoners and bringing them back here where they can get something to eat the French pins a meddle on them and sometimes they do it if you don't do nothing but die only then of course they send it to your family so as they will have something to show their friends besides snapshots of Mich. City.

Well we was kidding back and fourth about it today and one of the smart alex in our Co. a bird named Johnny Alcock that is always trying to kid somebody all the time he said to me "Well I suppose they will half to build more tonnages to carry all the meddles you will win back to the states." So I said "Well I guess I will win as many of them as you will win." That shut him up for a wile but finely he says "You have got enough chest to wear a whole junk shop on it." So I said "Well I am not the baby that can't win them." So he says "If you ever happen to be snooping around the bosh trenchs when Fritz climbs over the top you will come back so fast that the Kaiser will want to know who was that speed merchant that led the charge and decorate you with a iron cross." So I said "I will decorate you right in the eye one of these days." So he had to shut up and all the other boys give him the laugh.

Well Al jokeing to one side if I half to go back home without a meddle it will be because they are playing favorites but I guess I wouldn't be left out at that because I stand ace high with most of the Frenchmens around here because they like a man that's always got a smile or a kind word for them and they would like me still better yet if they could understand more English and get my stuff better but it don't seem like they even try to learn and I suppose its because they figure the war is in their country so everybody should ought to talk their language but when you get down to cases they's a big job on both our hands and if one of us has got to talk the others language why and the he——ll should they pick on the one that's hard to learn it and besides its 2 to 1 you might say because the U. S. and the English uses the same language and they's nobody only the French that talks like they do because they couldn't nobody else talk that way so why wouldn't it be the square thing for them to forget theirs and tackle ours and it would prolongate their lifes to do it because most of their words can't be said without straining yourself and no matter what kind of a physic you got its bound to wear you down in time.

But I suppose the French soldiers figure they have got enough of a job on their hands remembering their different uniforms and who to salute and etc. and they have got a fine system in the French army Al because you wear whatever you was before you got to be what you are that is sometimes. For inst. suppose you use to be in the artillery and now you are a aviator you still wear a artillery uniform part of the time and its like I use to pitch for the White Sox and I guess I would be a pretty looking bird if I waddled around in the mire here a wile with my old baseball unie on me and soon people would begin to think I was drafted from the Toledo Mud Hens.

Seriously Al sometimes you see 4 or 5 French officers comeing along and they haven't one of them got the same color uniform on but they are all dressed up like a Roman candle you might say and if their uniforms run when they got wet a man could let them drip into a pail and drink it up for a pussy cafe.

Well Al the boys in our regt. is going to get out a newspaper and get it out themself and it will be just the news about our regt. and a few gags and comical storys about the different boys and they are going to get it out once per wk.

Corp. Pierson from our Co. that use to work on a newspaper somewheres is going to be the editor and he wants I should write them up something about baseball and how to pitch and etc. but I don't believe in a man waisting their time on a childs play like writeing up articles for a newspaper but just to stall him I said I would try and think up something and give it to him when I had it wrote up. Well him waiting for my article will be like me waiting for mail because I don't want nobody to take me for a newspaper man because I seen enough of them in baseball and one time we was playing in Phila. and I had them shut out up to the 8th inning and all of a sudden Weaver and Collins got a stroke of paralysis and tipped their caps to a couple ground balls that grazed their shoe laces and then Rube Oldring hit one on a line right at Gandil and he tried to catch it on the bounce off his lap and Bill Dinneen's right arm was lame and he begin calling everything a ball and first thing you know they beat us 9 to 2 or something and Robbins one of the Chi paper reporters that traveled with us wired a telegram home to his paper that Phila. was supposed to be a town where a man could get plenty of sleep but I looked like I had set up all the nights we was there and of course Florrie seen it in the paper and got delirious and I would of busted Robbins in the jaw only I wasn't sure if he realy wrote it that way or the telegraph operator might of balled it up.

So they won't be no newspaper articles in mine Al but I will be anxious to see what Pierson's paper looks like when it comes out and I bet it will be a fine paper if our bunch have the writeing of it because the most of them would drop in a swoon if you asked them how to spell their name.

Your pal,   Jack.

Somewheres in France, March 9.

Friend Al: Well Al I guess I all ready told you about them getting up a newspaper in our regt. and Joe Pierson asked me would I write them up something for it and I told him no I wouldn't but it seems like he overheard me and thought I said I would so any way he was expecting something from me so last night I wrote them up something and I don't know if the paper will ever get printed or not so I will coppy down a part of what I wrote to give you a idear of what I wrote. He wanted I should write them up something about the stragety of baseball and where it was like the stragety in the war because one night last month I give them a little talk at one of their entertainments about how the man that used their brains in base-ball was the one that win just like in the army but I guess I all

ready told you about me giveing them that little talk and afterwards I got a skinfull of the old grape and I thought sure they
would have me up in front of the old court marshall but they never
knowed the difference on acct. of the way I can handle it and you
take the most of the boys and if they see a cork they want to kiss
the Colonel. Well any way here is the article I wrote up and I called
it War and Baseball 2 games where brains wins.

"The gen. public that go out to the baseball park and set
through the games probably think they see everything that is going
on on the field but they's a lot of stuff that goes on on the baseball
field that the gen. public don't see and don't know nothing about
and I refer to what we baseball boys calls inside baseball.

"No one is in a better position to know all about inside baseball
then a man like I who have been a pitcher in the big league because
it is the pitchers that has to do most of the thinking and pull off the
smart plays that is what wins ball games. For inst. I will write down
about a little incidents that come off one time 2 yrs. ago when the
Boston club was playing against the Chicago White Sox where I was
one of the stars when the U. S. went into the war and then I
dropped baseball and signed up a contract with Uncle Sam to play
for my country in the big game against the Kaiser of Germany. This
day I refer to I was in there giveing them the best I had but we was
in a tight game because the boys was not hitting behind me though
Carl Mays that was pitching for the Boston club didn't have nothing
on the ball only the cover and after the ball left his hand you could
have ran in the club house and changed your undershirt and still be
back in time to swing when the ball got up there.

"Well it come along the 9th. inning and we was tied up with
the score 2 and 2 and I had Larry Gardner swinging like a ham-
mock all day but this time he hit a fly ball that either Weaver or
Jackson ought to of caught in a hollow tooth but they both layed
down and died on it and Gardner got on second base. Well they
was 2 men out and Hoblitzel was the next man up and the next
man after he was Scott their shortstop that couldn't take the ball in

his hand and make a base hit off a man like I so instead of me give-ing Hobby a ball to hit I walked him as we call it and then of course it was Scott's turn to bat and Barry their mgr. hesitated if he should send Ruth up to hit for Scott or not but finely he left Scott go up there and he was just dragging his bat off his shoulder to swing at the first strike when I whizzed the third one past him.

"That is what we call inside baseball or stragety whether its in baseball or war is walking a man like Hoblitzel that might be lucky enough to hit one somewheres but if you don't give him nothing to hit how can he hit it and then I made Scott look like he had been sent for but couldn't come. Afterwards in the 11th. inning Duffy Lewis hit a ball that he ought to of been traded for even swinging at it because it come near clipping his ear lob but any way he swang at it and hit it for three bases because Jackson layed down and died going after it and Lewis scored on a past ball and they beat us 3 to 2.

"So that is what we call stragety on the baseball field and it wins there the same like in war and this war will be win by the side that has gens. with brains and use them and I figure where a man that has been in big league baseball where you can't never make a success out of it unless you are a quick thinker and they have got a big advantage over men that's been in the other walks of life where its most all luck and I figure the army would be a whole lot better off if all the officers and gens. had of played baseball in the big leagues and learned to think quick, but of course they ain't every-body that have got the ability to play baseball and stand the gaff but the man that has got the ability and been through the ropes is just that much ahead of the rest of them and its to bad that most of our gens. is so old that they couldn't of knew much about baseball since it become a test of brains like it is now.

"I am afraid I have eat up a lot of space with my little Article on War and Baseball so I will end this little article up with a little comical incidents that happened dureing our training trip down in Mineral Wells, Tex. a year ago this spring. The first day we was out for practice they was a young outfielder from a bush league and Mgr. Rowland told him to go out in right field and shag and this was his reply. 'I haven't never been in this park before so you will half to tell me which is right field.' Of course right field is the same field in all parks and that is what made the incidents so comical and some of the boys is certainly green when they first break in and we have manys the laugh at their expense."

That is what I wrote up for them Al and I wound it up with that little story and I was reading over what I wrote and Johnny Alcock seen me reading it and asked me to leave him see it so I showed it to him and he said it was great stuff and he hadn't never dreamt they was that much stragety in baseball and he thought if some of the officers seen it they would pop their eyes out and they would want to talk to me and get my idears and see if maybe they couldn't some of them be plied to war fair and maybe if I showed them where it could I would get promoted and stuck on to the gen. staff that's all made up from gens. that lays out the attacks and etc.

Well Al Alcock is a pretty wise bird and a fine boy to if you know how to take him and he seen right off what I was getting at in my article and its true Al that the 2 games is like the other and quick thinking is what wins in both of them. But I am not looking for no staff job that you don't half to go up in the trenchs and fight but just lay around in some office somewheres and stick pins in a map while the rest of the boys is sticking bayonets in the Dutchmen's maps so I hope they don't none of the gens. see what I wrote because I come over here to fight and be a soldier and carry a riffle instead of a pin cushion.

But it don't hurt nothing for me to give them a few hints once in a wile about useing their brains if they have got them and if I can do any good with my articles in the papers why I would just as leaf wear my fingers to the bone writeing them up.

Your pal,   Jack.

Somewheres in France, March 13.

FRIEND AL: Well Al I bet you will pretty near fall over in a swoon when you read what I have got to tell you. Before you get this letter you will probably all ready of got a coppy of the paper I told you about because it come out the day before yesterday and I sent you a coppy with my article in it only they cut a part of it out on acct. of not haveing enough space for all of it but they left the best part of it in.

Well Al somebody must of a sent a coppy to Gen. Pershing and marked up what I wrote up so as he would be sure and see it and probably one of the officers done it. Well that's either here or there but this afternoon when we come in they was a letter for me and who do you think it was from Al. Well you can't never even begin to guess so I will tell you. It was from Gen. Pershing Al and it come from Paris where he is at and I have got it here laying on the table and I would send it to you to look at only I wouldn't take no chances of looseing it and I don't mean you wouldn't be care-full of it Al but of course the mail has got to go across the old pond and if the Dutchmens periscoped the boat the letter was on it it would be good night letter and a letter like this here is something to be proud of and hold onto it and keep it for little Al till he grows up big enough to appreciate it. But they's nothing to prevent me from copping down the letter so as you can read what it says and here it is.

PRIVATE KEEFE,

DEAR SIR: My attention was called today to an article writ-ten by you in your regimental paper under the title War and Baseball: Two Games Where Brains Wins. In this article you state that our generals would be better able to accomplish their task if they had enjoyed the benefits of strategic train-ing in baseball. I have always been a great admirer of the na-tional game of baseball and I heartily agree with what you say. But unfortunately only a few of us ever possessed the ability to play your game and the few never were proficient enough to play it professionally. Therefore the general staff is obliged to blunder along without that capacity for quick thinking which is acquired only on the baseball field.

But I believe in making use of all the talent in my army, even among the rank and file. Therefore I respectfully ask whether you think some of your baseball secrets would be of strategic value to us in the prosecution of this war and if so whether you would be willing to provide us with the same.

If it is not too much trouble, I would be pleased to hear from you along these lines, and if you have any suggestion to make regarding a campaign against our enemy, either offensive or defensive, I would be pleased to have you outline it in a letter to me.

By the way I note with pleasure that our first names are the same. It makes a sort of bond between us which I trust will be further cemented if you can be of assistance to me in my task.

I shall eagerly await your reply.

Sincerely,
BLACK JACK PERSHING,
Folies Bergere, Paris, France.

That is the letter I got from him Al and I'll say its some letter and I bet if some of these smart alex officers seen it it would reduce some of the swelling in their chest but I consider the letter confidential Al and I haven't showed it to nobody only 3 or 4 of my buddys and I showed it to Johnny Alcock and he popped his eyes out so far you could of snipped them off with a shears. And he said it was a cinch that Pershing realy wrote it on acct. of him signing it Black Jack Pershing and they wouldn't nobody else sign it that way because it was a private nickname between he and some of his friends and they wouldn't nobody else know about it.

So then he asked was I going to answer the letter and I said of course I was and he says well I better take a whole lot of pains with my answer and study up the situation before I wrote it and put some good idears in it and if my letters made a hit with Gen. Pershing the next thing you know he would probably summons me to Paris and maybe stick me on the war board so as all I would half to do would be figure up plans of attacks and etc. and not half to go up in the trenchs and wrist my life and probably get splattered all over France.

So I said "Well I am not looking for no excuse to get out of the trenchs but its just the other way and I am nuts to get in them." So he says "You must be." But he showed me where it would be a great experience to set in at them meetings even if I didn't have much to say and just set there and listen and hear their plans and what's comeing off and besides I would get a chance to see something of Paris and it don't look like none of us only the officers would be give leave to go there but of course I would go if Black Jack wanted me and after all Al I am here to give Uncle Sam the best I have got and if I can serve the stars and strips better by sticking pins in a map then getting in the trenchs why all right and it takes more than common soldiers to win a war and if I am more use to them as a kind of adviser instead of carrying a bayonet why I will sacrifice my own feelings for the good of the cause like I often done in baseball.

But they's another thing Alcock told me Al and that is that the war board they have got has got gens. on it from all the different countrys like the U. S. and England and France and Spain and of course they are more French gens. than anything else on acct. of the war being here in France so probably they do some of their talking in French and Alcock says if he was I he would get busy and try and learn enough French so as I could make myself understood when I had something to say and of course they probably won't nothing come out of it all but still and all I always say its best to be ready for whatever comes off and if the U. S. had of been ready for this war I wouldn't be setting here writeing this letter now but I would be takeing a plunge in one of them Berlin brewry vats.

Any way I have all ready picked enough French so as I can talk it pretty good and I would be O. K. if I could understand it when they are talking it off but to hear them talk it off you would think they seen their dinner at the end of the sentence.

Well Al I will tell you how things comes out and I hope Black Jack will forget all about it and lay off me so as I can get into the real fighting instead of standing in front of a map all the wile like a school teacher or something and I all most wished I hadn't never wrote that article and then of course the idear wouldn't of never came to Black Jack that I could help him but if he does take me on his staff it will be some pair of Jacks eh Al and enough to open the pot and if the Germans is sucker enough to stay in they will get their whiskers cinched.

Your pal,   Jack.

Somewheres in France, March 14.

FRIEND AL: Well this is the second letter I have wrote today and the other one is to Gen. Pershing and I have still got the letter here yet Al and I will coppy it down and tell you what I wrote to him.

GEN. JACK PERSHING,
Care Folies Bergere, Paris, France

DEAR GEN: You can bet I was supprised to get a letter from you and when I wrote that article I didn't have no idear that they would something come out of it. Well Gen. I come into the army expecting to fight and lay down my life if nessary and I am not one of the kind that are looking for an out and trying to hide behind a desk or something because I am afraid to go into the trenchs but I guess if you know something about baseball you won't accuse me from not having the old nerve because they can't no man hold onto a job in the big leagues unless a man is fearless and does their best work under fire and especially a pitcher. But if you figure that I can serve old glory better some other way then in the rank and files I am willing to sacrifice myself like I often done in baseball. Anything to win Gen. is the way I look at it.

You asked me in your letter did I think some of my idears would help out well gen. a man don't like to sound like they was bragging themself up but this isn't no time for monking and I guess you want the truth. Well gen. I don't know much about running a army and their plans but stragety is the same if its on the battle field or the baseball diamond you might say and it just means how can we beat them and I often say that the men that can use their brains will win any kind of a game except maybe some college Willy boy game like football or bridge whist.

Well gen. without no bragging myself up I learned a whole lot about stragety on the baseball field and I think I could help you in a good many ways but before I tried to tell you how to do something I would half to know what you was trying to do and of course I know you can't tell me in a letter on acct. of the censors and of course they are Americans to but they's a whole lot of the boys that don't mean no harm but they are gabby and can't keep their mouth shut and who knows who would get a hold of it and for the same reason I don't feel like I should give you any of my idears by mail but if I could just see you and we could have a little talk and talk things over but I don't suppose they's any chance of that unless I could get leave off to run down to Paris for a wile and meet you somewheres but they won't give us no leave to go to Paris but of course a letter from you that I could show it to Capt. Seeley would fix it up and no questions asked.

So I guess I better wait till I hear from you along these lines and in the mean wile I will be thinking the situation over and see what I can think up and I all ready got some idears that I feel like they would work out O. K. and I hope I will get a chance in the near future to have a little chat with you.

I note what you say about our name being both Jack and I was thinking to myself that lots of times in a poker game a pair of jacks is enough to win and maybe it will be the same way in the war game and any way I guess the 2 of us could put up a good bluff and bet them just as if we had them. Eh gen?

Respy,
Jack Keefe.

That's what I wrote to him Al and he will get it some time to-morrow or the next day and I should ought to hear from him back right away and I hope he will take my hint and leave me stay here with my regt. where I can see some real action. But if he summonses me I will go Al and not whine about getting a raw deal.

Well I happened to drop into a estaminet here yesterday and that's kind of a store where a man can buy stuff to take along with him or you can get a cup of coffee or pretty near anything and they was a girl on the job in there and she smiled when I come in and I smiled at her back and she seen I was American so she begin talking to me in English only she has got some brogue and its hard to make it out what she is trying to get at. Well we talked a wile and all of a sudden the idear come to me that I and her could hit it off and both do the other some good by her learning me French and I could learn her English and so I sprung it on her and she was tickled to death and we called it a bargain and tomorrow we are going to have our first lessons and how is that Al for a bargain when I can pick up French without it costing me a nickle and of course they won't be

139

only time for 1 or 2 lessons before I hear from Black Jack but I can learn a whole lot in 2 lessons if she will tend to business but the way she smiled at me when I come out and the looks she give me I am afraid if she seen much of me it would be good night so I will half to show her I won't stand for no foolishness because I had enough flirtations Al and the next woman that looks X eyed at me will catch her death of cold.

Your pal,   Jack.

Somewheres in France, March 16.

FRIEND AL: Well old pal it looks like they wouldn't be no front line trenchs for this baby and what I am getting at is that the word was past around today that Black Jack himself is comeing and they isn't no faulse alarm about it because Capt. Seeley told us himself and said Gen. Pershing would be here in a day or 2 to overlook us and he wanted that everybody should look their best and keep themself looking neat and clean and clean up all the billets and etc. because that was what Gen. Pershing was comeing to see, how we look and how we are getting along and etc.

Well Al that's what Capt. Seeley said but between you and I they's another reason why he is comeing and I guess he figures they will be a better chance to talk things over down here then if I was to go to Paris and I am not the only one that knows why he is comeing because after supper Alcock called me over to 1 side and congratulated me and said it looked like I was in soft.

Well I will be ready for him when he comes and I will be ready to pack up and blow out of here at a minute's notice and I can't help from wondring what some of these smart alex officers will say when they see what's comeing off. So this won't be only a short letter Al because I have got a lot to do to get ready and what I am going to do is write down some of my idears so as I can read them off to him when he comes and if I didn't have them wrote down I might maybe get nervous when I seen him and maybe forget what I got to say because the boys says he's a tough bird for a man to see for the first time till you get to know him and he acts like he was going to eat you alive but he's a whole lot like a dog when you get to know him and his bark is worse then a bite.

Well Al how is that for news and I guess you will be prouder then ever of your old pal before this business gets over with and I would feel pretty good with everything breaking so good only I am getting worried about Ernestine that little French gal in the estaminet and I wished now I hadn't never seen her or made no bargain with her and I didn't do it so much for what I could learn off of her but these French gals Al has had a tough time of it and if a man can bring a little sunshine into their life he wouldn't be a man unless he done it. So I was just trying to be a good fellow and here is what I get for it because I caught her today Al with that look in her eye that I seen in so many of them and I know what it means and I guess about the best thing for me to do is run away from Gen. Pershing and go over the top or something and leave the boshs shoot my nose off or mess me up some way and then maybe I won't get pestered to death every time I try and be kind to some little gal.

I guess the French lessons will half to be cut out because it wouldn't be square to leave her see me again and it would be different if I could tell her I am married but I don't know the French terms for it and besides it don't seem to make no difference to some of them and the way they act you would think a wife was just something that come out on you like a sty and the best way to do was just to forget it.

Well Al as I say I caught her looking at me like it was breaking her heart and I wouldn't be supprised if she cried after I come away, but what can a man do about it Al and I have got a good notion to wear my gas mask everywhere I go and then maybe I will have a little peace once in a wile.

I must close now for this time and get busy on some idears so as Black Jack won't catch me flat footed but I guess they's no danger of that eh Al?

Your pal,   Jack.

Somewheres in France, March 18.

FRIEND AL: Well old pal I am all set for Gen. Pershing when he comes and I have got some of my idears wrote down just the bear outlines of them and when he asks me if I have got any I can just read them off from my notes like 1 was a lecture and here is a few of the notes I have got wrote down so you can get some idear of what I am going to spring on him.

1

In baseball many big league mgrs. before a game they talk it over in the club house with their men and disgust the weakness of the other club and how is the best way to beat them and etc. For inst. when I was pitching for the White Sox and suppose we was going to face a pitcher that maybe he was weak on fielding bunts so before the game Mgr. Rowland would say to us "Remember boys this baby so and so gets the rabbis if you lay down bunts on him." So we would begin laying them down on him and the first thing you know he would be frothing at the mouth and triping all over himself and maybe if he did finely get a hold of the ball he would throw it into the Southren League or somewheres and before the other mgr. could get another bird warmed up they would half to hire a crossing policeman to straiten out the jam at the plate. And the same thing would be in war like in baseball and instead of a army going into it blind you might say, why the gens. ought to get together before the battle and fix it up to work on the other side's weakness. For inst. suppose the Germans is weak on getting out of

142

the way of riffle bullets why that's the weapon to use on them and make a sucker out of them.

2

Getting the jump on your oppts. is more then ½ the battle whether its in the war or on the baseball field and many a game has been win by getting the jump on your oppts. For inst. that reminds me of a little incidents that happened one day when we was playing the Washington club and I was pitching against the notorious Walter Johnson and before they was a man out Geo. McBride booted one and Collins and Jackson got a couple hits and we was 2 runs to the good before they was a man out. Well Johnson come back pretty good and the rest of the game the boys acted like they was scared of him and kept one foot in the water bucket but we would of win the game at that only in the 9th. inning Schalk dropped a third strike on me and Judge and Milan hit a couple of fly balls that would of been easy outs only for the wind but the wind raised havioc with the ball and they both went for hits and they beat us 3 to 2 and that's the kind of luck I genally always had against the Washington club.

3

In baseball of course they's only nine men on a side and that is where a gen. in the war has got the advantage on a mgr. in baseball because they's no rules in war fair to keep a man from useing all the men he feels like so it looks to me like a gen. had all the best of it because suppose the other side only had say 50 thousand men in a certain section they's nothing to prevent a gen. from going after them with a 100 thousand men and if he can't run them ragged when you got to them 2 to 1 its time to enlist in the G. A. R. All though as I say a mgr. can't only use nine men at a time in baseball, but at that I know of incidents where a mgr. has took advantage of the oppts. being shy of men and one time the St. Louis club came to Chi and Jones was all crippled up for pitchers but the game was on our home grounds so it was up to Mgr. Rowland to say if the game should be played or if he should call it off on acct. of cold weather because it was in the spring. But he knowed Jones was shy of pitchers so he made him play the game and Jones used big Laudermilk to pitch against us and they beat us 5 and 2.

4

Another advantage where a gen. got it on a baseball mgr. because in baseball the game begins at 3 o'clock and the other club knows when its going to begin just the same as your club so they can't neither club beat the other one to it and start the game wile the other club is looking out the window.

But a gen. don't half to tell the other side when he is going to attack them but of course they have observers that can see when you are going to get ready to pull something. But it looks to me like the observers wouldn't be worth a hoop and he——ll if the other gen. made his preparations at night when it was dark like bringing up the troops and artilery and supplys and etc. and in that way you could take them by supprise and make them look like a fool, like in baseball I have often crossed the batter up and one day I had Cobb 3 and 2 and he was all set to murder a fast one and I dinked a slow one up there to him and the lucky stiff hit it on the end of his bat just inside third base and 2 men scored on it.

That's about the idears I am going to give him Al only of course I can talk it off better then I can write it because wile I am talking I can think up a lot more incidents to tell him and him being a baseball fan he will set there pop eyed with his mouth open as long as I want to talk. But now I can't hardly wait for him to get here Al and it seems funny to think that here I am a $30 dollar a mo. doughboy and maybe in a few days I will be on the staff and they don't have nobody only officers and even a lieut. gets 5 or 6 times as much as a doughboy and how is that for a fine nickname Al for men that all the dough they are getting is a $1 per day and the pollutes only gets 2 Sues a day and that's about 2 cents so I suppose we ought to call them the Wall St. crowd.

Well Al you should ought to be thankfull you are there at home with your wife where you can watch her and keep your eyes on her and find out what she is doing with her spare time though I guess at that they wouldn't be much danger of old Bertha running a muck and I don't suppose she would half to wear bob wire entanglements to keep Jack the Kisser away but when a man has got a wife like Florrie and here I am over here and there she is over there well Al a man don't get to sleep no quicker nights from thinking about it and I lay there night after night and wonder what and the he——ll can she be doing and she might be doing most anything Al and they's only the one thing that its a cinch she ain't doing and that's writeing a letter to me and a man would pretty near think she had forgot my first name but even at that she could set down and write to me and start it out Dear Husband.

But the way she acts why even if they was any fun over here I wouldn't be haveing it and suppose I do get on Gen. Pershing's staff and get a lieut. or something and write and tell her about it, why she would probably wait till a legal holiday to answer me back and then she would write about 10 words and say she went to the Palace last week and when she come out after the show it was raining.

Well Al you can't blame a man for anything he pulls off when their wife acts like that and if I give that little Ernestine a smack the next time she bulges her lips out at me whose fault is it Al? Not mine.

Your pal,   Jack.

Somewheres in France, March 20.

FRIEND AL: Well Al the sooner the Germans starts their drive let them come and I only hope we are up there when they start it and believe me Al if they come at us with the gas I will dive into it with my mouth wide open and see how much of it I can get because they's no use Al of a man trying to live with the kind of luck I have got and I'm sick in tired of it all.

Wait till you hear what come off today Al. In the first place my feet's been going back on me for a long wile and they walked us all over France yesterday and this A. M. I couldn't hardly get my shoes on and they was going out for riffle practice and I don't need no riffle practice Al and besides that I couldn't of stood it so I got excused and I set around a wile after the rest of the bunch was gone and finely my feet got feeling a little better and I walked over to the es-taminet where that little gal's at to see if maybe I couldn't brighten things up a little for her and sure enough she was all smiles when she seen me and we talked a wile about this in that and she tried to get personal and called me cherry which is like we say dearie and finely I made the remark that I didn't think we would be here much longer and then I seen she was going to blubber so I kind of petted her hand and stroked her hair and she poked her lips out and I give her a smack Al but just like you would kiss a kid or something after they fell down and hurt themself. Well Al just as this was comeing off the door to the other part of the joint opened up and in come her old man and seen it and I thought all French-mens talked fast Al but this old bird made them sound like a im-pediment and he come at me and if he hadn't been so old I would of crowned him but of course I couldn't do nothing only let him rave and finely I felt kind of sorry for him and I had a 20 frank note on me so I shoved it at him and it struck him dumb Al and I got out of there and come back to the Ark and it seems like I had been away a whole lot longer then I meant to and any way I hadn't hardly no more then got my shoes off and layed down when in come some of the boys.

Well Al what do you think? Gen. Pershing was out there to the riffle practice to overlook them and I suppose he heard we was going to be out there and he went out there to be sure and catch me and he was makeing a visit around the camp and instead of him stopping here he went out there to see us and instead of me being out there Al, here I was mixed up in a riot with an old goof over nothing you might say and Black Jack wondring where and the he——ll could I be at because Alcock told me he noticed him looking around like he mist somebody. And now he's on his way back to Paris and probably sore as a boil and I can't do nothing only wait to hear from him and probably he will just decide to pass me up.

And the worst of it is Al that when they brought us the mail they was 2 letters for me from Florrie and I couldn't of asked for nicer letters if I had wrote them myself only why and the he——ll couldn't she of wrote them a day sooner and I would of no more thought of getting excused today then fly because if I had knew how my Mrs. mist me and how much she cares I wouldn't of been waisting no time on no Ernestine but its to late now and Black Jack's gone and so is my 20 franks and believe me Al 20 frank notes is tray pew over here. I'll say they are.

Your pal,   Jack.

Decorated

Somewheres in France, April 2.

FRIEND AL: Well Al yesterday was April Fool and you ought to seen what I pulled on 1 of the boys Johnny Alcock and it was a screen and some of the boys is still laughing over it yet but he is 1 of the kind that he can't see a joke at their own expenses and he swelled up like a poison pup and now he is talking about he will get even with me, but the bird that gets even with me will half to get up a long time before revelry eh Al.

Well Al I will tell you what I pulled on him and I bet you will bust your sides. Well it seems like Johnny has got a girl in his home town Riverside, Ill. near Chi and that is he don't know if he has got her or not because him and another bird was both makeing a play for her, but before he come away she told him to not worry, but the other bird got himself excused out of the draft with a cold sore or something and is still there in the old town yet where he can go and call on her every night and she is libel to figure that maybe she better marry him so as she can have some of her evenings to herself and any way she might as well of told Johnny to not scratch himself over here as to not worry because for some reason another the gal didn't write to him last month at lease he didn't get no letters and maybe they got lost or she had writers cramps or something but any way every time the mail come and nothing for him he looked like he had been caught off second base.

Well the day before yesterday he was reading 1 of the letters he got from this baby 5 or 6 wks. ago on acct. of not haveing nothing better to read and he left the envelope lay on the floor and I was going to hand it back to him but I happened to think that yesterday would be April Fool so I kept a hold of the envelope and I got a piece of paper and wrote April Fool on it and stuck it in the envelope and fixed it up so as it would look like a new letter and I handed it to him yesterday like it was mail that had only just came for him and you ought to see him when he tore it open and didn't find nothing only April Fool in it. At first he couldn't say nothing but finely he says "That's some comedy Keefe. You ought to be a end man in the stretcher bearers minstrels" and he didn't crack a smile so I said "What's the matter with you can't you take a joke?" So he said "What I would like to take is a crack at your jaw." So I said "Well it's to bad your arms is both paralyzed." Well Al they's nothing the matter with his arms and I was just kidding him because as far as him hitting anybody is conserned I was just as safe as the gen. staff because he ain't much bigger than a cutie and for him to reach my jaw he would half to join the aviation.

Well of course he didn't start nothing but just said he would get back at me if it took him till the duration of the war and I told some of the other boys about putting it over on him and they couldn't hardly help from smileing but he acts like a baby and don't speak to me and I suppose maybe he thinks that makes me feel bad but I got to be 25 yrs. old before I ever seen him and if his head was blowed off tomorrow A. M. I would try and show up for my 3 meals a day if you could call them that.

But speaking about April Fool Al I just stopped writeing to try and light a cigarette with 1 of these here French matchs and every one of them is a April Fool and I guess the parents of the kids over here don't never half to worry about them smokeing to young because even if they had a box of cigarettes hid in their cradle they would be of age before they would run across a match that lit and I wouldn't be scared to give little Al a bunch and turn him loose in a bbl. of gasoline.

Well Al I suppose you been reading in the papers about the Dutchmens starting a drive vs. the English up in the northren part of the section and at first it looked like the English was going to leave them walk into the Gulf Stream and scald themself to death, but now it seems like we have got them slowed up at lease that's

149

the dope we get here but for all the news we get a hold of we might as well of jumped to the codfish league on the way over and once in a wile some of the boys gets a U. S. paper a mo. old but they hog onto it and don't leave nobody else see it but as far as I am con-serned they can keep it because I haven't no time to waist reading about the Frisco fair or the Federal League has blowed up and etc. And of course they's plenty of newspapers from Paris but all printed in la la la so as every time you come to a word you half to rumage through a dictionary and even when you run it down its libel to mean 20 different articles and by the time you figured out whether they are talking about a st. car or a hot bath or a raisin or what and the he——ll they are talking about they wouldn't be no more news to it then the bible and it looks to me Al like it would be a good idear if you was to drop me a post card when the war is over so as I can tell Capt. Seeley or he will still be running us ragged to get in shape a couple of yrs. after the last of the Dutch-mens lays molting in the grave.

Jokeing to 1 side Al you probably know what's going on a long wile before we do and the only chance we would have to know how a battle come out would be if we was in it and they's no chance of that unless they send us up to the northern part of the section to help out because Van Hindenburg must have something under his hat besides bristles and he ain't a sucker enough to start driveing vs. the front that we are behind it unless he is so homesick that he can't stand it no longer in France.

Your pal,   Jack.

Somewheres in France, April 6.

FRIEND AL: Well Al 1 of the Chi newspapers is getting out a paper in Paris and printed in English and I just seen a copy of it where the Allys has finely got wise to themself and made 1 man gen. of all the Allys and it was a sucker play to not do that long ago only it looks to me like they pulled another boner by makeing a French-man the gen. and I suppose they done it for a complement to the Frenchmens on acct. of the war being here, but even suppose this here Foch is a smart gen. and use his brains and etc. it looks to me like it would of been a whole lot better to of picked out a man that can speak English because suppose we was all in a big battle or something and he wanted we should go over the top and if he said it in French why most of the boys hasn't made no attempts to mas-ter the language and as far as they was conserned he might as well be telling them to wash their neck. Or else they would half to be interpeters to translate it out in English what he was getting at and by the time he give the orders to fire and the interpeter looked it up and seen what it meant in English and then tell us about it the Dutchmens would be putting peep holes through us with a bayo-net and besides the French word for fire in English is feu in French and you say it like it was few and if Gen. Foch yelled few we might think he was complaining of the heat.

But at that its better to have 1 man running it even a French-man then a lot of different gens. telling us to do this in that and the other thing every one of them different and suppose they done that in baseball Al and a club had 3 or 4 mgrs. and suppose for inst. it come up to the 9th. inning and we needed some runs and it was Benz's turn to hit and 1 mgr. would tell him to go up and hit for himself and another mgr. would tell Murphy to go up and hit for him and another mgr. would send Risberg up and an-other would send Russell and the next thing you know they would be 2 of them swinging from 1 side of the plate and 2 from the other side and probably busting each other in the bean with their bats but you take most bird's beans and what would break would be Mr. Bat. But its the same in war like in baseball and you got to have 1 man running it. With a lot of different gens. in command, 1 of them might tell the men to charge while another was telling them to pay cash.

Jokeing to 1 side Al some of our boys have overtook a section up along the Moose river and I wouldn't dast write about it only its been printed in the papers all ready so I am not giveing away no secrets to the Dutchmens. At lease they don't mind us writeing something that's came out in the papers though as far as I can see how would the Dutchmens know it any more if it was in the papers or not, because they ain't so choked with jack over in Germany that they are going to spend it on U. S. papers a mo. old and even when they got them they would half to find somebody that could read English and hadn't been killed for it and it would be like as if I should spend part of my $15 a mo. subscribeing to the Chop Suey Bladder that you would half to lay on your stomach and hold it with your feet to get it right side up and even then it wouldn't mean nothing. But any way the Dutchmens is going to know sooner or later that we are in the war and what's the differents if they meet us at the Moose or the Elks? Jokeing a side Al I guess you won't be supprised to hear how I have picked up in the riffle practice and I knew right along that I couldn't hardly help from being a A No. 1 marksman because a man that had almost perfect control in pitching you might say would be bound to shoot straight when they got the hang of it and don't be supprised if I write you 1 of these days that I been appointed a snipper that sets up in a tree somewheres and picks off the boshs whenever they stick their head up and they call them snippers so pretty soon my name is libel to be Jake Snipe instead of Jack Keefe, but seriously Al I can pick off them targets like they was cherrys or something and maybe I won't half to go in the trenchs at all.

I guess I all ready told you about that little trick I pulled on Johnny Alcock for a April Fool gag and at first he swelled up like a poison pup and wouldn't talk to me and said he wouldn't never rest till he got even. Well he finely got a real letter from the gal back home and she is still waiting for him yet so he feels O. K. again and I and him are on speaking turns again and I am glad to not be scraping with him because I don't never feel right unless I am pals with everybody but they can't nobody stay sore at me very long and even when some of the boys in baseball use to swell up when I pulled 1 of my gags on them it wouldn't last long because I would just smile at them and they would half to smile back and be pals and I always say that if a man can't take a joke he better take acid or something and make a corps out of himself instead of a monkey.

Your pal,   Jack.

Somewheres in France, April 11.

FRIEND AL: Well Al I don't suppose you knew I was a detective but when it comes to being a dick it looks like I don't half to salute Wm. Burns or Shylock or none of them.

Seriously Al I come onto something today that may turn out to be something big and then again it may not but it looks like it was something big only of course it has got to be kept a secret till I get the goods on a certain bird and I won't pull it till I have got him right and in that way he won't suspect nothing until its to late. But I know you wouldn't breath a word about it and besides it wouldn't hurt nothing if you did because by the time you get this letter the whole thing will be over and this bird to who I refer will probably own a peace of land in France with a 2 ft. frontidge and 6 ft. deep. But you will wonder what am I trying to get at so maybe I better explain myself.

Well Al they's a big bird in our Co. name Geo. Shaffer and that's a German name because look at Schaefer that use to play ball in our league and it was spelt different but they called him Germany and he thought he was funny and use to pull gags on the field but I guess he didn't feel so funny the day Griffith sent him up to hit against me in the pinch 1 day at Washington and if the ball he hit had of went straight out instead of straight up it would of pretty near cleared the infield. But any way this bird Shaffer in our

Co. is big enough to have a corporal to himself and they must of
spent the first Liberty Loan on his uniform and he hasn't hardly
said a word since we been in France and for a wile we figured it
was just because he was a crab and to grouchy to talk, but now I
wouldn't be supprised Al if the real reason was on acct. of him
being a Dutchman and maybe can't talk English very good. Well I
would feel pretty mean to be spying on most of the boys that's
been good pals with me, but when a man is a pro German spy himself they's no question of friendship and etc. and whatever I can do
to show this bird up I won't hesitate a minute.

Well Al this bird was writeing a letter last night and he didn't
have no envelope and he asked me did I have 1 and I said no and
he wouldn't of never spoke only to say Gimme but when I told him
I didn't have no envelope he started off somewheres to get 1 and
he dropped the last page out of the letter he had been writeing and
it was laying right there along side of me and of course I wouldn't
of paid no tension to it only it was face up so as I couldn't help from
seeing it and what I seen wasn't no words like a man would write in
a letter but it was a bunch of marks like a x down at the bottom and
they was a whole line of them like this

x x x x x x x x x x x

Well that roused up my suspicions and I guess you know I am
not the kind that reads other people's letters even if I don't get
none of my own to read but this here letter I kind of felt like they
was something funny about it like he was writeing in ciphers or
something so I picked the page up and read it through and sure
enough they was parts of it in ciphers and if a man didn't have the
key you couldn't tell what and the he——ll he was getting at.

Well Al I was still studing the page yet when he come back in
and they wasn't nothing for me to do only set on it so as he wouldn't
see I had it and he come over and begin looking for it and I asked
him had he lost something to throw him off the track and he said
yes but he didn't say what it was and that made it all the more
suspicious so he finely give up looking and went out again.

Well I have got it put away where he can't get a hold of it because I showed it to Johnny Alcock this A. M. and asked him if it didn't look like something off color and he said yes it did and if he was me he would turn it over to Capt. Seeley but on 2d thoughts he said I better keep it a wile and at the same time keep a eye on Shaffer and get more evidents vs. him and then when I had him dead to rights I could turn the letter and the rest of the evidents over to Capt. Seeley and then I would be sure to get the credit for showing him up.

Well Al I figure this 1 page of his letter is enough or more then enough only of course its best to play safe and keep my eyes pealed and see what comes off and I haven't got time to copy down the whole page Al and besides they's a few sentences that sounds O. K. and I suppose he put them in for a blind but you can't get away from them x marks Al and I will write down a couple other sentences and I bet you will agree that they's something fishy about them and here is the sentences to which I refer:

"In regards to your question I guess I understand O. K. In reply will say yes I. L. Y. more than Y. L. M. Am I right."

"Have you saw D. Give him a ring and tell the old spinort I am W. C. T. U. outside of a little Vin Blank."

Can you make heads or tales out of that Al? I guess not and neither could anybody else except they had the key to it and the best part of it is his name is signed down at the bottom and if he can explain that line of talk he is a wonder but he can't explain it Al and all as he can do is make a clean brest of the whole business and Alcock thinks the same way and Alcock says he wished he had of been the 1 that got a hold of this evidents because whoever turned it over to Capt. Seeley along with what other facts I can get a hold of will just about get a commission in the intelligents dept. and that's the men that looks after the pro German spys Al and gets the dope on them and shows them up and I would probably have my head quarters in Paris and get good money besides my expenses and I would half to pass up the chance to get in the trenches and fight but they's more ways of fighting then 1 and in this game Al a man has got to go where they send you and where they figure they would do the most good and if my country needs me to track after spys I will sacrifice my own wishs though I would a whole lot rather stay with my pals and fight along side of them and not snoop round Paris fondleing door nobs like a night watchman. But Alcock says he would bet money that is where I will land and he says "You ought to feel right at home in the intelligents dept. like a camel in Lake Erie" and he says the first chance I get I better try and start up a conversation with Shaffer and try and lead him on and that is the way they trap them is to ask them a whole lot of questions and see what they have got to say and if you keep fireing questions at them they are bound to get balled up and then its good night.

Well I don't suppose it seems possible to you stay at homes that they could be such a thing like a pro German spy in the U. S. army and how did he get there and why did they leave him in and etc. Well Al you would be supprised to know how many of them has slipped in and Alcock says that at first it amounted to about 200% but the intelligents officers has been on their sent all the wile and most of them has been nailed and when they get them they shoot them down like a dog and that's what Shaffer will get Al and he is out of luck to be so big because all as the fireing squad would half to do would be look at their compass and see if he was east or west of them and then face their riffle in that direction and let go.

I will write and let you know how things comes along.

Your pal,   Jack.

Somewheres in France, April 14.

Friend Al: Well Al I am closeing the net of evidents around Shaffer and I guess I all ready got enough on him to make out a case that he couldn't never wrinkle out of it but Capt. Seeley is away and I can't do nothing till he gets back.

I had my man on the grill today Al and I thought he would be a fox and not criminate himself but I guess I went at him so smooth he didn't never suspect nothing till along towards the finish and then it was to late. I don't remember all that was said but it run along these lines like as follows: In the first place I asked him where he lived and he said Milwaukee Ave. in Chi and I don't know if you know it or not Al but that's a st. where they have got traffic policemens at the corners to blow their whistles once for the Germans to go north and south and twice for them to go east and west. So then I said was he married and he says no. So then I asked him where he was born and he said "What and the he——ll are you the personal officer?" So I laughed it off and said "No but I thought maybe we come from the same part of the country." So he says something about everybody didn't half to come from the country but he wouldn't come out and say where he did come from so then I kind of led around to the war and I made the remark that the German drive up on the north side of France didn't get very far and he says maybe they wasn't through. How was that for a fine line of talk Al and he might as well have said he hoped the Germans wouldn't never be stopped.

Well for a minute I couldn't hardly help from takeing a crack at him but in these kind of matters Al a man has got to keep a hold of themself or they will loose their quarry so I kind of forced a smile and said "Well I guess they would have kept going if they could of." And then he says "Yes but they half to stop every once in a wile to bring up Van Hindenburg." So I had him traped Al and quick is a flash I said "Who told you their plans?" And he says "Oh he——ll my mother in law" and walked away from me.

Well Al it was just like sometimes when they are trying a man for murder and he says he couldn't of did it because he was over to the Elite jazing when it come off and a little wile later the lawyer asks him where did he say he was at when the party was croked and he forgets what he said the 1st. time and says he was out to Lincoln Pk. kidding the bison or something and the lawyer points out to the jury where his storys don't jib and the next thing you know he is dressed up in a hemp collar a couple sizes to small.

And that's the same way I triped Shaffer getting him to say he wasn't married and finely when I have him cornered he busts out about his mother in law. Well Al I don't know of no way to get a mother in law without marrying into one. So I told Alcock tonight what had came off and he says it looked to him like I had a strong case and if he was me he would spill it to Capt. Seeley the minute he gets back. And he said "You lucky stiff you won't never see the inside of a front line trench." So I asked him what he meant and he repeated over again what he said about them takeing me in the intelligents dept. So it looks like I was about through being a dough-boy Al and pretty soon I will probably be writeing to you from Paris but I don't suppose I will be able to tell you what I am doing because that's the kind of a job where mum is the word.

Your pal,   Jack.

Somewheres in France, April 16.

FRIEND AL: Well old pal don't be supprised if I write you the next time from Paris. I have got a date to see Capt. Seeley tomorrow and Lieut. Mather fixed it up for me to see him but I had to convince the lieut. that it wasn't no monkey business because they's always a whole lot of riffs and raffs asking Capt. Seeley can they have a word with him and what they want is to borry his knife to pair their finger nails.

But I guess he won't be sorry he seen me Al not when I show him the stuff I have got on this bird and he will probably shake me by the hand and say "Well Keefe Uncle Sam is proud of you but you are waisting your time here and I will be sorry to loose you but it looks like you belong in other fields." And he will wire a telegram to the gen. staff reccomending me to go to Paris.

I guess I all ready told you some of the stuff I have got on this bird but I have not told you all because the best one didn't only

happen last night. Well on acct. of I and Alcock being friends he
has kind of been keeping a eye pealed on Shaffer to help me out
and he found a letter last night that Shaffer had wrote and this
time it was the whole letter with the address and everything and
who do you suppose it was to? Well Al it was to Van Hindenburg
himself and I have got it right here where I can keep a eye on it
and believe me it's worth watching and I wished I could send it to
you so you could see for yourself what kind of a bird we are deal-
ing with. But that's impossible Al but they's nothing to keep me
from copping it off.

Well the letter is wrote in German and to show you what a foxy
bird he is he wrote it out in printing so as if it got found by somebody they couldn't prove he wrote it because when words is wrote
out in printing it looks just the same who ever wrote it and you
can't tell. But he wasn't foxy enough to not sign G. S. down to the
bottom of it and that stands for his name George Shaffer and he is
the only G. S. in the Co. so it looks like we had him up in a tree.
Here is what the letter says:

> "Field Marshall Van Hindenburg, c/o Die Vierten Dachs-
> hunds, Deutscher Armee, Flanders. 500,000 U. S. Soldaten
> schon in Frankreich doch. In Lauterbach habe Ich mein
> Strumpf verloren und ohne Strumpf gehe Ich nicht heim.
> xxxxxxx G. S."

Notice them x marks again Al like in the other letter and the
other letter was probably to Van Hindenburg to and I only wished I
knew what the x marks means but maybe some of the birds that's
all ready in the intelligents dept. can figure it out. But they's no
mystery about the rest of it Al because Alcock understands German and he translated it out what the German words means and
here is what it means:

500,000 United States soldiers in France all ready yet. Will advise you when to attack on this front.

How is that Al for a fine trader and spy to tell the gen. of the German army how many soldiers we got over here and to not attack till Shaffer says the word and he was probably going to say it wile we was all asleep or something. But thanks to me Al he will be the one that is asleep and it will be some sleep Al and it will make old Rip and Winkle look like they had the colic and when the boys finds out what I done for them I guess they won't be nothing to good for me. But it will be to late for them to show their appreciations because I won't be here no more and the boys probably won't see me again till its all over and we are back in the old U. S. because Alcock was talking to a bird that's in the int. dept. and he says 1 of their dutys was to keep away from everybody and not leave them know who you are. Because of course if word got out that you was a spy chaser the spys wouldn't hardly run up and kiss you on the st. but they would duck when they seen you and you would have as much chance to catch them as though you was trolling for wales with a grass hopper.

And from this bird's dope that Alcock was talking to I will half to leave off my uniform and wear plain close and maybe wear false whiskers and etc. so as people who see me the 1st. time I will look different to them the next time they see me and maybe I will half to let my mustache grow and grease it so as they will think maybe I am a Dutchman and if they are working for the Kaiser I could maybe pump them.

But they's 1 thing I don't like about it Al because Alcock says Paris is full of women that isn't exactly spys but they have been made a fool out of and they are some German's duke but the Dutchmens tells them a whole lot of things that Uncle Sam would like to know and I would half to find them things out and the only way to do that would be to get them stuck on me and I guess that wouldn't be no chore but when a gal gets stuck on you they will tell you everything they know and wile with most gals I ever seen they could do that without dropping another nickle still and all it would be different with these gals in Paris that's been the tools of some

Dutchmens because you take a German and he don't never stop braging till he inhales a bayonet.

But it don't seem fair to make love to them and pertend like I was nuts over them and then when I had learned all they was to know I would half to get rid of them and cast them to 1 side and god knows how many wounds I will leave behind me but probably as many as though I was a regular soldier or snipper but then I wouldn't feel so bad about it because it would be men and not girlies but everything goes in war fair as they say Al and if Uncle Sam and Gen. Pershing asks me to do it I will do whatever they ask me and they can't nobody really hold it vs. me because of why I am doing it.

But talking about snippers Al I noticed today that I wasn't near as good as usual in the riffle practice and it was like as if I was have-ing a slump like some of the boys does in baseball when they go along 5 or 6 days without finding out who is umpireing the bases and I am afraid that is how it would be with me in snipping I would be O. K. part of the time and the rest of the time I couldn't hit Eu-rope and maybe I would fall down when they was depending on me and then I would feel like a rummy so I guess I better not try and show up so good in practice even when I do feel O. K. because they might make a snipper out of me without knowing my weak-ness and I figure its something the matter with my eyes. Besides Al it don't seem like its a fair game to be pecking away at somebody that they can't see you and aren't looking for no supprise and its a whole lot different then fighting with a bayonet where its man to man and may the best man win.

Well Al I guess I have told you all the news and things is going along about as usual and they don't seem to be no prospects of us overtakeing a section up to the front but its just train and train and train and if the ball clubs had a training trip like we been haveing they would be so tired by the 1 of May that they wouldn't run out a base on balls. Yesterday we past by a flock of motor Lauras that was takeing wounded back to a base hospital somewheres and Alcock was talking to 1 of the drivers and he said that over 100% of the birds that's getting wounded and killed these days is the snippers and the boshs don't never rest till they find out where there nests is at and then they get all their best marksmens and aim at where they think the snipper has got his nest and then its good night snipper and he is either killed right out or looses a couple of legs or something. I certainly feel sorry for the boys that's wounded Al and every time we see a bunch of them all us boys is crazy to get up there to the front and get even for what they done.

Well old pal I will half to get busy now and overlook the dope I have got on Shaffer so as I will have everything in order for Capt. Seeley and I will write and let you know how things comes out.

Your pal,   Jack.

Somewheres in France, April 18.

FRIEND AL: Well Al they's a whole lot of birds that thinks they are wise and always trying to pull off something on somebody but once in a wile they pick out the wrong bird to pull it on and then the laugh is on the smart Alex themself.

Well Alcock and some of them thought they was putting up a game on me and was going to make me look like a monkey but before I get through with them Al they will be the suckers and I will be giveing them the horse laugh but what I ought to do is bust them in the jaw and if I was running this war every bird that tried to pull off some practical joke to put a man in bad, I would give a lead shower in their honor some A. M. before breakfast.

Alcock was trying to make me believe that 1 of the boys in the Co. name Geo. Shaffer was a German spy or something and they framed up a letter like as if he wrote it to Van Hindenburg giveing away secrets in German about our army and etc. but they made the mistake of signing his initials to the letter so when I come to think it over I seen it must be a fake because a bird that was a real spy wouldn't never sign their own name to a letter but they would sign John Smith or something.

But any way I had a hold of this letter and a peace of another letter that Shaffer really did write it and I thought I would show them to Capt. Seeley and play it safe because they might be something in them after all and any way it would give him a good laugh. So yesterday I went and seen him and he says "Well Keefe what can I do for you?" So I said "You can't do nothing for me sir but this time I can do something for you. What would you think if I told you they was a trader and a German spy in your Co." So he says "I would think you were crazy." So I said "I am afraid you will half to think so then but maybe you won't think I am so crazy when I show you the goods."

So then Al I pulled that 1st. peace of a letter on him and showed it to him and he read it and when he got through he says "Well it looks suspicious all right. It looks like the man that wrote it was hacking up a big plot to spring a few dependents on his local board the next time they draft him." So I said "The bird that wrote that letter is a Dutchman name Geo. Shaffer." So Capt. Seeley says "Well I wish him all the luck in the world and a lot of little Shaffers." So I said "Yes but what about them x marks and all them letters without no words to them?" So he said "Didn't you never correspond with a girl and put some of them xs down to the bottom of your letter?" So I says "I have wrote letters to a whole lot of girls but I never had to write nothing in ciphers because I wasn't never ashamed of anything I wrote." So he said "Well your lady friends was all cheated then because this is ciphers all right but its the kind of messages they love to read because it means kisses."

Well Al of course I knew it meant something like that but I didn't think a big truck horse like Shaffer would make such a mushmellow out of himself. But anyway I said to Capt. Seeley I says "All right but what about them other initials without no words to go with them?" And he says "Well that's some more ciphers but they's probably a little gal out in Chi that don't half to look at no key to figure it out."

So then I pulled the other letter on him the 1 in German and he also smiled when he read this one and finely he says "Some of your pals has been playing a trick on you like when you come over on the ship and the best thing you can do is to tear the letters up and keep it quite and don't leave nobody know you fell for it. And now I have got a whole lot to tend to so good by."

So that's all that was said between us and I come away and come back to quarters and Alcock and 2 or 3 of the other boys was there and Alcock knew where I had been and I suppose he had told the other birds and they was all set to give me the Mary ha ha but I beat them to it.

"Well Alcock" I says when I come in "you are some joke Smith but you wouldn't think you was so funny if I punched your jaw." So he turned kind of pail but he forced a smile and says "Well I guess the Vin Blank is on you this time." So I said "You won't get no Vin Blank off me but what you are libel to get is a wallop in the jaw." So he says "You crabbed at me a wile ago for not takeing a joke but it looks like you was the one that couldn't take them now." So I said "What I would like to take is a poke at your nose." So that shut him up and they didn't none of them get their laugh because I had them scared and if they had of laughed I would of made them swallow it.

So after all Al the laugh is on them because their gag fell dead and I guess the next time they try and pull some gag they will pick out some hick from some X roads to pull it on and not a bird that has traveled all over the big leagues and seen all they is to see.

Well Al I am tickled to death I won't half to give up my uniform and snoop around Paris like a white wings double crossing women and spying and etc. and even if the whole thing hadn't of been just a joke I was going to ask Capt. Seeley to not reccomend me to no int. dept. but jest leave me be where I am at so as when the time comes I can fight fair like man to man and not behind no woman's skirts like a cur.

So you see Al everything is O. K. after all and the laugh is on Alcock and his friends because they was the ones that expected to do all the laughing but instead of that I made a monkey out of them.

Your pal,   Jack.

Somewheres in France, April 23.

FRIEND AL: Well Al if you would see my face you would think I had been attending a barrage or something or else I had been in a bar room fight only of course if it was a fair fight I wouldn't be so kind of marred up like I am. But I had a accident Al and fell over a bunk and lit on the old bean and the result is Al that I have got a black eye and a bad nose and my jaw is swole a little and my ears feels kind of dull like so I guess the ladys wouldn't call me Handsome Jack if they seen me but it will be all O. K. in a few days and I will be the same old Jack.

But I will tell you how it come off. I was setting reading a letter from Florrie that all as she said in it was that she had boughten herself a new suit that everybody says was the cutest she ever had on her back just like I give a dam because by the time I see her in it she will of gave it to little Al's Swede. But any way I was reading this letter when in come Shaffer the bird that was mixed up in that little gag about the fake spy and he come up to me and says "Well you big snake who's male are you reading now?" Well Al him calling me big is like I would say hello Jumbo to a flee. But any way I says "My own male and who and the he——ll male would I be reading?" So he said "Well its hard to tell because you stole some of mine and read it and not only that but you showed it to the whole A. E. F. so now stand up and take what's comeing to you."

Wel Al I thought he was just kidding so I says "I come over here to fight Germans and not 1 of my own pals." So he says

"Don't call me no pal, but if you come to fight Germans now is your chance because you say I'm 1 of them."

Well he kind of made a funny motion like he wanted to spar or wrestle or something and I thought he meant it in a friendly way like we sometimes pull off a rough house once in a wile so I stood up but before I had a chance to take holds with him he cut loose at me with his fists doubled up and I kind of triped or something and fell over a bench and I must have hit something sharp on the way down and I kind of got scratched up but they are only scratchs and don't amt. to nothing. Only I wished I knew he had of been serious and I would of made a punching bag out of him and you can bet that the next time he wants to start something I won't wait to see if he is jokeing but I will tear into him and he will think he run into a Minnie Weffers.

Well I suppose Alcock was sore at me for getting the best of him and not falling for his gag and he was afraid to tackle me himself and he told big Shaffer a peck of lies about some dam letter or something and said I stole it and it made Shaffer sore and no wonder because who wouldn't be sore if they thought somebody was reading their male. But a man like Shaffer that if he stopped a shell the Dutchmens would half to move back a ways so as they would be room enough in France to bury him hasn't got no right to pick on a smaller man especially when I wasn't feeling good on acct. of something I eat but at that Al size don't make no difference and its the bird that's got the nerve and knows how that can knock them dead and if Shaffer had of gave me any warning he would of been the 1 that is scratched up instead of I though I guess he is to lucky to trip over a kit bag and fall down and cut himself.

But my scratchs don't really amt. to nothing Al and in a few days I will be like new.

Your pal,   Jack.

Somewheres in France, April 25.

FRIEND AL: Well old pal I have got some big news for you now. We been ordered up to the front and its good by to this Class D burg and now for some real actions and I am tickled to death and I only hope the Dutchmens will loose their minds and try and start something up on the section where we are going to and I can't tell you where its at Al but you keep watching the papers and even if the boshs don't start nothing maybe we will start something on our own acct. and the next thing you know you will read where we have got them on the Lincoln highway towards Russia and believe me Al we won't half to stop every little wile to bring up no Van Hindenburg but we will run them ragged and they say the Germans is the best singers and when they all bust out with Comrades they will make the Great Lakes band sound like the Russia artillery.

Well Al I am so excited I can't write much and I have got a 100 things to tend to so I will half to cut this letter short.

Well some of the other birds like Alcock and them is pertending like they was tickled to death to but believe me Al if the orders was changed all of a sudden and they told us we was going to stay here till the duration of the war we wouldn't half to call on the Engrs. to dam their tear ducks. But they pertend like they are pleased and keep whistleing so as they won't blubber and today they all laughed their heads off at something that come out in the Co. paper that some of the boys gets out but they laughed like they was nervous instead of enjoying it.

Well what come out in the paper was supposed to be a joke on me and if they think its funny they are welcome and I would send the paper to you that its in only I haven't got only the 1 copy so I will copy it down and you can see for yourself what a screen it is. Well they's 1 peace that's got up to look like it was the casuality list in some regular newspaper and it says:

WOUNDED IN ACTION
Privates
Jack Keefe, Chicago, Ill. (Very)

And then they's another peace that reads like this:

DECORATED

"The Company has won its first war honors and Private Jack Keefe is the lucky dog. Private Keefe has been decorated by Gen. George Shaffer of the 4th. Dachshunds for extreme courage and cleverness in showing up a dangerous nest of spies. Keefe was hit four times by large caliber shells before he could say surrender. He was decorated with the Order of the Schwarz Auge, the Order of the Rot Nase and the Order of the Blumenkohl Ohren, besides which a Right Cross was hung on his jaw. Private Keefe takes his honors very modestly, no one having even heard him mention them except in stifled tones during the night."

Well Al all right if they can find something to amuse themself and they need it I guess. But they better remember that they's plenty of time for the laugh to be on the other foot before this war is over.

Your pal,   Jack.

Sammy Boy

In the Trenchs, May 6.

FRIEND AL: Well Al I haven't wrote you no letter for a long wile and I suppose maybe you think something might of happened to me or something. Well old pal they hasn't nothing happened and I only wished they would because anything would be better than laying around here and I would rather stop a shell and get spread all over Europe then lay around here and die a day at a time you might say.

Well I would of wrote you before only we was on the march and by the time night come around my dogs fret me so bad I couldn't think of nothing else and when they told us we was comeing up here I thought of course they would send us up in motor Lauras or something and not wear us all out before we got here but no it was drill every ft. of the way and I said to Johnny Alcock the night we got here that when they was sending us up here to die they might at lease give us a ride and he says no because when they send a man to the electric chair they don't push him up there in a go cart but they make him get there on his own dogs. So I said "Yes but he travels light and he don't half to go far and when he gets there they's a chair waiting for him to set down in it but they load us up like a troop ship and walk us ½ way to Sweden and when we finely get here we can either remain standing or lay down in a mud puddle and tuck ourself in."

And another thing Al I thought they meant we was going right in the front line trenchs where a man has got a chance to see some fun but where we are at is what they call the reserve trenchs and we been here 3 days all ready and have got to stay here 7 days more that is unless they should something happen to the regt. that's up ahead of us in the front line and if they get smashed up or something and half to be sent back to the factory then we will jump right in and take their place and I don't wish them no bad luck but I wished they would get messed up tonight at lease enough so as they would half to come out for repairs but it don't look like they was much chance of that as we are on a quite section where they hasn't been nothing doing since the war begin you might say but of course Jerry is raising he——ll all over the front now and here is where he will probably pick on next and believe me Al we will give him a welcome.

But the way things is mapped out now we will be here another wk. yet and then up in the front row for 10 days and then back to the rest billets for a rest but they say the only thing that gets a rest back there is your stomach but believe me your stomach gets a holiday right here without going to no rest billets.

Well I thought they would be some excitement up here but its like church but everybody says just wait till we get up in front and then we will have plenty of excitement well I hope they are telling the truth because its sure motonus here and about all as we do is have inspections and scratch. As Johnny Alcock says France may of lose a whole lot of men in this war but they don't seem to of been no casualitys amist the cuties.

Well Al they's plenty of other bugs here as well as the kinds that itchs and I mean some of the boys themselfs and here is where it comes out on them is where they haven't nothing to do only lay around and they's 1 bird that his name is Harry Friend but the boys calls him the chicken hawk and its not only on acct. of him loveing the ladys but he is all the wile writeing letters to them and he is 1 of these fancy writers that has to wind up before he comes down on the paper with a word and between every word he sores up and swoops down again like he was over a barn yard and sometimes the boys set around and bets on how many wirls he will take before he will get within writeing distants of the paper.

Well any way he must get a whole lot of letters wrote if he answers all the ones that comes for him because every time you bump into him he pulls one on you that he just got from some gal that's nuts about him somewheres in the U. S. and its always a different 1 and I bet the stores that sells service stars kept open evenings the wk. this bird enlisted in the draft. But today it was a French gal that he had a letter from her some dame in Chalons and he showed me her picture and she's some queen Al and he is pulling for us to be sent there on our leave after we serve our turn up here and I don't blame him for wanting to be where she's at and I wished they was some baby doll that I could pal around with in what ever burg they ship us to. But I don't know nobody Al and besides I'm a married man so no flirting with the parley vous for me and I suppose I will spend most of my time with the 2 Vin sisters and a headache.

Your pal,   Jack.

In the Trenchs, May 9.

FRIEND AL: Well Al I was talking to 1 of the boys Jack Brady today and we was talking about Harry Friend and I told Jack about him getting a letter from this French girlie at Chalons and how he was pulling for us to go there on our leave so as he could see her so Jack said he didn't think we would go there but they would probably send us to 1 of the places where we could get a bath as god knows we will need one and they will probably send us to Aix les Bains or Nice or O. D. Cologne. So I said I didn't care where we was sent as they wouldn't be no gal waiting for me in none of them towns so Jack says it was my own fault if they wasn't as all these places was full of girlies that was there for us to dance with them and etc. and the officers had all their names and addresses and the way to do was write to 1 of them and tell her when you was comeing and would she like to show you around and he said he would see 1 of the lieuts. that he stands pretty good with him and see what he could do for me. Well Al I told him to go ahead as I thought it was just a joke but sure enough he showed up after a wile and he said the lieut. didn't only have 1 name left but she was a queen and he give me her name and address and its Miss Marie Antoinette 14 rue de Nez Rouge, O. D. Cologne.

Well Al I didn't have nothing else to do so I set down and wrote her a note and I will coppy down what I wrote:

"DEAR MISS ANTOINETTE: I suppose you will be supprised to hear from me and I hope you won't think I am some fresh bird writeing you this letter for a joke or something but I am just 1 of Uncle Sam's soldiers from the U. S. A. and am now in the trenchs fighting for your country. Well Miss Antoinette we expect to be here about 2 wks. more and then we will have a leave off for a few days and some of the boys thinks we may spend it in your city and I thought maybe you might be good enough to show me around when we get there. I was a baseball pitcher back in the U. S. A. tall and athletic build and I don't suppose you know what baseball is but thought maybe you would wonder what I look like. Well if you aren't busy when we get there I will hope to see you and if you are agreeable drop me a line here and I will sure look you up when I get there."

So then I give her my name and where to reach me and of course they won't nothing come out of it Al only a man has got to amuse yourself some way in a dump like this or they would go crazy. But it would sure be a horse on me if she was to answer the letter and say she would be glad to see me and then of course I would half to write and tell her I was a married man or else not write to her at all but of course they won't nothing come out of it and its a good bet we won't never see Cologne as that was just a guess on Brady's part.

Well Al things is going along about like usual with nothing doing only inspections and etc. and telling us how to behave when we get up there in the front row and not to stick our head over the top in the day time and you would think we was the home guards or something and at that I guess the home guards is seeing as much of the war as we are in this old ditch but they say it will be different when we get up in front and believe me I hope so and they can't send us there to soon to suit me.

Your pal,   Jack.

In the Trenchs, May 11.

FRIEND AL: Well Al here we are up in the front line trenchs and we come in here 2 days ahead of time but that's the way they run everything in the army except feed you but they don't never do nothing when they say they are going to and I suppose they want a man to get use to haveing things come by supprise so as it won't interfere with your plans if you get killed a couple days before you was looking for it.

Well Al we are looking for it now most any day and this may be the last letter you will ever get from your old pal and you may think I am kidding when I say that but 1 of the boys told me a wile ago that he heard Capt. Seeley telling 1 of the lieuts. that the reason we come in here ahead of time was on acct. of them expecting the Dutchmans to make their next drive on this section and the birds that we are takeing their place was a bunch of yellow stiffs that was hard of hearing except when they was told to retreat and Gen. Pershing figured that if they was up here when Jerry made a attack they would turn around and open up a drive on Africa and the bosh has been going through the rest of the line like it was held by the ladies aid and Gen. Foch says they have got to be stopped so we are elected Al and you know what that means and it means we can't retreat under no conditions but stay here till we get killed. So you see I wasn't kidding Al and it looks like it was only a question

173

of a few days or maybe not that long but at that I guess most of the boys would just as leave stop a Dutch bayonet as to lay around in this he———ll hole. Believe me Al this is a fine resort to spend 10 days at what with the mud and the perfume and a whole menajery useing you for a parade grounds.

Well Capt. Seeley wants us to get all the rest we can now on acct. of what's comeing off after a wile but believe me I am not going to oversleep myself in this he———ll hole because suppose Jerry would pick out the time wile you was asleep to come over and pay us a visit and they's supposed to be some of the boys on post duty to watch all night and keep their eye pealed and wake us up if they's something stiring but I have been in hotels a lot of times and left a call with some gal that didn't have nothing to do only pair her finger nails and when the time come ring me up but even at that she forgot it so what chance is they for 1 of these sentrys to remember and wake everybody up when maybe they's 5 or 6 Dutchmens divideing him into building lots with their bayonet or something. So as far as I am conserned I will try and keep awake wile I can because it looks like when we do go to sleep we will stay asleep several yrs. and even if we are lucky enough to get back to them rest billets we can sleep till the cows come home a specially if they give us some more of them entertainments like we had in camp.

Well Al before we got here I thought they would be so much fire-ing back and 4th. up here that a man couldn't hear themself think but I guess Jerry is saveing up for the big show though every little wile they try and locate our batterys and clean them out and once in so often 1 of our big guns replys but as Johnny Alcock says you couldn't never accuse our artillrys from being to gabby and I guess we are lucky they are pretty near speechless as they might take a notion to fire short but any way a little wile ago 1 of our guns sent a big shell over and Johnny says what and the he———ll can that be and I said its a shell from 1 of our guns and he says he thought they fired 1 yesterday.

Well as I say here we are with 10 days of it stareing us in the eye and the cuties for company and the only way we can get out of here ahead of time is on a stretcher and I wouldn't mind that Al but as I say I want to be awake when my time comes because if I am going to get killed in this war I want to have some idear who done it.

Your pal,   Jack.

In the Trenchs, May 14.

FRIEND AL: Well Al I got the supprise of my life today when Jack Brady handed me a letter that had came for me and that's supprise enough itself but all the more when I opened it up and seen who it was from. Well it was from that baby in Cologne and I will coppy it down as it is short and you can see for yourself what she says. Well here it is:

> "DEAR MR. KEEFE: Your letter just reached me and you can bet I was glad to get it. I sure will be glad to see you when you come to Cologne and I will be more than glad to show you the sights. This is some town and we sure will have a time when you get here. I am just learning to write English so please excuse mistakes but all I want to say is don't disappoint me but write when you will come so I can be all dressed up comme un cheval. Avec l'amour und kussen.

> "Marie Antoinette."

You see Al they's part of it wrote in French and that last part means with love and kisses. Well I guess that letter I wrote her must have went over strong and any ways it looks like she didn't exactly hate me eh Al? Well it looks like I would half to write to her back and tell her I am a married man and they can't be no flirting between her and I but if she wants to be a good pal and show me around O. K. and no harm done. Well I hope she takes it that way because it sure will seem good to talk to a gal again that can talk a little English and not la la la all the wile but of course its a good bet that I won't never see her because we are just as libel to go somewheres else as Cologne though Brady seems to think that's where we are headed for. Well time will tell and in the mean wile we are libel to get blowed to he————ll and gone and then of course it would be good by sweet Marie but I was supprised to hear from her as I only wrote to her in fun and didn't think nothing would come from it but I guess Harry Friend isn't the only lady killer in the U. S. army and if I was 1 of the kind that shows off all their letters I guess I have got 1 now to show.

A side from all that Al we was supposed to have our chow a hr. ago but no chow and some of the boys says its on acct. of our back arears being under fire and you see the kitchens is way back of the front lines and the boys on chow detail is supposed to bring our food up here but when the back arears is under fire they are scared to bring it up or they might maybe run into some bad luck on the way. How is that for fine dope Al when a whole regt. starves to death because a few yellow stiffs is afraid that maybe a shell might light near them and spill a few beans. Brady says maybe they are trying to starve us so as we will get mad and fight harder when the time comes like in the old days when they use to have fights between men and lions in Reno and Rome and for days ahead they wouldn't give the lions nothing to eat so as they would be pretty near wild when they got in Reno and would make a rush at the gladaters that was supposed to fight them and try and eat them up on acct. of being so near starved. Well Al I would half to be good and hungry before I would want to eat a Dutchman a specially after they been in the trenchs a wile.

But any way it don't make a whole lot of differents if the chow gets here or not because when it comes its nothing only a eye dropper full of soup and coffee and some bread that I would hate to have some of it fall on my toe and before we left the U. S. everybody was trying to preserve food so as the boys in France would have plenty to eat but if they sent any of the preserves over here the boat they come on must of stopped a torpedo and I hope the young mackerels won't make themselfs sick on sweets.

Jokeing to 1 side this is some climate Al and they don't never a day pass without it raining and I use to think the weather profits back home had a snap that all they had to do was write down rain or snow or fair and even if they was wrong they was way up there where you couldn't get at them but they have got a tough job when you look at a French weather profit and as soon as he learns the French for rain he can open up an office and he don't half to hide from nobody because he can't never go wrong though Alcock says they have got a dry season here that begins the 14 of July and ends that night but its a holiday so the weather profit don't half to monkey with it. Any way its so dark here all the wile that you can't hardly tell day and night only at night times the Dutchmens over across the way sends up a flare once in a wile to light things up so as they can see if they's any of us prowling around Nobody's Land and speaking about Nobody's Land Brady says its the ground that lays between the German trenchs and the vermin trenchs but jokeing to 1 side if it wasn't for these here flares we wouldn't know they was anybody over in them other trenchs and when we come in here they was a lot of talk about Jerry sending over a patrol to find out who we was but it looks like he wasn't interested. But all and all Al its nothing like I expected up here and all we have seen of the war is when a shell or 2 busts in back of us or once in a wile 1 of their areoplanes comes over and 1 of ours chases them back and sometimes they have a battle but they always manage to finish it where we can't see it for the fear we might enjoy ourselfs.

Well it looks like we would half to go to bed on a empty stomach if you could call it bed and speaking about stomach Brady says they's a old saying that a army travels on their stomach but a cutie covers a whole lot more ground. But as I say when you don't get your chow you don't miss much only it kills a little time and everybody is sick in tired of doing nothing and 1 of the boys was saying tonight he wished the Dutchmens would attack so as to break the motley and Alcock said that if they did attack he hoped they would do it with gas as his nose needed a change of air.

Your pal,   Jack.

In the Trenchs, May 16.

FRIEND AL: Well old pal I come within a ace you might say of not being here to write you this letter and you may think that's bunk but wait till you hear what come off. Well it seems our scout planes brought back word yesterday that the Dutch regt. over across the way had moved out and another regt. had took their place and it seems when they make a change like that our gens. always trys to find out who the new rivals is so the orders come yesterday that we was to get up a patrol party for last night and go over and take a few prisoners so as we would know what regt. we was up vs. Well as soon as the news come out they was some of the boys volunteered to go in the patrol and they was only a few going so I didn't feel like noseing myself in and maybe crowding somebody out that was set on going and besides what and the he——ll do I care what regt. is there as long as its Germans and its like you lived in a flat and the people across the hall moved out and some people moved in why as long as you knowed they wasn't friends of yours you wouldn't rush over and ring their door bell and say who the he——ll are you but you would wait till they had time to get some cards printed and stick 1 in the mail box. So its like I told Alcock that when the boys come back they would tell the Col. that the people opp. us was Germans and the Col. would be supprised because he probably thought all the wile that they was the Idaho boy scouts or something. But at that I pretty near made up my mind at the last minute to volunteer just to break the motley you might say but it was to late and I lost out.

Well Al the boys that went didn't come back and I hope the Col. is satisfied now because he has lost that many men and he knows just as much as he did before namely that they's some Germans across the way and either they killed our whole bunch or took them a prisoner and instead of us learning who they are they found out who we are because the boys that's gone is all from our regt. and its just like as if we went over and give them the information they wanted to save them the trouble of comeing over here and getting it.

Well it don't make a man feel any happier to think about them poor boys and god only knows what happened to them if they are prisoners or dead and some of them was pals of mine to but the worst part of it is that the word will be sent home that they are missing in actions and their wifes won't know what become of them if they got any and I can't help from thinking I might of been with them only for not wanting to crowd somebody out and if I had of went my name would be in the casuality list as missing in actions but I guess at that if Florrie picked up the paper and seen it she wouldn't know it was her husband its so long since she wrote it on a envelop.

Well Al they's other gals in the world besides Florrie and of course its to late to get serious with them when a man has got a wife and kid but believe me I am going to enjoy myself if they happen to pick out Cologne to send us to and if the little gal down there is 1 of the kind that can be good pals with a man without looseing her head over me I will sure have a good time but I suppose when she sees me she will want to begin flirting or something and then I will half to pass her up before anybody gets hurt. Well any way I wrote her a friendly letter today and just told her to keep me in mind and I stuck a few French words in it for a gag but I will coppy down what I wrote the best I can remember it so you will know what I wrote. Here it is:

MON CHER MARIE: Your note recd. and you can bet I was mighty glad to hear from you and learn you would show me around Cologne. That is if they send us there and if we get out of here alive. Well you said you was just learning English well I will maybe be able to help you along and you can maybe help me with the French so you see it will be 50 50. Well I sure hope they send us to Cologne and I will let you know the minute I find out where they are going to send us and maybe even if its somewheres else couldn't you visit there at the same time and maybe I could see you. Well girlie we will be out of here in less then a wk. now if we don't have no bad luck and you can bet I won't waist no time getting to where ever they send us and I hope its Cologne. So in the mean wile don't take no wood nickles and don't get impatient but be a good girlie and save up your loving for me. Tres beaucoup from

Your Sammy Boy,
Jack Keefe.

That's what I wrote her Al and I bet she can't hardly wait to hear if I'm comeing or not but I don't suppose they's any chance of them sending us there and a specially if they find out that anybody wants to go there but maybe she can fix it to meet me somewheres else and any ways they won't be no lifes lost if I never see her and maybe it would be better that way. But a man has got to write letters or do something to keep your mind off what happened to them poor birds that went in the patrol and a specially when I come so near being 1 of them.

Your pal,   Jack.

In the Trenchs, May 18.

FRIEND AL: Well Al if I am still alive yet its not because I laid back and didn't take no chances and I wished some of the baseball boys that use to call me yellow when I was in there pitching had of seen me last night and I guess they would of sang a different song only in

the 1st. place I was where they couldn't nobody see me and sec-
ondly they would of been so scared they would of choked to death
if they tried to talk let alone sing. But wait till you hear about it.

Well yesterday P. M. Sargent Crane asked me how I liked life in
the trenchs and I said O. K. only I got tired on acct. of they not
being no excitement or nothing to do and he says oh they's plenty
to do and I could go out and help the boys fix up the bob wire in
front of the trenchs like we done back in the training camp. So I
said I didn't see how they could be any fixing needed as they hadn't
nothing happened on this section since the war started you might
say and the birds that was here before us had plenty of time to fix it
if it needed fixing. So he says "Well any ways they's no excitement
to fixing the wire but if you was looking for excitement why didn't
you go with that patrol the other night?' So I said "Because I didn't
see no sence to trying to find out who was in the other trenchs
when we know they are Germans and that's all we need to know.
Wait till they's a real job and you won't see me hideing behind nobody." So he says "I've got a real job for you tonight and you can go
along with Ted Phillips to the listening post."

Well Al a listening post is what they call a little place they got
dug out way over near the German trenchs and its so close you can
hear them talk sometimes and you are supposed to hear if they are
getting ready to pull something and report back here so as they
won't catch us asleep. Well I was wild to go just for something to do
but I been haveing trouble with my ears lately probably on acct. of
the noise from so much shell fire or something but any ways I have
thought a couple times that I was getting a little deef so I thought I
better tell him the truth so I said "I would be tickled to death to go
only I don't know if I ought to or not because I don't hear very
good even in English and of course Jerry would be telling their
plans in German and suppose I didn't catch on to it and I would
feel like a murder if they started a big drive and I hadn't gave my
pals no warning." So he says "Don't worry about that as Phillips
has got good ears and understands German and he has been there

before only in a job like that a man wants company and you are going along for company."

Well before we snuck out there Sargent Crane called us to 1 side and says "You boys is takeing a big chance and Phillips knows what to do but you want to remember Keefe to keep quite and not make no noise or talk to each other because if Jerry finds out you are there we probably won't see you again."

Well Al it finely come time for us to go and we went and if anybody asks you how to spend a pleasant evening don't steer them up against a listening post with a crazy man. Well I suppose you think its pretty quite there at home nights and I use to think so to but believe me Al, Bedford at 2 o'clock in the A. M. is a bowling alley along the side of 1 of these here listening posts. It may sound funny but I would of gave a month's pay if somebody would of shot off a fire cracker or anything to make a noise. There was the bosh trench about 20 yds. from us but not a sound out of them and a man couldn't help from thinking what if they had of heard us out there and they was getting ready to snoop up on us and that's why they was keeping so still and it got so as I could feel 1 of their bayonets burrowing into me and I am no quitter Al when it comes to fighting somebody you can see but when you have got a idear that somebody is cralling up on you and you haven't no chance to fight back I would like to see the bird that could enjoy themself and besides suppose my ears had went back on me worse then I thought and the Dutchmens was realy makeing a he———ll of a racket but I couldn't hear them and maybe they was getting ready to come over the top and I wouldn't know the differents and all of a sudden they would lay a garage and dash out behind it and if they didn't kill us we would be up in front of the court's marshal for not warning our pals.

Well as I say I would of gave anything for some one to of fired off a gun or made some noise of some kind but when this here Phillips finely opened up his clam and spoke I would of jumped a mile if they had of been any room to jump anywheres. Well the sargent had told us not to say nothing but all of a sudden right out

loud this bird says this is a he——ll of a war. Well I motioned back
at him to shut up but of course he couldn't see me and he thought I
hadn't heard what he said so he said it over again so then I thought
maybe he hadn't heard the sargent's orders so I whispered to him
that he wasn't supposed to talk. Well Al they wasn't no way of
keeping him quite and he says "That's all bunk because I been out
here before and talked my head off and nothing happened." So I
says well if you have got to talk you don't half to yell it. So then he
tried to whisper Al but his whisper sounded like a jazz record with
a crack in it so he says I'm not yelling I am whispering so I said yes
I have heard Hughey Jennings whisper like that out on the lines.

So he shut up for a wile but pretty soon he busted out again
and this time he was louder then ever and he asked me could I sing
and I said no I couldn't so then he says well you can holler can't
you so I said I suppose I could so he says "Well I know how we
could play a big joke on them square heads. Lets the both of us
begin yelling like a Indian and they will hear us and they will think
they's a whole crowd of us here and they will begin bombing us or
something and think they are going to kill a whole crowd of Americans but it will only be us 2 and we can give them the laugh for
waisting their ammunitions."

Well Al I seen then that I was parked there with a crazy man
and for a wile I didn't say nothing because I was scared that I might
say something that would encourage him some way so I just shut
up and finely he says what is the matter ain't you going to join me?
So I said I will join you in the jaw in a minute if you don't shut your
mouth and then he quited down a little, but every few minutes he
would have another swell idear and once he asked me could I imi-
tate animals and I said no so he says he could mew like a cow and
he had heard the boshs was so hard up for food and they would
rush out here thinking they was going to find a cow but it wouldn't
be no cow but it would be a horse on them.

Well you can imagine what I went through out there with a bird
like that and I thought more then once I would catch it from him

and go nuts myself but I managed to keep a hold of myself and the happiest minute of my life was when it was time for us to crall back in our dug outs but at that I can't remember how we got back here.

This A. M. Sargent Crane asked me what kind of a time did we have and I told him and I told him this here Phillips was squirrel meat and he says Phillips is just as sane as anybody usualy only everybody that went out on the listening post was effected that way by the quite and its a wonder I didn't go nuts to.

Well its a wonder I didn't Al and its a good thing I kept my head and kept him from playing 1 of those tricks as god knows what would of happened and the entire regt. might of been wipped out. But I hope they don't wish no more listening post on me but if they do you can bet I will pick my own pardner and it won't be no nut and no matter what Sargent Crane says if this here Phillips is sane we're stopping at Palm Beach.

Your pal,   Jack.

In the Trenchs, May 19.

FRIEND AL: Well old pal don't say nothing about this not even to Bertha what I am going to tell you about as some people might not understand and a specially a woman and might maybe think I wasn't acting right towards Florrie or something though when a man is married to a woman that he has been in France pretty near 4 mos. and she has wrote him 3 letters I don't see where she would have a sqawk comeing at whatever I done but of course I am not going to do nothing that I wouldn't just as leave tell her about it only I want to tell her myself and when I get a good ready.

Well I guess I told you we was only supposed to stay here in the front line 10 days and then they will somebody come and releive us and take our place and then we go to the rest billets somewheres and lay around till its our turn to come up here again.

Well Al we been in the front line now eight days and that means we won't only be here 2 days more so probably we will get out of here the day after tomorrow night. Well up to today we didn't have no idear where we was going to get sent as they's several places where the boys can go on leave like Aix le Bains and Nice and etc. and we didn't know which 1 it would be. So today we was talking about it and I said I wished I knew for sure and Jack Brady stands pretty good with 1 of the lieuts. so he says he would ask him right out. So he went and asked him and the lieut. told him Cologne.

Well Al I hadn't no sooner found out when 1 of the boys hands me a letter that just come and it was a letter from this baby doll that I told you about that's in Cologne and I will coppy down the letter so you can see for yourself what she says and here it is Al:

DEAR SAMMY BOY:

I was tres beaucoup to get your letter and will sure be glad to see you and can hardly wait till you get here. Don't let them send you anywhere else as Cologne is the prettiest town in France and the liveliest and we will sure have some time going to shows etc. and I hope you bring along beaucoup francs. Well I haven't time to write you much of a letter as I have got to spend the afternoon at the dress-maker's. You see I am getting all dolled up for my Sammy Boy. But be sure and let me know when you are going to get here and when you reach Cologne jump right in a Noir et Blanc taxi and come up to the house. You know the number so come along Sammy and make it toot sweet.

Yours with tres beaucoup,
Marie.

So that's her letter Al and it looks like I was going to be in right in old O. D. Cologne and it sure does look like fate was takeing a hand in the game when things breaks this way and when I wrote to this gal the first time I didn't have no idear of ever seeing her but the way things is turning out it almost seems like we was meant to meet each other. Well Al I only hope she has got some sence and won't get to likeing me to well or of course all bets is off but if we can just be good pals and go around to shows etc. together I don't see where I will be doing anything out of the way. Only as I say don't say nothing about it to Bertha or nobody else as people is libel to not understand and I guess most of them women back in the U. S. thinks that when a man has been up at the front as long as we have and then when he gets a few days leave he ought to take a running hop step and jump to the nearest phonograph and put on a Rodeheaver record.

Your pal,   Jack.

In the Trenchs, May 20.

FRIEND AL: Well Al just a line and it will probably be the last time I will write you from the trenchs for a wile as our time is up tomorrow night and the next time I write you it will probably be from Cologne and I will tell you what kind of a time they show us there and all about it. I just got through writeing a note to the little gal there telling her I would get there as soon as possible but I couldn't tell her when that would be as I don't know how far it is or how we get there but Brady said he thought it was about 180 miles so I suppose they will make us walk.

Well talk about a quite section and they hasn't even been a gun went off all day or no areoplanes or nothing and here we thought we was going to see a whole lot of excitement and we haven't fired a shot or throwed a grenade or even saw a German all the wile we was here and we are just like when we come only for those poor birds that went on that wild goose chase and didn't come back and they's been some talk about sending another patrol over to get revenge for those poor boys but I guess they won't nothing come of it. It would be like sending good money after bad is the way I look at it.

Several of the boys has been calling me Sammy Boy today and I signed my name that way in 1 of the notes I wrote that little gal and I suppose who ever censored it told some of the boys about it and now they are trying to kid me. Well Al I don't see where a censor has got any license to spill stuff like that but they's no harm done and they can laugh at me all they want to wile we are here as I will be the 1 that does the laughing when we get to Cologne. And I guess a whole lot of them will wish they was this same Sammy Boy when they see me paradeing up and down the blvd. with the bell of the ball. O you sweet Marie.

Your pal,   Jack.

In the Trenchs, May 22.

FRIEND AL: Well Al its all off and we are here yet and what is more we are libel to be here till the duration of the war if we don't get killed and believe me I would welcome death rather then stay in this he——ll hole another 10 days and from now on I am going to take all the chances they is to take and the sooner they finish me I will be glad of it and it looks like it might come tonight Al as I have volunteered to go along with the patrol that's going over and try and get even for what they done to our pals.

Well old pal it was understood when we come up here that we would be here 10 days and yesterday was the 10th. day we was here. Well I happened to say something yesterday to Sargent Crane about what time was we going and he says where to and I said I thought our time was up and we was going to get relieved. So he says "Who is going to releive us and what and the he——ll do you want to be releived of?" So I said I understood they didn't only keep a regt. in the front line 10 days and then took them out and sent them to a rest billet somewheres. So he says what do you call this but a rest billet? So then I asked him how long we had to stay here and he said "Well it may be a day or it may be all summer. But if we get ordered out in a hurry it won't be to go to no rest billet but it will be to go up to where they are fighting the war."

So I made the remark that I wished somebody had of tipped me off as I had fixed up a kind of a date thinking we would be through here in 10 days. So he asked me where my date was at and I said Cologne. So then he kind of smiled and said "O and when was you planing to start?" So I said "I was figureing on starting tonight." So he waited a minute and then he said "Well I don't know if I can fix it for you tonight or tomorrow night, but they's some of the boys going to start in that direction one of them times and I guess you can go along."

Well Al I suppose Alcock and Brady and them has been playing another 1 of their gags on me and I hope they enjoyed it and as far as I am conserned they's no harm done. Cologne Al is way back of the German lines and when Sargent Crane said they was some of the boys starting in that direction he meant this here patrol. So I'm in on it Al and they didn't go last night but tonight's the big night. And some of the boys is calling me Sammy Boy and trying to make a monkey out of me but the smart Alex that's doing it isn't none of them going along on this raid and that's just what a man would expect from them. Because they's a few of us Al that come across the old puddle to fight and the rest of them thinks they are at the Young Peoples picnic.

Your pal,   Jack.

Simple Simon

In the Trenchs, May 29.

FRIEND AL: Well Al we have been haveing a lot of fun with a bird name Jack Simon only the boys calls him Simple Simon and if you seen him you wouldn't ask why because you would know why as soon as you seen him without asking why as he keeps his mouth open all the wile so as he will be ready to swallow whatever you tell him as you can tell him anything and he eats it up. So the boys has been stuffing him full of storys of all kinds and he eats them all up and you could tell him the reason they had the bob wire out in front was to scratch yourself on it when the cuties was useing you for a race track and he would eat it up.

Well when we come in here and took over this section this bird was sick and I don't know what ailed him only it couldn't of been brain fever but any way he didn't join us in here till the day before yesterday but ever since he joined us the boys has been stuffing him full and enjoying themself at his expenses. Well the 1st. thing he asked me was if we had saw any actions since we been here and I told him about a raid we was on the other night before he come and we layed down a garage and then snuck over to the German trenchs and jumped into them trying to get a hold of some prisoners but we couldn't find head or tale of no Germans where our bunch jumped in as they had ducked and hid somewheres when they found out we was comeing. So he says he wished he could of been along as he might of picked up some souvenirs over in their trenchs.

That's 1 of his bugs Al is getting souvenirs as he is 1 of these here souvenir hounds that it don't make no differents to him who wins the war as long as he can get a ship load of junk to carry it back home and show it off. So I told Johnny Alcock and some of the other boys about Simon wishing he could of got some souvenirs so they framed up on him and begin selling him junk that they told him they had picked it up over in the German trenchs and Alcock blowed some cigarette smoke in a bottle and corked it up and told him it was German tear gas and Simon give him 8 franks for it and Jack Brady showed him a couple of laths tied together with a peace of wire and told him it was a part of the areoplane that belonged to Guy Meyer the French ace that brought down so many Dutchmans before they finely got him and Brady said he hated to part with it as he had took it off a German prisoner that he brought in but if Simon thought it was worth 20 franks he could have it. So Simon bought it of him and wanted to know all about how Brady come to get the prisoner and of course Brady had to make it up as we haven't saw a German let alone take them a prisoner since we was back in the training arears and wouldn't know they was any only for their artillery and throwing up rockets at night and snipping at a man every time you go out on a wire party or something.

But any way Simon eats it up whatever you pull on him and some times I feel sorry for him and feel like tipping him off but the boys fun would be spoiled and believe me they need some kind of sport up here or pretty soon we would all be worse off then Simon and we would be running around fomenting at the mouth.

Well Al I wished you would write once in a wile if its only a line as a man likes to get mail once in a wile and I haven't heard from Florrie for pretty near a month and then all as she said was that the reason she hadn't wrote was because she wasn't feeling the best and I suppose she got something in her eye but anything for an excuse to not write and you would think I had stepped outdoors to wash the windows instead of being away from her since last December.

Your pal,   Jack.

In the Trenchs, June 4.

FRIEND AL: Well Al nothing doing as usual only patching things up once in a wile and it would be as safe here as picking your teeth if our artillery had a few brains as the Germans wouldn't never pay no tension to us if our batterys would lay off them but we don't no sooner get a quite spell when our guns cuts loose and remind Fritz that they's a war and then of course the Dutchmens has got to pay for their board some way and they raise he———ll for a wile and make everybody cross but as far as I can see they don't nobody never get killed on 1 side or the other side but of course the shells mess things up and keeps the boys busy makeing repairs where if our artillery would keep their mouth shut why so would theirs and the boys wouldn't never half to leave their dice game only for chow.

But from all as we hear I guess they's no dice game going on up on some of the other sections but they's another kind of a game going on up there and so far the Dutchmens has got all the best of it but some of the boys says wait till the Allys gets ready to strike back and they will make them look like a sucker and the best way to do is wait till the other side has wore themself out before you go back at them. Well I told them I have had a lot of experience in big league baseball where they's stragety the same like in war but I never heard none of the big league managers tell their boys to not try and score till the other side had all the runs they was going to get and further and more it looked to me like when the Germans did get wore out they could rest up again in the best hotel in Paris. So Johnny Alcock says oh they won't never get inside of Paris because the military police will stop them at the city limits and ask them for their pass and then where would they be? So I says tell that to Simple Simon and he shut up.

Speaking about Simple Simon what do you think they have got him believeing now. Well they told him Capt. Seeley had sent a patrol over the other night to find out what ailed the Germans that they never showed themself or started nothing against us and the patrol found out that Van Hindenburg had took all the men out of the section opp. us and sent them up to the war and left the trenchs opp. us empty so Simon asked him why we didn't go over there and take them then and they told him because our trenchs was warmer on acct. of being farther south. I suppose they will be telling him the next thing that Capt. Seeley and Ludendorf married sisters and the 2 of them has agreed to lay off each other.

Well Al I am glad they have got somebody else to pick on besides me and of course they can have a lot more fun with Simon as they's nothing to raw that he won't eat it up wile in my case I was to smart for them and just pretended like I fell for their gags as they would of been disappointed if I hadn't of and as I say somebody has got to furnish amusement in a he——ll hole like this or we would all be squirrel meat.

Your pal,   Jack.

In the Trenchs, June 7.

FRIEND AL: Well Al here is a hot 1 that they pulled on this Simon bird today and it was all as I could do to help from busting out laughing while they was telling it to him.

Well it seems like he must of been thinking that over what they told him about they not being no Germans in the trenchs over opp. to where we are at and it finely downed on him that if they wasn't nobody over there why who was throwing up them flares and rockets every night. So today he said to Brady he says "Didn't you birds tell me them trenchs over across the way was empty?" So Brady says yes what of it. So Simon says "Well I notice they's somebody over there at night times or else who throws up them flares as they don't throw themselfs up." So Brady says they had probably left a flare thrower over there to do that for them. But Simon says they must of left a lot of flare throwers because the flares come from different places along the line.

So then Alcock cut in and says "Yes but you will notice they don't come from different places at once and the bird that throws them gos from 1 place to another so as we will think the trenchs is full of Germans." So Simon says "They couldn't nobody go from 1 place to another place as fast as them flares shoots up from different places." So Alcock says "No they couldn't nobody do it if they walked but the man that throws them flares don't walk because he hasn't got only 1 leg as his other leg was shot off early in the war. But Van Hindenburg is so hard up for men that even if you get a leg shot off as soon as the Dr. mops up the mess and sticks on the court plaster they send the bird back in the war and put him on a job where you don't half to walk. So they stuck this old guy in the motorcycle dept. and now all as he does is ride up and down some quite section like this here all night and stop every so often and throw up a flare to make us think the place is dirty with Germans."

Well Al Simon thought it over a wile and then asked Alcock how a man could ride a motorcycle with only 1 leg and Alcock says "Why not because you don't half to peddle a motorcycle as they run themself." So Simon says yes but how about it when you want to get off? So Alcock says "What has a man's legs got to do with him getting off of a motorcycle as long as you have got your head to light on?"

That is what they handed him Al and they hadn't hardly no sooner then got through with that dose when Brady begun on the souvenirs. First he asked him if he had got a hold of any new ones lately and Simon says no he hadn't seen nobody that had any for sale and besides his jack was low so Brady asked him how much did he have and he says about 4 franks. So Brady says "Well you can't expect anybody to come across with anything first class for no such chicken's food as that." So Simon says well even if he had a pocket full of jack he couldn't buy nothing with it when they wasn't nothing to buy. Then Brady asked him if he had saw the German speegle Ted Phillips had picked up and Simon says no so Brady went and got Phillips and after a wile he come back with him and Phillips said he had the speegle in his pocket and he would show it to us if we promised to be carefull and not jar it out of his hands wile he was showing it as he wouldn't have it broke for the world. So Simon stood there with his eyes popping out and Phillips pulled the speegle out of his pocket and it wasn't nothing only a dirty little looking glass that you could pretty near crall through the cracks in it and all the boys remarked what a odd little speegle it was and they hadn't never saw 1 like it before and etc. and finely Simon couldn't keep his clam shut no longer so he asked Phillips how much he would take for it. Well Phillips says it wasn't for sale as speegles was scarce in Germany on acct. of the war and that was why the Dutchmens always looked like a bum when you took them a prisoner. So Simon asked him what price he would set on it suppose he would sell it and Phillips says about 8 franks. Well Simon got out all his jack and they wasn't only 4 franks and he showed it to Phillips and said if he would take 10 franks for the speegle he would give him 4 franks down and the other 6 franks when he got hold of some jack so Phillips hummed and hawed a wile and finely said all right Simon could have it but he wouldn't never sell it to him only that it kept worring him so much to carry it in his pocket for the fear he would loose it or break it.

Well Al Phillips has got Simon's last 4 franks and Simon has got Phillips's speegle and I suppose now that the boys sees how soft it is they will be selling him stuff on credit and he will owe them his next months pay before they get through with him and I suppose the next thing you know they will keep their beard when they shave and sell it to him for German tobacco. Well I would half to be pretty hard up before I went in on some skin game like that and I would just as leave go up to 1 of them cripples that use to spraddle all over the walk along 35 st. after the ball game and stick my heel in their eye and romp off with their days receipts.

Your pal,   Jack.

In the Trenchs, June 11.

FRIEND AL: Well Al it seems like Capt. Seeley is up on his ear because they haven't took our regt. out of here yet because it seems

Gen. Pershing told Gen. Foch that he was to help himself to any part of the U. S. army and throw them in where ever they was needed and they's been a bunch of the boys throwed in along the other parts of the front to try and stop the Germans and Capt. Seeley is raveing because they keep us here and don't take us where we can get some actions. Any way 1 of the lieuts. told some of the boys that if we didn't get took out of here pretty quick Capt. Seeley would start a war of our own on this section and all the officers was sore because we hadn't done nothing or took no prisoners or nothing you might say only make repairs in the wire and etc. Well Al how in the he———ll can we show them anything when they don't never send us over the top or nowheres else but just leave us here moldering you might say but at that I guess we have showed as much life as the birds that's over there opp. us in them other trenchs that hasn't hardly peeped since we come in here and the boys says they are a Saxon regt. that comes from part of Germany where the Kaiser is thought of the same as a gum boil so the Saxons feels kind of friendly towards us and they will leave us alone as long as we leave them alone and visa and versa. So I don't see where Capt. Seeley and them other officers has got a right to pan us for not showing nothing but I don't blame them for wishing they would take us out of here and show us the war and from all as we hear they's plenty of places where we could do some good or at lease as much good as the birds that has been there.

Well Al they have been stringing poor Simon along and today they give him a song and dance about some bird name Joe in the regt. that was here ahead of us that got a collection of souvenirs that makes Simon's look rotten and they said the guy's pals called him Souvenir Joe on acct. of him haveing such a fine collection. So Brady says to Simon "All you have got is 5 or 6 articles and the next thing you know they will be takeing us out of here and you might maybe never get another chance to pick up any more rare articles so if I was you I would either get busy and get a real collection or throw away them things you have got and forget it."

So Simon says "How can I get any more souvenirs when I haven't no more jack to buy them and besides you birds haven't no more to sell." So Brady says "Souvenir Joe didn't buy his collection but he went out and got them." So Simon asked him where at and Brady told him this here Joe use to crall out in Nobody's Land every night and pick up something and Simon says it was a wonder he didn't get killed. So Brady says "How would he get killed as the trenchs over across the way was just as empty when he was here as they are now and Old 1 Legged Mike and his motorcycle was on the job then to, so Joe would wait till Mike had throwed a few flares on this section and then he would sneak out and get his souvenirs before Mike come back again on his rounds."

Well then Simon asked him where the souvenirs was out there and Brady says they was in the different shell holes because most of Joe's souvenirs was the insides of German shells that had exploded and they was the best kind of souvenirs as they wasn't no chance of them being a fake.

Well Al I had a notion to take Simon to 1 side and tell him to not pay no tension to these smart alex because the poor crum might go snooping out there some night after the insides of a shell and get the outsides and all and if something like that happened to him I would feel like a murder though I haven't never took no part in makeing a monkey out of him, but I thought well if the poor cheese don't know no more then that he is better off dead so let him go.

Your pal,   Jack.

In the Trenchs, June 13.

FRIEND AL: Just a line Al as I am to excited to write much but I knew you would want to know the big news. Well Al I have got a daughter born the 18 of May. How is that for a supprise Al but I guess you won't be no more supprised than I was when the news come as Florrie hadn't gave me no hint and a man can't guess a thing like that when you are in France and the lady in question is back in old Chi. But it sure is wonderfull news Al and I only wished I was somewheres where I could celebrate it right but you can't even whistle here or somebody would crown you with a shovle.

Well Al the news come today in a letter from Florrie's sister Marie Allen and she has been down in Texas but I suppose Florrie got her to come up and stay with her though as far as I can see its bad enough to have a baby without haveing that bird in the house to, but they's 1 consolation we haven't got rm. in the apt. for more than 2 kids and 3 grown ups so when I get home if sweet Marie is still there yet we will either half to get rid of the Swede cook or she, and when it comes to a choice between a ski jumper that will work and a sister that won't why Florrie won't be bothered with no family ties.

Any way I haven't no time to worry about no Allen family now as I am feeling to good and all as I wish is that somebody wins this war dam toot sweet so as I can get home and see this little chick Al and I bet she is as pretty as a picture and she couldn't be nothing else you might say and I have wrote to Florrie to not name her or nothing till I have my say as you turn a woman loose on nameing somebody all alone and they go nuts and look through a seed catalog.

Well old pal I know you would congratulate me if you was here and I am only sorry I can't return the complement and if I was you and Bertha I would adopt 1 of these here Belgium orphans that's lost their parents as they's nothing like it Al haveing a kid or 2 in the house and I bet little Al is tickled to death with his little sister.

Well Al I have told all the boys about it and they have been haveing a lot of fun with me but any way they call me Papa now which is a he——ll of a lot better then Sammy Boy.

Your pal,   Jack.

In the Trenchs, June 14.

FRIEND AL: I am all most to nervous to write Al but anything is better then setting around thinking and besides I want you to know what has came off so as you will know what come off in the case something happens.

Well Al Simple Simon's gone. We don't know if he's dead or alive or what the he——ll and all as we know is that he was here last night and he ain't here today and they hasn't nobody seen or heard of him.

Of course Al that isn't all we know neither as we can just about guess what happened. But I have gave my word to not spill nothing about what the boys pulled on him or god knows what Capt. Seeley would do to them.

Well Al I got up this A. M. feeling fine as I had slept better then any time for a wk. and I dreamt about the little gal back home that ain't never seen her daddy or don't know if she's got 1 or not but in my dream she knowed me O. K. as I dreamt I had just got home and Florrie wasn't there to meet me as usual but I rung the bell and the ski jumper let me in and I asked her where Florrie was and she said she had went out somewheres with little Al so I was going out and look for them but the Swede says the baby is here if you want to see her and I asked her what baby and she says why your new little baby girl.

So then I heard a baby crying somewheres in the house and I went in the bed rm. and this little mite jumped right up out of bed and all of a sudden she was 3 yrs. old instead of a mo. and she come running to me and hollered daddy. So then I grabbed her up and we begin danceing around but all of a sudden it was I and Florrie that was danceing together and little Al and the little gal was danceing around us and then I woke up Al and found I was still in this he——ll hole but the dream was so happy that I was still feeling good over it yet and besides it looked like the sun had forgot it was in France and was going to shine for a while.

Well pretty soon along come Corp. Evans and called me to 1 side and asked me what I knew about Simon. So I says what about him. So Corp. Evans says he is missing and they hasn't nobody saw him since last night. So I says I didn't know nothing about him but if anything had happened to him they was a lot of birds in this Co. that ought to pay for it. So Corp. Evans asked me what was I driveing at and I started in to tell him about Alcock and Brady and them kidding this poor bird to death and Corp. Evans says yes he knew all about that and the best thing to do was to shut up about it as it would get everybody in bad. He says "Wait a couple days any way and maybe he will show up O. K. and then they won't be no sence in spilling all this stuff." So I says all right I would wait a couple days but these birds ought to get theirs if something serious has happened and if he don't show up by that time I won't make no promise to spill all I know. So Corp. Evans says I didn't half to make no promise as he would spill the beans himself if Simon isn't O. K.

Well Al of course all the boys had heard the news by the time I got to talk to them and they's 2 or 3 of them that feels pretty sick over it and no wonder and the bird that feels the sickest is Alcock and here is why. Well it seems like yesterday while I was telling all the boys about the news from home Simon was giveing Alcock a ear full of that junk Brady had been slipping him about Souvenir Joe and Simon asked Alcock if he thought they was still any of them souvenirs worth going after out in them shell holes. So Alcock says of course they must be as some of the holes was made new since we been here. But Alcock told him that if he was him he wouldn't waist no time collecting the insides of German shells as the Germans was so hard up for mettle and etc. now days that the shells they was sending over was about ½ full of cheese and stuff that wouldn't keep. So Alcock says to him "What you ought to go after is a Saxon because you can bet that Souvenir Joe didn't get none and if you would get 1 all the boys would begin calling you Souvenir Simon instead of Simple Simon and you would make Souvenir Joe look like a dud."

Well Al Simon didn't know a Saxon from a hang nail so he asked Alcock what they looked like and Alcock told him to never mind as he couldn't help from knowing 1 if he ever seen it so then Simon asked him where they was libel to be and Alcock told him probably over in some of the shell holes near the German trench.

That's what come off yesterday wile I was busy telling everybody about the little gal as you can bet I would of put Simon wise had I of been in on it and now Al he's gone and they don't nobody know what's became of him but they's a lot of us that's got a pretty good idear and as I say they's 2 or 3 feels pretty sick and one a specially. But I guess at that they don't no one feel no worse then me though they can't nobody say I am to blame for what's happened but still in all I might of interfered because I am the only 1 of them that has got a heart Al and the only reason Alcock and Brady is so sick now is that they are scared to death of what will happen to them if they get found out. Because their smartness won't get them nothing up in front of the Court Marshall as he has seen to many birds just like them.

Well Al I am on post duty tonight and maybe you don't know what that means. Well old pal its no Elks carnivle at no time and just think what it will be tonight with your ears straining for a cry from out there. And if the cry comes Al they won't only be the 1 thing to do and I will be the 1 to do it.

So this may be the last time you will hear from me old pal and I wanted you to know in the case anything come off just how it happened as I won't be here to write it to you afterwards.

All as I can think about now Al is 2 things and 1 of them is that little gal back home that won't never see her daddy but maybe when she gets 4 or 5 yrs. old she will ask her mother "Why haven't I got a daddy like other little girls?" But maybe she will have 1 by that time Al. But what I am thinking about the most is that poor ½ wit out there and as Brady says he isn't nothing but a Mormon any way and ought never to of got in the army but still and all he is a man and its our duty to fight and die for him if needs to be.

Your pal,   Jack.

The Real Dope

In the Hospital, July 20.

FRIEND AL: You will half to excuse this writeing as I am proped up in a funny position in bed and its all as I can do to keep the paper steady as my left arm ain't no more use then the Russian front.

Well Al yesterday was the 1st. time they left me set up and I wrote a letter to Florrie and told her I was getting along O. K. as I didn't want she should worry and this time I will try and write to you. I suppose you got the note that the little nurse wrote for me about 2 wks. ago and told you I was getting better. Well old pal the gal that wrote you that little note is some baby and if you could see the kid that wrote you that little note you would wished you was laying here in my place. No I guess you wouldn't wished that Al as they's nobody that would want to go through what I have been through and they's very few that could stand it like I have and keep on smileing.

Well old pal they thought for a wile that it was Feeney for yrs. truly as they say over here and believe me I was in such pain that I would of been glad to die to get rid of the pain and the Dr. said it was a good thing I was such a game bird and had such a physic or I couldn't of never stood it. But I am not strong enough yet to set this way very long so if I am going to tell you what happened I had better start in.

Well Al this is the 20 of July and that means I have been in here 5 wks. as it was the 14 of June when all this come off. Well Al I can remember writeing to you the day of the night it come off and I guess I told you about this bird Simon getting lost that was always after the souvenirs and some of the boys told him they wasn't no Germans over in the other trenchs but just a bird name Motorcycle Mike that went up and down the section throwing flares so as we would think they was Germans over there. So they told him if he wanted to go out in Nobody's Land and spear souvenirs it was safe if you went just after Mike had made his rounds so as the snippers wouldn't get you.

201

Well old pal I was standing there looking out over Nobody's Land that night and I couldn't think of nothing only poor Simon and listening to hear if I couldn't maybe hear him call from somewheres out there and I don't know how long I had been standing there when I heard a kind of a noise like somebody scrunching and at the same time they was a flare throwed up from our side and I seen a figure out there cralling on the ground quite a ways beyond our wire. Well Al I didn't wait to look twice but I called Corp. Evans and told him. So he says who did I think it was and I said it must be Simon. So he says "Well Keefe its up to 1 of us to go get him." So I said "Well Corp. I guess its my job." So he says "All right Keefe if you feel that way about it." So I says all right and I'll say Al that he give up his claims without a struggle.

Well I started and I was going without my riffle but the Corp. stopped me and says take it along and I says "What for, do you think I am going to pick Simon up with a bayonet." So he says who told me it was Simon out there. Well Al that's the 1st. time I stopped to think it might maybe be somebody else.

Well Florrie use to say that I couldn't get up in the night for a drink of water without everybody in the bldg. thinking the world serious must of started but I bet I didn't knock over no chairs on this trip. Well Al it took me long enough to get out there as you can bet I wasn't trying for no record and every time they was a noise I had to lay flat and not buge. But I got there Al to where I thought I had saw this bird moveing around but they hadn't no rockets went up since I started and it was like a troop ship and I couldn't make out no figure of a man or nothing else and I was just going to whisper Simon's name when I reached out my hand and touched him. Well Al it wasn't Simon.

Well old pal we had some battle this bird and me and the both of us forgot bayonets and guns and everything else. I would of killed him sure only he got a hold of my left hand between his teeth and I couldn't pry it loose. But believe me Al he took a awful beating with my free hand and I will half to hand it to him for a game bird only what chance did he have? None Al and the battle couldn't only end the 1 way and I was just getting ready to grab his wind pipe and shut off the meter when he left go of my other hand and let out a yell that you could hear all over the great lakes and then all of a sudden it seemed like everybody was takeing a flash light and then the bullets come whizzing from all sides it seemed like and they got me 3 times Al and never pinked this other bird once. Well Al it wasn't till 2 wks ago that I found out that my opponent was Johnny Alcock.

Just 2 wks. ago yesterday Johnny come in and seen me and told me the whole story and it was the 1st. day they left me see anybody only the Dr. and the little nurse and was the 1st. day Johnny was able to be up and around. How is that Al to put a man in the hospital for 3 wks. without useing no gun or knife or nothing on him only 1 bear fist. Some fist eh Al.

Well it seems like he had been worring so about Simon that he finely went out there snooping around all by himself looking for him and he was the 1 I seen when that flare went up and of course we each thought the other 1 was a German and finely it was him yelling and the rockets going up at the same time that drawed the fire and I got all of it because I was the bird on top.

But listen Al till you hear the funny part of it. Simple Simon the bird that we was both out there looking for him showed up in our trench about a ½ hr. after we was brought in and he showed up with a Saxon all right but the Saxon was dead. Well Al Simon told them that he had ran into this guy over near their wire and that he was alive when he got him, but Alcock says that Brady said Simon hadn't only been gone 24 hrs. and the Saxon had been gone a he——ll of a lot longer than that.

Well they's no hard feeling between Alcock and I and I guess I more then got even with him for eating out of my hand as they say but Johnny said it was a shame I couldn't of used some of my strength on a German instead of him but any way its all over now and the Dr. says my leg is pretty near O. K. and I can walk on it in a couple wks. but my left arm won't be no use for god knows how long and maybe never and I guess I'm lucky they didn't half to clip it off. So I don't know when I will get out of here or where I will go from here but I guess they's 1 little party that ain't in no hurry to see me go and I wished you could see her look at me Al and you would say its to bad I am a married man with 2 kids.

Your pal,   Jack.

Somwheres in France, Aug. 16.

FRIEND AL: Well Al I don't suppose this will reach you any sooner then if I took it with me and mailed it when I get home but I haven't nothing to do for a few hrs. so I might as well be writeing you the news.

Well old pal I am homewards bound as they say as the war is Feeney as far as I am conserned and I am sailing tonight along with a lot of the other boys that's being sent home for good and when I look at some of the rest of them I guess I am lucky to be in as good a shape as I am. I am O. K. only for my arm and wile it won't never be as good as it was I can probably get to use it pretty good in a few months and all as I can say is thank god it is my left arm and not the old souper that use to stand Cobb and them on their head and it will stand them on their head again Al as soon as this war is over and I guess I won't half to go begging to Comiskey to give me another chance after what I have done as even if I couldn't pitch up a alley I would be a money maker for them just setting on the bench and showing myself after this.

Well we are saying good by to old France and I don't know how the rest of the boys feels but I am not haveing no trouble controlling myself and when it comes down to cases Al the shoe is on the other ft. and what I am getting at is that France ought to be the 1 that hates to see us leave as I doubt if they will ever get a bunch of spenders like us over here again.

Well Al it certainly seems quite down here in this old sea port town after what we have been through and it seems like I can still hear them big guns roar and them riffles crack and etc. and I feel like I ought to keep my head down all the wile and keep out of the snippers way and I could all most shut my eyes and imagine I was back there again in that he——ll hole but I know I'm not Al as I don't itch.

Well Al my wounds isn't the only reason I am comeing home but they's another reason and that is that they want some of us poplar idles to help rouse up the public on this here next Liberty Loan and I don't mind it as they have promised to send me home to Chi and I can be with Florrie and the kids. I will do what I can Al though I can't figure where the public would need any rouseing up and they certainly wouldn't if they had of been through what I have been through and maybe some of the other boys to. It takes jack to run a war Al even if us boys don't get none of it or what we do get they either send it home to our wife or take it away from us in a crap game.

Well old pal I left the hospital the day before yesterday and that was the only time I felt like crying since they told me I was going home and it wasn't so much for myself Al but that poor little nurse and you would of felt like crying to if you could of seen the look she give me. Her name is Charlotte Warren and she lives in Minneapolis and expects to go right back there after she is through over here but that don't do me no good as a married man with a couple children has got something better to do besides flirting with a pretty little nurse and besides I won't never pitch ball in Minneapolis as I expect to quit the game when I am about 40.

Well Al some of the boys wants to say their farewells to the Vin Rouge and the la la las and I will half to close and I will write again as soon as I get home and tell you what the baby gal looks like though they's only the 1 way she could look and that's good.

Well here is good by to France and good luck to all the boys that's going to stay over here and Simple Simon with the rest of them and I suppose I ought to of got a few souvenirs off him to bring home with me. But I guess at that I will be carrying a souvenir of this war for a long wile Al and its better than any of them foney ones he has got as the 1 I have got shows I was realy in it and done my bit for old Glory and the U. S. A.

Your pal,   Jack.

Chicago, Aug. 29.

FRIEND AL: Well Al here I am back in old Chi and feeling pretty good only for my arm and my left leg is still stiff yet and I caught a mean cold comeing across the old pond but what is a few little things like that as the main thing is being home.

Well old pal they wasn't nothing happened on the trip across the old pond only it took a whole lot to long and believe me old N. Y. looked good but believe me I wouldn't waist no time in N. Y. only long enough to climb outside a big steak and the waiter had to cut it up for me but even the waiters treated us fine and every-wheres we showed up the people was wild about us and cheered and clapped and it sounded like old times when I use to walk out there to warm up.

Well we hit N. Y. in the A. M. and left that night and got here last eve. and I didn't leave Florrie know just when I was comeing as I wanted to supprise her. Well Al I ought to of wired ahead and told her to go easy on my poor old arm because when she opened the door and seen me she give a running hop step and jump and dam near killed me. So then she seen my arm in a sling and cried and cried and she says "Oh my poor boy what have you been through." So I says "Well you have been through something your-self so its 50 50 only I got this from a German."

Well Al little Al was the cutest thing you ever seen and he grabbed me by the good hand and rushed me in to where the little stranger was laying and she was asleep but we broke the rules for once and all and all it was some party and she is some little gal Al and pretty as a picture and when you can say that for a 3 mos. old its going some as the most of them looks like a French breakfast.

Well I finely happened to think of Sister Marie and I asked where she was at and Florrie says she went back to Texas so I says tough luck and Florrie says I needn't get so gay the 1st. evening home and she says "Any way we have still got a Marie in the house as that is what I call the baby." So I says "Well you can think of her that way but her name ain't going to be that as I don't like the name." So she says what name did I like and I pretended like I was thinking a wile and finely I says what is the matter with Charlotte. Well Al you will half to hand it to the women for detectives as I hadn't no sooner said the name when she says "Oh no you can't come home and name my baby after none of your French nurses." And I hadn't told her nothing about a nurse.

Well any way I says I had met a whole lot more Maries then Charlottes in France and she says had I met any Florries and I said no and that was realy the name I had picked out for the kid. So she says well she didn't like the name herself but it was the only name I could pick out that she wouldn't be suspicious of it so the little gal is named after her mother Al and if she only grows up ½ as pretty as her old lady it won't make no differents if she has got a funny name.

Well Al have you noticed what direction the Dutchmens is makeing their drive in now? They started going the other way the 18 of July and it was 2 days ahead of that time that our regt. was moved over to the war and now they are running them ragged. Well Al I wished I was there to help but even if I was worth a dam to fight I couldn't very well leave home just now.

Your pal,   Jack.

The Busher Reënlists

Chi, Dec. 2.

FRIEND AL: Well Al I was down to see the Dr. for the last time today as he said they wasn't no use in me comeing down there again as my arm is just as good is new though of course its weak yet on acct. of being in a sling all this wile and I haven't used it and I suppose if it was my right arm it would take me a long wile to get it strenthened up again to where I could zip the old ball through there the way like I use to but thank god its the left arm that the Dutchmens shot full of holes. But at that it wouldn't make no differents if it was the left arm or the old souper either one as I have gave up the idear of going back in to the old game.

I bet you will be surprised to hear that Al as I am still a young man just a kid you might say compared to some of the other birds that is still pitching yet and getting by with it and I figure that if I would stick in the game my best yrs. is yet to come. But that isn't the point Al but the point is that after a man has took part in the war game all the other games seems like they was baby games and after what I went through acrost the old pond how could a man take any interest in baseball and it would be like as if a man set up all night in a poker game with the sky for the limit and when they come home their wife asked them to play a hand of jack straws to see which one of them had to stick the ice card in the window. No man can do themself justice Al if you don't take your work in ernest whether its pitching baseball or takeing a bath.

Besides that Al I figure that even a man like I am that's put up like a motor Laura you might say can't last forever in baseball and why not quit wile you are young and have still got the old ambition to start out in some other line of business that a man can last in it all their life and probably by the time I got to be the age where I would half to give up pitching if I stuck at it, why by that time I can work myself up to the head of some business where I would be drawing $15000.00 per annum or something and no danger of getting kicked out of it when the old souper finely lays down on me.

And besides that when a man has got a wife and 2 kiddies that the whole 3 of them has got the world beat why should I go out and pitch baseball and be away from home ½ the year around where if I hooked up good in some business here in Chi I wouldn't never half to leave except maybe a run down to N. Y. city once or twice a yr. So in justice to them and myself I don't see nothing to it only give up the game for good in all and get in to something permerant.

Well Al I suppose you will be saying to yourself that I haven't never had no experience in business and what kind of business could I get in to that would pay me the right kind of money. Well old pal if you will stop and think I haven't never tackled no job yet where I didn't make good and in the 1st. place it was pitching base-ball and I hadn't only been pitching a little over 2 yrs. when I was in the big league and then come the war game and I was made a corporal a few wks. after I enlisted and might of stayed a corporal or went higher yet only I would rather pal around with the boys and not try and lord it over them and you can bet it won't be no dif-ferent in whatever business I decide to take up because they isn't nothing that can't be learned Al if a man goes at it the right way and has got something under their hat besides scalp trouble.

As for getting in to the right kind of a place I guess I can just about pick out what kind of a place I want to start in at as everybody that reads the papers knows who I am and how I went in the war wile most of the other baseball boys kept the home fires burning though I had a wife and a kid to look out for besides the baby that came since I went in and for all as I knew might of been here a long wile before that. So it looks like when I make up my mind what business I want to tackle I can just go to whoever is at the head of the business and they will say "You bet your life we will find a place for you after what you done both in baseball and for the stars and strips." Because they won't no real man turn a soldier down Al a specially 1 that erned his wound strips acrost the old pond.

So they won't be no trouble about me landing when I decide what I want to go in to and the baseball men can offer me whatever kind of a contract they feel like and I will give them 1 of my smiles and tell them they are barking the wrong tree.

Regards to Bertha.

Your pal,   Jack.

Chi, Dec. 8.

FRIEND AL: Well Al this is a fine burg where a lot of the business men don't know they's been a war or read the papers or nothing only set in front of the cash register and watch how the money rolls in or else they must of bet 20 cents on the Kaiser and have got a grudge against the boys that stopped him.

The other night I was with a couple of friends of mine that's White Sox fans and we was histing a few and 1 of them is asst. mgr. down to 1 of the big dept. stores so I told him I was going to quit the game and try and bust in to some business where I could work up to something worth wile and he says they was shy of a floor man down to their store and he would speak to the mgr. about me and if I come down maybe I could land the job, as the floor man has to be a man that can wear clothes and carry themself as most of the customers is ladys and you half to give them a smile and make them feel at home and the job pays pretty good jack.

Well I didn't think much of the job only this bird is a kind of an admire of mine on acct. of baseball so I didn't want to be nasty to him so I went down there yesterday and he introduced me to the mgr. and his name is suppose to be Kelly but I guess Heinz would be closer to what his name is. Well he asked me had I had any experience in dept. stores and I said yes I had had all the experience I wanted the times I had been in there with Florrie shoping and my feet was still sore yet where all the women in Chi had used them for a parade grounds. So he said he meant did I ever have any experience working in a store so I said do I look like a counter jumper or something? I said "I have had the kind of experience that I guess a whole lot of men would give their right eye if they could brag about it, playing in the big league in baseball and the big league in war and I guess that's enough of experience for a man of my age." So he said "Well our floor men is not suppose to hit the customers with a bat or tickle them with a bayonet either one so I don't see how we can use you right now." So I said "I have got a charge acct. here and here is where my wife does pretty near all her shoping." So he said "Well if we was to give jobs to all our customers why as soon as they had all reported for work in the A. M. we could close the doors and get along without a floor man." Well Al all as I could do was walk away from him as I couldn't very well take a wallop at his jaw on acct. of his asst. being my pal.

Well as long as I was down town I thought I might as well look up some of my other friends so I happened to remember a pal of mine that use to work in the Gas Co. so I dropped in there and asked for him but he wasn't there no more so I asked for whoever was in charge and they showed me to an old bird that must of began to work for them the day they struck gas and I told him my name and who I was and he said about the only thing open was meter readers so I said "Read them yourself" and come away.

That's the kind of birds we have got here Al but they can't all be that way and the next time I will wait for them to come to me before I go around and lay myself libel to insults from a bunch of pro German spys or whatever you have a mind to call them.

Well they's a saloon on Adams St. that it use to be a big hang out for the fans so I dropped in there before I started home but they wasn't nobody in there that I knew them or they knew me and the bunch that was in there didn't even know their own name but they was all trying to sing tenor and that's about the way it is in all the saloons you drop in to these days and they all seem to think that every day is June 30. Well I couldn't stand for the noise and everybody with their arm around each other tearing off Smiles so I come home and Florrie asked me how I had came out and I told her and she says it looked like I better go back in to baseball. So I said if I do go back it will be because they give me a $5000.00 contract in the stead of the $2500.00 I was getting when I quit and enlisted and between you and I Al that's the lowest figure I would sign up for and of course I wouldn't have no trouble getting that if I give Comiskey the word that I was thinking about pitching baseball again. But nothing doing in baseball for me Al when I know I can get in to some big business with a future in it and won't never half to worry about my arm or catching cold in it or nothing and be home every night with the kiddies. But if I did sign up to a $5000.00 contract in baseball it would mean our income would be around $8000.00 per annum as Florrie is kicking out pretty close to $250.00 per mo. clear profit in her beauty parlor.

Well Florrie said if I couldn't get no $5000.00 from the White Sox or find no job that suited me she would give me a job herself so I said "What doing pairing finger nails over in your studio?" So she said "No indeed I would hire you as nurse for little Al and the baby in place of the one we have got." So I said I wouldn't mind being a nurse for little Al as I and him can have a fine time playing together and I would make a man out of him but I wouldn't sign no contract to take care of little Florrie for no amt. of money as it would mean I would half to stay awake 24 hrs. per day as this little bird don't never close her eyes and I only wished they was a few umpires like her in the American League and maybe a man could get something like a square deal. I have often heard people that had babys brag about how good they was and slept all the wile except when they was getting their chow but little Florrie ain't no relation to them or neither is little Al as he was just as bad when he was a baby and when I hear these storys about these here perfect babys I begin to think that the husbands and wifes that owns them is the same kind that never had a cross word since they been married.

But jokeing to 1 side Al I don't see how the Swede stands it being up all day and then up again all night and sometimes I wished I could help her out by walking the floor with the kid nights but the Dr. said I wasn't to do nothing that might strain my bad arm till I was sure it was O. K.

Your pal,   Jack.

Chi, Dec. 12.

FRIEND AL: Well Al yesterday was the American League meeting and I happened to be down town so I dropped in to the hotel where the meeting was at just to see some of the boys as they's always a bunch of them hangs around in the hopes that 1 of the club owners will smile at them or something and any way I dropped in the lobby and the 1st. bird I seen was Bobby Roth that was with us a few yrs. ago and played the outfield for Cleveland last yr. So I says "Hello Bobby." So he said "Hello Jack." Well it was the 1st. time I seen him since I quit baseball for the army but I guess he hadn't never heard that I was in the war or something and any way he didn't say nothing about it but finely he said he supposed I would be back with the White Sox next yr. so then I told him I had made it up in my mind to quit the game and go in to business and he said he was sorry to hear it. So I said "Yes you are because when you was with the Cleveland club I always made you look like a monkey." So he said "I never had a chance to hit against you as they had me batting 4th. at Cleveland and by the time it come my turn to hit you was took out of the game." So I said "Yes I was" and he didn't have nothing more to say.

Well I walked around a wile and run in to some of the other boys Artie Hofman and Charley O'Leary and Jim Archer and Joe Benz but not a 1 of them mentioned about the war or me being over there and I finely figured it out that it was a kind of a sore subject with them so I walked away from them and all of a sudden I seen Rowland the mgr. and I thought sure he would ask me about signing up but I guess Bobby or somebody must of tipped him off about me going in to business so he didn't want to take a chance of me turning him down or maybe he thought he would have a better chance of landing me if he didn't say nothing at this time but just sent me a big fat contract when the time comes. Any way we didn't talk contract but he had heard about me getting shot in the left arm and he mentioned about it and smiled and said it was lucky I wasn't a left hander so you see he has got me on his mind and I suppose the contract will come along in a few days and then I will half to send it back to them and tell them I am through even if the contract meets my figure which is $5000.00 because I wouldn't go back and pitch baseball even for that amt. when I can go in to business and maybe not do that well right at the start but work myself up in to something worth wile.

Well after I left Rowland I bumped in to Hy Pond that I was with him down in the Central League and he asked me to come in and have a drink so I went with him and histed a couple beers but it was a mad house and besides wile we was over there takeing the fight out of the Germans the people that stayed home done the same thing to the beer and the way they have got it fixed now you could drink all they have got left without feeling like shock troops so finely I told Hy to make my excuses to the boys and I come along home.

Well I have had 2 or 3 pretty good chances so far to break in to some line of business and 1 of them was an ad I seen in the paper today where they wanted a young man of good appearances to represent them in Detroit with $5000.00 per annum to start out but they didn't say what line of business it was and besides I don't feel like moveing to Detroit so I decided to not answer the ad but wait till something showed up where I could stay here in Chi as they's no use of a man rushing in to something blind folded you might say when all as I half to do is play the waiting game and let them come to me with all their offers and then pick out the one that suits me best. Get them bidding against each other for you is the system Al.

Your pal,   Jack.

Chi, Dec. 23.

FRIEND AL: Well Al I just come back from down town where I and Florrie has been all P. M. buying xmas presents and she has been saying ever since I come back from France how lonesome she was all the wile I was away but from the number of xmas presents she had to buy for people I never seen or heard of they couldn't of been more than a couple hours of the time I was over there when she wasn't busy saying please to meet you. But whenever I would raise a holler about the jack she was spending she would swell up and tell me she would pay for it out of her own money so of course I couldn't say nothing though when the bills comes in they will be addressed to me and her check book will of probably got halled away with the garbage.

Well when we got through buying for the city directory she said she was through except for the baby as she had fixed up for little Al last time she was down so she asked me what could I suggest for little Florrie so I said why get her a new rattle as what else is they for a 6 mos. old baby so she said the baby wasn't going to be 6 mos. old all her life. How is that for a bright remark Al but of course a woman can't expect to have the looks and everything else with it, but any way she said she had a idear that she heard about a friend of hers doing it that had a little baby girl and that was to start a pearl necklace for her and 1st. buy the chain and a few pearls and then add a couple pearls every yr. so as when she got old enough to wear it she would have something.

Well I said why not wait till some xmas when we have got a little more jack say in 7 or 8 yrs. and then get enough pearls to make up for the yrs. we passed up and then give them to the little girl and tell her we started buying them before she was a yr. old and she wouldn't know the differents and in the mean wile we could get her something that if she busted it we wouldn't be out no real jack. So Florrie said "You don't suppose I am going to leave her get a hold of the necklace now do you or even show it to her?" So I said "That is a fine way to give a person a xmas present is to buy something and hide it and if that is the system why don't you buy her a couple new undershirts my size and I can wear them and when I have wore them out you can put them away somewheres till she gets old enough to have some sence and then you can hall them out and show them to her and tell her that was what we give her for xmas in 1918."

Well you know how much good it done to argue and finely she picked out a little gold chain and 4 little pearls to go with it and it cost $47.50 but what and the he——ll is $47.50 as long as the baby has a merry xmas.

Well we was shoping all the P. M. but you can bet we didn't go in that smart Alex store where that smart Alex mgr. got so fresh when they offered me that cheap job and we use to spend a lot of jack in there at that but never again and if they want to know why they haven't got no big bill against us like they usually have around xmas time I will tell them and then maybe Mr. Smart will wished he hadn't of been so smart but at that when I seen them floor men on the job today I was tickled to death I turned that job down because the way them women jousled them around I couldn't of never stood for it and I would of felt like busting them in the eye if it had of been me and of course I don't mean that Al as I wouldn't think of hitting a woman but I would of certainly gave them the elbow or accidently parked my heel on a few of their best toes.

Well of course I couldn't buy Florrie no present wile she was along and I half to go back down again tomorrow and try and find something and I haven't the lease idear what will it be and all as I know is that it won't be no pearl necklace for adults. She says she has all ready boughten my present and wait till I see it. Well I suppose it will be a corset or maybe she will give me a set of false teeth and hide them away somewheres till I come of age to put them on.

Well Al we are sending xmas cards to you and Bertha and I only wished it could be something more but we kind of feel this yr. like we shouldn't ought to spend a whole lot of money what with some of the boys still over in France yet and another liberty loan come-ing along some time soon and all and all it don't seem hardly right to be blowing jack for xmas presents but maybe next yr. everything will be different and in the mean wile merry xmas to you and Bertha from the both of us.

Your pal,   Jack.

Chi, Dec. 31.

FRIEND AL: Well Al they's not much news to write as everything has been going along about like usual and I haven't made it up in my mind yet what line of business to take up though I have got several good offers hanging in the fire you might say and am just playing the waiting game till I decide which 1 looks best as I would be sorry to get in to 1 thing and then find out they was something else opened up that I would like a whole lot better.

One of the things I have got in mind is takeing up newspaper work and writing articles about baseball or maybe army life and when the baseball season opens maybe I would go out and see the games and write up the reports and you can bet my articles would be different then some of these birds that's reporting the games as I would at lease know what I was writeing about wile you take the most of these here reporters and all the baseball they know you could carry it around in a eye dropper.

But I don't know whether the papers would pay me the kind of money I would want and if not why I am in a position to laugh at them.

Well I got tired of setting around the house today as Florrie was over to her looks garage and the Swede had both the kiddies out to get the air so I walked around a wile and then I hopped on to a 35th. St. car and rode over west and I happened to look out of the window and we was just passing the ball pk. so I didn't have nothing else to do so I give the conductor the highball and jumped off and went up in the office to see if they wasn't maybe some mail for me that some of the boys wrote from France not knowing my home address.

Well they wasn't no mail so I set down and fanned a wile with Harry the secty. of the club and he asked me all about what I seen over acrost the pond and we had quite a talk and finely I thought maybe Comiskey would be sore if he heard I had been up there and hadn't paid my respects but Harry said he wasn't in so then I thought maybe he might of left some word about me and wanted to know if I was going to come back and pitch baseball for him or not but Harry said he hadn't mentioned nothing about it so I guess when the time comes he will just send me my contract and then I will send it back and tell him I have decided to quit baseball and go in to some line of business where they's a future in it.

Because they's no use of a man killing himself pitching baseball and then when your arm gives out you haven't got no business to go in to because business men won't hire a man that's 33 or 34 yrs. old and no experience and besides if a man has got a family like mine why not stay home and enjoy them in the stead of traveling on the road ½ the yr. around you might say. So even if Comiskey should send me a contract calling for $4000.00 per annum I would send it back though that is the lease I would sign up for if I was going to sign at all.

Well Al xmas is over and I only wished you could of been here to see how little Al eat it up. Besides all the junk we give him all of Florrie's friends sent something and all together he must of got about 25 presents in the 1st. place and now he has got about a 100 as everything he got is broke in to 4 peaces and they also sent the baby a load of play things that means as much to her as the hit and run but Florrie says never mind they will be put away till some xmas when she is old enough to enjoy them and then we won't half to buy her nothing new. Well the idear is O. K. Al but it reminds me like when Sept. comes along and a man has got a straw Kelly that looks pretty good and you give it to your wife to take care of till next June and when it comes June you go and buy yourself a new hat.

Well Florrie's present to me was a phonograph and of course that's a mighty fine present and will cost her or whoever pays for it a bunch of jack but between you and I Al I wouldn't be surprised if she was thinking to herself when she bought it that maybe she might turn it on some times when I am not in the house. What I give her is 1 of these here patent shower bath attachments that you can have it put up on a regular bath tub and you can have a regular tub bath or a shower just as you feel like. They cost real money to Al but what's the differents when its your wife?

Your pal,   Jack.

Chi, Jan. 16.

Friend Al: Well Al I don't know if you have been reading the papers but if you have you probably seen the big news where Kid Gleason has been appointed mgr. of the White Sox. Well old pal that peace of news makes all the differents in the world to your old pal. As you know I had entirely gave up the idear of going back in to baseball and figured where I would take up some other line of business and work myself up to something big and I was just about makeing it up in my mind to accept 1 of the offers I got when this news come out.

Well old pal I haven't no idear how things will come out now as I guess you know what friends I and Gleason are. You know he was asst. mgr. when Callahan had the club and then again the yr. Rowland win the pennant and he seemed to take a fancy to me some way and I guess I may as well come out and say that I was his favorite of any man on the club and I always figured that it was because when he tried his kidding on me I always give him back as good as he sent wile the rest of the boys was a scared of him but he use to kid me just to hear what I would say back to him. Like 1 time we was playing a double header with the St. Louis club and Jim Scott lose the 1st. game and Callahan said I was to work the 2d. game so I was warming up and Gleason come out and stood behind me and I had eat something that didn't set very good so Gleason asked me how I felt and I said "Not very good. I'm not myself today." So he said "Well then it looks like we would break even on the afternoon." So I said "I will break your jaw in a minute."

But a side from all that he was the 1 man that ever give me the credit for the work I done and if he had of been mgr. of the club he would of pitched me in my regular turn in the stead of playing favorites like them other 2 birds and all as I needed was regular work and I would of made them forget Walsh and all the rest of them big 4 flushers.

Well Al Gleason lives in Philly in the winter so I expect he will either wire me a telegram and ask for my terms or else he will run out here and see me and if they give me $4000.00 per annum I am afraid they won't be nothing for me to do only sign up though I have got several chances to go in to some business at better money than that and with a future to it. But this here is a matter of friendships Al and after all Gleason done for me why if he says the word I can't hardly do nothing only say yes though of course I am not going to sacrifice myself or sign for a nickel less than $4000.00.

You see Al this will be Gleason's 1st yr. as a mgr. and he will want to finish up in the race and I don't care how good a mgr. is he can't win unless he has got the men and beleive me he will need all the pitching strenth he can get a hold of as Cleveland and N. Y. has both strenthened up and the Boston club with all their men back from the service has got enough good ball players to finish 1st. and 2d. both if they was room for all of them to play at once. So that is where friendships comes in Al and I figure that it is up to your old pal to pass up my business chances and show the Kid I am true blue and beleive me I will show him something and I will come pretty near winning that old flag single handed.

So all and all it looks like your old pal wouldn't go in to no business adventure this yr. but I will be out there on the old ball field giveing them the best I have got and I guess the fans won't holler their heads off when I walk out there the 1st. time after what I done in France.

Your pal,   Jack.

Chi, Feb. 13.

FRIEND AL: Well Al it says in the paper this A. M. that Gleason is comeing to Chi for a few days to see Comiskey and talk over the plans for the training trip and etc. but they's another reason why he is comeing to Chi and maybe you can guess what it is. Well Al that's the way to work it is to wait and let them come to you in the stead of you going to them as when you make them come to you you can pretty near demand whatever you want and they half to come acrost with it.

That's a fine story Al about him comeing to talk over plans for the training trip as I know Comiskey and you could talk to him for 3 wks. about the plans for the training trip and when you got all through talking he would tell you what the plans was for the training trip so you can bet that Gleason isn't comeing all the way out here from Philly to hear himself talk but what he is comeing for is to get some of the boys in line that lives here and when I say some of the boys I don't half to go no further eh Al?

And all the more because I dropped him a letter a couple wks. ago and said I had made all arrangements to go in to business but if he wanted me I would give up my plans and pitch for him provided he give me my figure which is $3600.00 per annum and I never got no answer to the letter and now I know why I didn't get no answer as he is 1 of the kind that would rather set down and do their talking face to face then set down and take the trouble of writeing a letter when he could just as well hop on the old rattler and come out here and see me personly.

Well Al he will be here next wk. and I have left my phone No. over to the ball pk. so as he will know how to get a hold of me and all they will be to it is he will ask me how much I want and I will tell him $3600.00 and he will say sign here.

Well Al Florrie says she don't know if she is glad or sorry that I am going to be back in the old game as she says she don't like to have me away from home so much but still and all she knows I wouldn't be happy unless I was pitching baseball but she also says that if I do get back in to harness and ern a liveing and they's another war breaks out she will probably half to go as she couldn't claim no exemptions on the grounds of a dependant husband. So I said "I guess they won't ask no women to go to war because the minute they heard 1 of them trench rats give their college yell they would all retreat to the equator or somewheres." So she said "They had women in the Russia army and they didn't retreat." So I said "Yes they did only the men retreated so much faster that the women looked like they was standing still."

Jokeing to 1 side Al I will let you know how I come out with Gleason but they's only 1 way I can come out and that is he will be tickled to death to sign me at my own figure because if he trys any monkey business with me I will laugh in his face and Comiskey to, and give up the game for good and take the best offer I have got in some other line.

Your pal,   Jack.

Chi, Feb. 20.

FRIEND AL: Well Al I have just came back from the ball pk. and had a long talk with Gleason and the most of it was kidding back and 4th. like usual when the 2 of us gets together but it didn't take no Wm. A. Pinkerton to see that he is anxious to have me back on the ball club and in a few days they will probably send me a contract at my own figures and then they won't be nothing to do only wait for the rattler to start for the sunny south land.

Well Gleason got in yesterday P.M. and I was expecting him to call up either last night or this A.M. but they didn't no call come and I figured they must of either lost my phone No. over to the office or else the phone was out of order or something and the way the phones has been acting all winter why he might of asked central to give him my No. and the next thing he knew he would be connected with the morgue so any way when they hadn't no call came at noon I jumped on a 35th St. car and went over to the pk. and up in the office and the secty. said Gleason was in talking to Comiskey but he would be through in a little while.

Well after about a hr. Gleason come out and seen me setting there and of course he had to start kidding right off of the real so he said "Well here is the big Busher and I hoped you was killed over in France but I suppose even them long distance guns fell short of where you was at." So I said "They reached me all right and they got me in the left arm and wasn't it lucky it wasn't my right arm?" So he said "Its to bad they didn't shoot your head off and made a pitcher out of you." So then he asked me all about the war and if I got in to Germany and I told him no that I got my wounds in June and was invalid home. So he said "You fight just like you pitch and they half to take you out in the 5th. inning." So I asked him if he got my letter and he said he got a letter that looked like it might of came from me so he didn't open it. So I said "Well I don't know if you opened it or not but I just as soon tell you right here what I said in the letter. I told you I was going in to some business but I would stay in baseball another yr. to help you out if you met my figure." So he asked what was my figure, so I told him $3000.00 per annum. So he said how much was I getting in the army and I told him I was getting about $30.00 per mo. most of the time. So he said "Yes you was getting $30.00 per mo to get up at 5 A.M. and work like a dog all day and eat beans and stew and sleep in a barn nights with a cow and a pig for your roomies and now you want $3000.00 a yr. to live in the best hotels and eat off the fat of the land and about once in every 10 days when we feel like we can afford to loose a ball game why you half to go out there and stand on your feet pretty near ½ the P. M. and if it happens to be July or Aug. you come pretty close to prespireing."

So I said "You are the same old Gleason always trying to kid somebody but jokeing a side I will sign up for $3000.00 or else I will go in to business." So he asked me what business I was going in to and I told him I had an offer from the Stock Yards. So he said "How much do they offer for you on the hoof?"

Well we kidded along back and 4th. like that for a wile and finely he said he was going out somewhere with Comiskey so I asked him if he wasn't going to talk business to me 1st. So he said "I will tell you how it is boy. They have cut down the limit so as each club can't only carry 21 men and that means we won't have no room for bench lizards. But the boss says that on acct. of you haveing went to France and wasn't killed why we will take you south if you want to go and you will get a chance to show if you are a pitcher yet or not and if you are like you use to be why maybe the Stock Yards will keep open long enough to take you when we are through with you and you can tell Armour and Swift and them that I will leave them know whether I want you or not about 3 days after we get to Texas." So I asked him how about salery and he said "The boss will send you a contract in a few days and if I was you I would be satisfied with it."

So it looks now like I was all set for the season Al and Gleason said I would be satisfied with the salery which is just as good as saying it will be $3000.00 as I wouldn't be satisfied with no less, so all I half to do now is wait for the contract and put my name on it and I will be back in the game I love and when a man's heart is in their work how are you going to stop him a specially with the stuff I've got.

Your pal,   Jack.

Chi, March 8.

FRIEND AL: Well Al I am through with baseball for good and am going in to business and I don't know just yet which proposition I will take that's been offered to me but they's no hurry and I will take the one that looks best when the proper time comes.

I suppose you will be surprised to hear that I have gave up the old game but maybe you won't be surprised when I tell you what come off today.

Well in the 1st. place when the mail man come this A.M. he brought me a contract from Comiskey and the figures amounted to $2400.00 per annum. How is that Al when I was getting $2500.00 per annum before I went to the war. Well at 1st. I couldn't hardly beleive my eyes but that was the figure all right and finely I thought they must be some mistake so I was going to call up Comiskey and demand an explanation but afterwards I thought maybe I better run over and see him.

Well Al I went over there and Harry said the boss was busy but he would find out would he see me. Well after a wile Harry come out and said I was to go in the inside office so I went in and Comiskey was setting at his desk and for a wile he didn't look up but finely he turned around and seen me and shook hands and said "Well young man what can I do for you?" So I said "I come to see you about this here contract." So he asked me if I had signed it and I said no I hadn't so he said "Well they's nothing to see me about then." So I said "Yes because I figure they must of been some mistake in the salery you offered me." So he said "Don't you think you are worth it?" So I said "This here contract calls for $2400.00 per annum and I was getting $2500.00 when I quit and enlisted in the war so it looks like you was fineing me $100.00 per annum for fighting for my country." I said "Gleason said he wanted me and would send me a contract that I would be satisfied with." Well Comiskey said "If Gleason said he wanted you he must of been kidding me when I talked to him but if he wants

227

you bad enough to pay the differents between what that contract calls for and what you want why he is welcome but that is up to him."

Well Al it was all as I could do to hold myself in and if he was a younger man it would of been good night Comiskey but I kept a hold of myself and asked him why didn't he trade me to some club where I could get real jack. So he said "Well I will tell you young man I have got just 1 chance to trade you and that is to Washington and if you think Griffith will pay you more money than I will why I will make the trade." Well I told him to not trouble himself as I was through with baseball any way and had decided to go in to some business so he said good luck and I started out but he said "Here you have left your contract and you better take it along with you because some times when you leave a contract lay around the house a few days the figures gets so big that you wouldn't hardly know them."

Well I seen he was trying to kid me so I said "All right I will take the contract home and tear it up" and I walked out on him.

Well Al that's all they is to it and I am tickled to death that it has came out the way it has and now I can take the best offer that comes along in some good business line and can stay right here in Chi and be home all the yr. around with Florrie and the kiddies.

As for the White Sox I wished them good luck and beleive me they will need it the way Gleason and Comiskey are trying to run things and they will do well to finish in the same league with Boston and Cleveland and N. Y. but at that I don't believe its Gleason that's doing it and the way I figure is that this is his 1st. yr. as mgr and he is a scared to open his clam and if he had his say he would give me the $2800.00 I am holding out for. But its Comiskey himself that's trying to make a monkey out of me. Well god help his ball club is all as I can say.

As for leaveing them trade me to Washington that would be a sweet club to pitch for Al where the only time they get a run is when the president comes out to see them and he's libel to be in France all summer.

Your pal,   Jack.

Chi, March 20.

FRIEND AL: Well Al this is the last letter you will get from me from Chi for a wile as I am leaveing for Texas with the White Sox tomorrow night. The scheme worked Al and by setting pretty in the boat and keeping my mouth shut I made them come to me.

I suppose you will be surprised to hear that I am going to get back in to harness but wait till I tell you what come off today and you will see where they wasn't no other way out.

Well I went over to the stores this A.M. and when I come back the Swede said some man had called me up on the phone. So of course I knew it must of been the ball pk. so I called them up and the secty. answered the phone and I asked him if anybody wanted to talk to me. So he said no but Gleason was there if I wanted to talk to him.

So I said put him on the wire and pretty soon I heard Gleason's voice and he said "Well Jack are you going along with us?" So I said "What about salery?" So he said "You have got your contract haven't you?" So I said "Yes but it don't call for enough jack." So he said "Well if you earn more jack than your contract calls for you will get it." So I said "If that's a bet I'm on."

So he told me to bring my contract along and come over there and I went over and there was a whole bunch of the boys getting ready for the get away and I wished you could of heard them when they seen me stride in to the office. Well Al they was hand shakes all around and you would of thought it was a family union or something.

Well the business was all tended to in a minute and I signed up and I am going to get $2400.00 which is the same money I was getting when I quit and that's going some Al when you think of the way they have been cutting salerys in baseball.

Well Al I am going to show them that they haven't made no mistake and I am going to work my head off for Gleason and Comiskey and the rest of the boys and wile I hate to be away from Florrie and the kiddies, still and all they's nobody on this ball club that lays awake all night crying for their bottle and if Texas don't do nothing else for me it will at lease give me a chance to get a little sleep.

Your pal,   Jack.

II

The Writer Goes to War

My Four Weeks in France

Dodging Submarines to Cover the Biggest Game of All

Wednesday, July 18. A Lake Michigan Port.

I KEPT an appointment to-day with a gentleman from Somewhere in Connecticut.

"How," said he, "would you like to go to France?"

I told him I'd like it very much, but that I was thirty-two years old, with a dependable wife and three unreliable children.

"Those small details," he said, "exempt you from military duty. But we want you as a war correspondent."

I told him I knew nothing about war. He said it had frequently been proved that that had nothing to do with it. So we hemmed and we hawed, pro and con, till my conscientious objections were all overruled.

"In conclusion," said he, "we'd prefer to have you go on a troopship. That can be arranged through the War Department. There'll be no trouble about it."

Monday, July 30. A Potomac Port.

To-day I took the matter up with the War Department, through Mr. Creel.

"Mr. Creel," I said, "can I go on a troopship?"

"No," said Mr. Creel.

There was no trouble about it.

Wednesday, August 1. An Atlantic Port.

The young man in the French Consulate has taken a great fancy to me. He will not visé my passport till I bring him two more autographed pictures of myself.

George W. Gloom of the steamship company said there would be a ship sailing Saturday.

"Are we convoyed through the danger zone?" I inquired.

"We don't guarantee it," said he. "There has never been an accident on this line," he added.

"What I was thinking about," said I, "wouldn't be classed as an accident." Further questioning developed the comforting fact that the ship I am taking has never been sunk.

I told him I wanted a cabin to myself, as I expected to work.

"You will be in with two others," he said.

"I would pay a little more to be alone," said I.

This evidently was not worth answering, so I asked him how long the trip would take.

"I know nothing about it," said he.

"I believe that," said I when I was well out of his ear-shot.

Wednesday, August 8. At Sea.

We left port at ten last night, a mere three and a half days behind schedule. The ship and I should be very congenial, as we are about the same age.

My roommates are a young man from Harvard and a young man from Yale, but so far I have managed to keep the conversation neutral. We suspect that they made ours a first-class cabin by substituting the word 1ère for 2ème on the sign, and I am very certain that my berth was designed for Rabbit Maranville.

Our passenger list includes a general, a congressman, a lady novelist and her artist husband, French; a songbird, also French; two or three majors, a Thaw, and numerous gentlemen of the consular service. The large majority on board are young men going into American Ambulance and Y. M. C. A. work.

After breakfast this morning there was life-boat drill, directed by our purser, who is permanently made up as Svengali. He sent us down to our cabins to get our life-belts and then assigned us to our boats. Mine, No. 12, is as far from my cabin as they could put it without cutting it loose from the ship, and if I happen to be on deck when that old torpedo strikes, believe me, I'm not going to do a Marathon for a life-belt. Shoes off, and a running hop, step and jump looks like the best system. Moreover, I'm going to disobey another of the rules, which is that each passenger must remain calm.

Next we had to fill out a form for the enlightenment of Svengali as to our destination, business, home address, foreign address, literary tastes, etc. One item was "the names of relatives or friends you lofh." This was unanswered, as nobody aboard seemed to know the meaning of the verb.

In the fumoir this afternoon a young American wanted a match. He consulted his dictionary and dug out "allumette." But he thought the *t*'s were silent and asked Auguste for "allumay." Auguste disappeared and returned in five minutes with a large glass of lemonade. The cost of that little French lesson was two francs.

I am elected to eat at the "second table." Our bunch has luncheon at twelve-thirty and dinner at seven. The first table crowd's hours are eleven and five-thirty. Breakfast is a free-for-all and we sit where we choose. My trough mates at the meals are two Americans, a Brazilian, and four Frenchmen. Ours is a stag table, which unfortunate circumstance is due to the paucity of women, or, as they are sometimes called, members of the fair sex. The Brazilian speaks nine or ten languages, but seems to prefer French. The two Americans are always engaged in sotto voce dialogue, and the four Frenchmen race with the Brazilian for the conversational speed championship of the high seas. This leaves me free to devote all my time to the proper mastication of food.

Thursday, August 9. Completely at Sea.

A gentleman on board is supplied with one of these newfangled one hundred dollar safety suits. The wearer is supposed to be able to float indefinitely. It is also a sort of thermos bottle, keeping one warm in cold water and cool in hot. I do not envy the gent. I have no ambition to float indefinitely. And if I didn't happen to have it on when the crash came, I doubt whether I could spare the time to change. And besides, if I ever do feel that I can afford one hundred dollars for a suit, I won't want to wear it for the edification of mere fish.

When Svengali isn't busy pursing, he is usually engaged in chess matches with another of the officers. The rest of the idle portion of the crew stand round the table and look on. Sometimes they look on for an hour without seeing a move made, but they never seem to lose interest. Every little movement brings forth a veritable torrent of français from the spectators. I can understand the fascination of chess from the player's end, but could get few thrills from watching, especially when there was standing room only.

Far more fascinating to look at is the game two of my French trough mates play at breakfast. The rules are simple. You take a muffin about the size of a golf ball. You drop it into your cup of chocolate. Then you fish for it, sometimes with a spoon, but more often with your fingers. The object is to convey it to your mouth without discoloring your necktie. Success comes three times in five.

The players are about evenly matched. One of them I suspect, is not in the game for sport's sake, but has a worthier object. Nature supplied him with a light gray mustache, and a chocolate brown would blend better with his complexion. If the muffins hold out, his color scheme will be perfect before we reach port.

The discovery has been made that there's a man on board who plays the cornet, so if we are subbed it will not be an unmitigated evil.

Friday, August 10.

Every morning one sees on the deck people one never saw before, and as we have not stopped at any stations since we started, the inference is that certain parties have not found the trip a continuous joy ride.

A news bulletin, published every morning, sometimes in English and sometimes in French, keeps us right up to date on thrilling events, thrillingly spelled. I have copied a sample:

It is now the tim for the final invaseon of the west by the eastren american league teams and before this clash is over it will be definitively known wether the two sox teams are to fight it out in a nip and tuk finish or wether the Chicago sox will have a comfortable margen to insure a world series betwean the two largest American citys Chicago and New York.

The French news deals exclusively with the developments in the world series Over There, which is, perhaps, almost as important.

A new acquaintance made to-day was that of the Gentleman from Louisiana. He introduced himself to scold me and another guy for not taking sufficient exercise. We told him we found little pleasure in promenading the deck.

"That's unnecessary," he said. "Get yourselves a pair of three-pound dumb-bells and use them a certain length of time every day."

So we are constantly on the lookout for a dumb-bell shop, but there seems to be a regrettable lack of such establishments in mid-ocean.

The Gentleman from Louisiana says he is going to join the Foreign Legion if they'll take him. He is only seventy years old.

"But age makes no difference to a man like I," says he. "I exercise and keep hard. All my friends are hard and tough. Why, one of my friends, an undertaker, always carries a razor in his boot."

Presumably this bird never allows psychological depression in his business.

The Gentleman from Louisiana continues:

"I've got a reputation for hardness, but I'm only hard when I know I'm right. I used such hard language once that they injected me from a committee. I was state senator then. But in all the time I held office I never talked more than two minutes."

We expressed polite regret that he was not a state senator still. And we asked him to have a lemonade.

"No, thank you. Even the softest drinks have a peculiar effect on me. They make my toes stick together."

We guaranteed to pry those members apart again after he had quenched his thirst, but he would not take a chance.

On the way cabinward from this fascinating presence, I was invited into a crap game on the salle à manger floor. The gentleman with the dice tossed a hundred-franc note into the ring and said: "Shoot it all." And the amount was promptly oversubscribed. So I kept on going cabinward.

Samedi, 11 Août.

The man back there in the steamship office can no more truthfully say: "There has never been an accident on this line."

I awoke at three-thirty this morning to find the cabin insufferably hot and opened the port-hole which is directly above my berth. The majority of the ocean immediately left its usual haunts and came indoors. Yale and Harvard were given a shower bath and I had a choice of putting on the driest things I could find and going on deck or drowning where I lay. The former seemed the preferable course.

Out there I found several fellow voyagers asleep in their chairs and a watchman in a red-and-white tam-o'-shanter scanning the bounding main for old Hans W. Periscope.

I wanted sympathy, but the watchman informed me that he ne comprended pas anglais, monsieur. So we stood there together and scanned, each in his own language.

My garçon de cabine promises he will have me thoroughly bailed out by bedtime to-night.

I sat at a different breakfast table, but there was no want of entertainment. At my side was a master of both anglais and français,

239

and opposite him an American young lady who thinks French is simply just impossible to learn.

"Mademoiselle," says he, "must find it difficult to get what she likes to eat."

"I certainly do," says she. "I don't understand a word of what's on the menu card."

"Perhaps I can help mademoiselle," says he. "Would she like perhaps a grapefruit?"

She would and she'd also like oatmeal and eggs and coffee. So he steered her straight through the meal with almost painful politeness, but in the intervals when he wasn't using his hands as an aid to gallant discourse, he was manicuring himself with a fork.

This afternoon they drug me into a bridge game. My partner was our congressman's secretary. Our opponents were a Standard Oil official and a vice-consul bound for Italy. My partner's middle name was Bid and Mr. Oil's was Double. And I was too shy to object when they said we'd play for a cent a point.

At the hour of going to press, Standard Oil had practically all the money in the world. And my partner has learned that a holding of five clubs doesn't demand a bid of the same amount.

Sunday, August 12.

The boat seems to be well supplied with the necessities of life, such as cocktails and cards and chips, but it is next to impossible to obtain luxuries like matches, ice-water and soap.

Yale and Harvard both knew enough to bring their own soap, but my previous ocean experiences were mostly with the Old Fall River Line, on which there wasn't time to wash. Neither Yale nor Harvard ever takes a hint. And "Apportez-moi du savon, s'il vous plaît," to the cabin steward is just as ineffectual.

All good people attended service this morning, and some bad ones played poker this afternoon.

In a burst of generosity I invited a second-class French young lady of five summers to have some candy. She accepted, and her acceptance led to the discovery that the ship's barber is also its candy salesman.

This barber understands not a syllable of English, which fact has added much to young America's enjoyment. The boys, in the midst of a hair cut, say to him politely: "You realize that you're a damn rotten barber?" And he answers smilingly: "Oui, oui, monsieur." Yesterday, I am told, a young shavee remarked: "You make me sick." The barber replied as usual, and the customer was sick all last night.

To-morrow afternoon there is to be a "concert" and I'm to speak a piece, O Diary!

Monday, August 13.

The concert was "au profit du Secours National de France. Œuvre fondée pour répartir les Secours aux Victimes de la Guerre."

Ten minutes before starting time they informed me that I was to talk on "The American National Game," and I don't even know how the White Sox came out a week ago to-morrow.

The afternoon's entertainment opened with a few well-chosen remarks by our congressman. The general, designated on the program as "chairman," though his real job was toastmaster, talked a while about this, that and the other thing, and then introduced the cornet player, using his real name. This gentleman and I blew at the same time, so I have no idea what he played. I got back in time for some pretty good harmonizing by three young Americans and a boy from Cincinnati. Then there was a Humorous Recitation (the program said so) by a gent with a funny name, and some really delightful French folk songs by the lady novelist. After which came a Humorous Speech (the program forgot to say so) by myself, necessarily brief, as I gave it in French. The French songbird followed with one of those things that jump back and forth between Pike's Peak and the Grand Cañon, and a brave boy played a ukelele, and the quartette repeated. In conclusion, we all rose and attempted *La Marseillaise.*

Some of the programs had been illustrated by the lady novelist's artist husband, and these were auctioned off after the show. I made my financial contribution indirectly, through better card players than myself. My bridge partner, I noticed, had recovered from his attack of the Bids.

Tuesday, August 14.

The concert, by the way, was given in the salon de conversation, which, I think, should be reserved for the Gentleman from Louisiana. He has now told me two hundred times that he won his election to the State Senate by giving one dollar and a half to "a nigger."

One of our young field-service men spoiled the forenoon poker game with a lecture on how to catch sharks. His remarkable idea is to put beefsteak on a stout copper wire and troll with it. He has evidently been very intimate with this family of fish, and he says they are simply crazy about beefsteak. Personally, I have no desire to catch sharks. There are plenty aboard. But I do wish he had not got to the most interesting part of his theory at the moment the dealer slipped me four sixes before the draw. Everybody was too busy listening to stay.

We have discovered that the man behind the gun in the fumoir bears a striking resemblance to Von Hindenburg, but no one has been found who will tell him so.

There was a track meet this afternoon, and the author of this diary was appointed referee. But the first event, a wheelbarrow race, was so exciting that he feared for his weak heart and resigned in favor of our general. There didn't seem to be much else to the meet but jujutsu, the sport in which skill is supposed to triumph over brawn. I noticed that a two-hundred-and-thirty-pound man was the winner.

We are in that old zone, and the second table's dinner hour has been advanced to half past six so that there need be no lights in the dining-room. Also, we are ordered not to smoke, not even to light a match, on deck after dark. The fumoir will be running for the last time, but the port-holes in it will all be sealed, meaning that after thirty-five smokers have done their best for a few hours the atmosphere will be intolerable. We can stay on deck smokeless, or we can try to exist in the airless fumoir, or we can go to bed in the dark and wish we were sleepy. And the worst is yet to come.

Wednesday, August 15.

The rules for to-night and to-morrow night provide for the closing of our old friend, the fumoir, at seven o'clock, and that witching hour is on you long before you expect it, for they jump the clock fifteen minutes ahead every time it's noon or midnight. The ship will not be lit up. The passengers may, if they do their shopping early.

There was another life-boat "drill" this afternoon. Every one was required to stand in front of his canoe and await the arrival of Svengali. When that gent appeared, he called the roll. As soon as you said "Here" or "Present," your part of the "drill" was over. When the time comes I must do my drifting under an alias, as Svengali insists on designating me as Monsieur Gardnierre. But No. 12 is at least honored with two second-class ladies. Many a poor devil on the ship is assigned to a life-boat that is strictly stag.

The Gentleman from Louisiana to-day sprang this one:

"You know when I part my hair in the middle I look just like a girl. Well, sir, during the Mardi Gras, two years ago, I put on a page's costume and parted my hair in the middle. And you know girls under a certain age must go home at nine o'clock in the evening. Well, sir, a policeman accosted me and told me I had to go home. I gave him the bawling out of his life. And maybe you think he wasn't surprised!"

Maybe I do think so.

The Gentleman strayed to the subject of Patti and wound up with a vocal imitation of that lady. He stopped suddenly when his voice parted in the middle.

We have seen no periscopes, but when I opened my suit-case this morning I met face to face one of those birds that are house pets with inmates of seven-room flats at twenty-five dollars per month. I missed fire with a clothes brush, and before I could aim again he had submerged under a vest. Looks as if the little fellow were destined to go with me to Paris, but when I get him there I'll get him good.

Thursday, August 16.

Great excitement last night when a small unlighted boat was sighted half a mile or so off our port. Our gunners, who are said to receive a bonus for every effective shot, had the range all figured out when the pesky thing gave us a signal of friendship. It may have been part of the entertainment.

To-day we persuaded the Gentleman from Louisiana to part his hair in the middle. The New Orleans policeman is not guilty.

It develops that while first- and second-class passengers were unable to read or smoke after dark, the third-class fumoir is running wide open and the Greeks have their cigarettes, libations and card games, while the idle rich bore one another to death with conversation.

Un Américain aboard is now boasting of the world's championship as a load carrier. It was too much trouble for him to pay Auguste for each beverage as it was served, so he ran a two days' charge account. His bill was one hundred and seventy-eight francs, or thirty-five dollars and sixty cents.

"Who got all the drinks?" he asked Auguste.

"You, monsieur," that gent replied.

"And what do you charge for a highball?"

"One franc, monsieur," said Auguste.

Which means, if Auguste is to be believed, that one hundred and seventy-eight highballs went down one throat in two days. And the owner of the throat is still alive and well. Also, he says he will hereafter pay as you enter.

As an appetizer for dinner to-night the captain told everybody to remain on deck, fully dressed and armed with a life-belt, this evening, until he gave permission to retire.

We're all on deck, and in another minute it will be too dark to write.

To-morrow night, Boche willing, we will be out of the jurisdiction of this Imp of Darkness.

I Get to Paris and Encounter
Some Strange Sights

Friday, August 17. A French Port.

IN obedience to the captain's orders we remained on deck last night, fully dressed, till our ship was past the danger zone and in harbor. There was a rule against smoking or lighting matches, but none against conversation.

The Gentleman from Louisiana and a young American Field Service candidate had the floor. The former's best was a report of what he saw once while riding along beside the Columbia River. An enormous salmon jumped out of the water and raced six miles with the train before being worn out. Whether the piscatorial athlete flew or rode a motorcycle, we were unable to learn.

The Gentleman from Louisiana yielded to his younger and stronger countryman. Some one had spoken of the lack of convoy. "Don't you think we haven't a convoy," the kid remarked.

I scanned the sea in all directions and saw nothing but the dark waters. "Where is it?" I inquired.

"There's one on each side of us," said Young America. "They're about twenty miles from the ship."

"I should think," said somebody, "that a very slender submarine might slip in between our side kicks and us and do its regular job."

"No chance," the youth replied. "The convoy boats are used as decoys. The sub would see them first and spend all its ammunition."

A little later he confided in me that the new American warships were two hundred and forty-five thousand horsepower. I had no idea there were that many horses left to measure by.

We spotted a shooting star. "That was a big one," I said.

"Big! Do you know the actual size of those things? I got it straight from a professor of astronomy. Listen. They're as small as a grain of sand."

"Why do they look so big?"

"Because they're so far away and they travel so fast."

Round ten o'clock, beckoning lights ashore told us we were close to safety. But the French gunners remained at their posts two hours longer. The captain's shouted order, relieving them from duty, was music to our ears.

After midnight, however, we turned a complete circle, and at once the deck was alive with rumors. We had been hit, we were going to be hit, we were afraid we would be hit, and so on. The fact was that our pilot from ashore was behind time and we circled round rather than stand still and be an easy target while awaiting him. We were in harbor and anchored at three. Many of us stayed up to see the sun rise over France. It was worth the sleep it cost.

They told us we would not dock until six to-night. Before retiring to my cabin for a nap, I heard we had run over a submarine and also that we had not. The latter story lacked heart interest, but had the merit, probably, of truth. Submarines have little regard for traffic laws, but are careful not to stall their engines in the middle of a boulevard.

I was peacefully asleep when the French officers came aboard to give us and our passports the Double O. They had to send to my cabin for me. I was ordered to appear at once in the salon de conversation. A barber hater addressed me through his beard and his interpreter: "What is Monsieur Laudanum's business in France?"

I told him I was a correspondent.

"For who?"

"Mark Sullivan."

"Have you credentials from him?"

"No, sir."

"Your passport says you are going to Belgium. Do you know there are no trains to Belgium?"

"I know nothing about it."

"Well, there are no trains. How will you go there?"

"I'll try to get a taxi," I said.

"Are you going from here to Paris?"

"Yes."

"And where are you going from Paris?"

"I don't know."

"Please explain that answer."

"I will go wherever the authorities permit me to go."

"That is not a satisfactory answer."

"I'm sorry."

"What is your real business in France?"

"To write."

"I'm afraid we'll have to keep your passport. You will appear to-morrow morning at nine o'clock at this address."

And they handed me a scary-looking card.

On the deck I met our congressman and told him my troubles.

"I know these fellows very well," he said. "If you like, I can fix it for you."

"No," I replied proudly. "I'd rather do my own fixing."

At the dock I got into a taxi and asked to be taken to the ——— Hotel. Not to my dying day will I forget that first ride in a French taxi. Part of the time we were on the right side of the street, part of the time on the left, and never once were we traveling under a hundred and fifty miles an hour. We turned twenty corners and always on one ear. We grazed dozens of frightened pedestrians, many of them men crippled in the war, or by taxis, and women too old to dodge quickly. We aimed at a score of rickety horse-drawn vehicles, but our control was bad and we bumped only one. In front of the hostelry we stopped with a jerk.

"Comme beaucoup?" I asked the assassin.

"Un franc cinquante," he said.

Only thirty cents, and I thought I knew why. When they get through a trip without killing any one, they feel they have not done themselves justice nor given you a square deal.

I found myself a seat at a sidewalk table and ordered sustenance. The vial they brought it in was labeled "Bière Ritten," but I suspect the adjective was misspelled.

Till darkness fell I watched the passing show—street-cars with lady motormen and conductors; hundreds of old carts driven by old women, each cart acting as a traveling roof for an old dog; wounded soldiers walking or hobbling along, some of them accompanied by sad-faced girls; an appalling number of women in black; a lesser number of gayly garbed and extremely cordial ones, and whole flocks of mad taxis, seeking whom they might devour.

By using great caution at the street crossings, I succeeded in reaching the telegraph office where I wrote a message informing Paris friends of my arrival. I presented it to the lady in the cage, who handed it back with the advice that it must be rewritten in French. I turned away discouraged and was starting out again into the gloom when I beheld at a desk the songbird of the ship. Would she be kind enough to do my translating? She would.

The clerk approved the new document, and asked for my passport. I told her it had been taken away. She was deeply grieved, then, but without it monsieur could send no message. Bonne nuit!

Back at the hotel I encountered the Yankee vice-consul, a gentleman from Bedford, Indiana. I told him my sad plight, and he said if matters got too serious his office would undertake to help.

With his assurances to comfort me, I have retired to my room to write, to my room as big as Texas and furnished with all the modern inconveniences.

Saturday, August 18. Paris.

It is Saturday night and they have hot water, but before I take advantage of it I must recount the thrilling experiences of the day.

After a sidewalk breakfast of "oofs" and so-called café in Bordeaux, I went to keep my engagement at court. It was apparent that I was not the only suspect. The walk outside and the room within were crowded with shipmates, most of them from the second cabin, all looking scared to death.

I stood in line till I realized that I must make it snappy if I wanted to catch the eleven-five for Paris; then I butted my way into the august presence of Him of the Beard.

He recognized me at once and told me with his hands to go up-stairs. In a room above I found the English-speaking cross-examiner, with the accent on the cross.

He waved me to a chair and began his offensive.

"Monsieur Laudanum," he said, "when I asked you yesterday how you expected to get to Belgium, you said something about a taxi. That answer was not satisfactory. You have not explained anything to us. I do not believe we can allow you to leave Bordeaux."

"All right, sir." I arose.

"Sit down!" he barked. "Now tell me if you have any explanations to make."

"Nothing beyond what I said yesterday. I have come here to write. I want to go to Paris, and when I arrive there I will find out where else I will be permitted to go."

"It seems very strange to me that you have no papers."

"Yes, sir."

"Have you any?"

I searched my pockets and produced a used-up check book on a Chicago bank. The ogre read every little stub and I felt flattered by his absorbed interest. When he had spent some five minutes on the last one, which recorded a certain painful transaction between me and a man-eating garage, he returned my book and said: "You don't satisfy me at all. You will have to stay here."

"Suppose," said I, "that the American consul vouches for me."

"That will make no difference. You do not seem to realize that we are at war."

"Not with America."

"I don't know your nationality."

"I thought," said I, "that my passport hinted at it."

"You will have to stay in Bordeaux," was his pertinent reply.

"Thank you, sir," I said, and arose again.

"Sit down," said he, "and wait a minute."

He was out of the room five years.

"If he ever does come back," I thought, "it will be in the company of five or six large gendarmes."

But when he came back he came alone.

"Here," he said abruptly, "is your passport. You will be permitted to go to Paris. We will keep track of you there." And he bowed me out of the joint.

The crowd down-stairs seemed as great as ever, and as scared. I picked my way through it with my head held high, a free man.

I decided on a fiacre for my trip from hotel to station. It would be safer, I thought. But I learned, on our interminable way, that defensive fighting in the streets of Bordeaux is far more terrifying, far more dangerous than the aggressive taxi kind. We were run into twice and just missed more times than I could count, and besides my conveyance was always on the verge of a nervous breakdown. 'Spite all the talk of periscopes and subs, the journey across the ocean was parlor croquet compared to my fiacre ride in Bordeaux.

While awaiting my turn at the ticket window I observed at the gate a French soldier wearing a large businesslike bayonet. "Probably to punch tickets with," I thought, but was mistaken. Another gentleman attended to that duty, and the soldier did not give me so much as the honor of a glance.

Outside on the platform were a few of the Red Cross and Y. M. C. A. men of our ship, and I learned from them that one of their number had suffered a sadder fate than I. He had tried to get by on a Holland passport, viséed at the French consulate in New York, and been quietly but firmly persuaded to take the next boat back home.

I shared a compartment on the train with a native of the Bronx, and a French lady who just couldn't make her eyes behave, and two bored-looking French gentlemen of past middle age, not to mention in detail much more baggage than there was room for. The lady and the two gentlemen wore gloves, which made the Bronxite and me feel very bourgeois.

Our train crew, with the possible exception of the engineer and fireman whom I didn't see, was female, and, thinking I might some time require the services of the porter, I looked in my dictionary for the feminine of George.

To try my knowledge of française, I had purchased at the station a copy of *Le Cri de Paris*. I found that I could read it very easily by consulting the dictionary every time I came to a word.

But the scenery and the people were more interesting than *Le Cri*, the former especially. Perfect automobile roads, lined with trees; fields, and truck gardens in which aged men and women, young girls and little boys were at work; green hills and valleys; winding rivers and brooks, and an occasional château or a town of fascinating architecture—these helped to make us forget the heat and dust of the trip and the ear-splitting shrieks of our engines. No wonder the boche coveted his neighbor's house.

We stopped for some time at one particularly beautiful town and went out for air. I wondered audibly concerning the name of the place. An American companion looked at the signs round the station.

"It's Sortie," he said.

But it wasn't. It was Angoulême, and I wouldn't mind moving thither. My American friend was probably from Exit, Michigan.

The discovery was made and reported that one might go into the dining-car and smoke as much as one liked without asking permission from the maiden with the dreamy eyes. This car was filled with French soldiers and officers going back to the front after their holiday. There seemed to be as many different uniforms as there were men, and the scenery indoors was almost as brilliant as that outside.

It was about eight-thirty in the evening when we reached Paris. The sophisticated soldiers engaged their "redcaps" before they left the train, calling to them through the open windows. The demand was much greater than the supply, and I was among the unfortunates who had to carry their own baggage. I staggered to a street where a whole flotilla of taxis was anchored, but when I asked for one the person in charge said "No, no, no, no, no," meaning "No," and pointed around the corner. I followed his directions and landed on a boulevard along which there was a steady procession of machines, but it was fully twenty minutes before one came that was going slow enough to stop.

Our city is not all lit up like a church these nights, and it was impossible to see much of what we passed on the way to the hotel.

At the desk an English clerk, dressed for a noon wedding, gave me a blank to fill out. All the blank wanted to know was my past family history. It is to be sent, said the clerk, to the prefect of police. I had no idea he was interested in me.

Sunday, August 19. Paris.

When I get back to Chicago I shall insist that my favorite restaurant place tables out on the walk. It is more hygienic and much more interesting.

But Chicago, I'm afraid, can't provide half as much sidewalk entertainment as Paris. As I remember the metropolis of Illinois, there is a sad lack there of demonstrative affection on the streets. In fact, I fear that a lady and gentleman who kissed each other repeatedly at the corner of Madison and Dearborn would be given a free ride to Central Station and a few days in which to cool off. Such an osculatory duel on Paris's Grand Boulevard—also known by a dozen other names—goes practically unnoticed except by us Illinois hicks.

An American officer and I—at the former's expense—lunched sur curb to-day. The food was nothing to boast about, but we got an eyeful of scenery. Soldiers—French, British and American—strolled by constantly, accompanied by more or less beautiful brunettes, and only a few were thoughtless enough not to stop and kiss a few times in full view of our table. We also observed the inmates of passing taxis. No matter how wide the back seat, the lady occupant invariably sat on her escort's lap. A five-passenger car in America is a ten-passenger car in Paris, provided the chauffeur has a girl of his own.

When the American officer was tired of buying, I left him and sought out the *Chicago Tribune* office, conveniently located above Maxim's. The editor was there, but he was also broke, so I went back to the Ritz and got ready for bed.

The express office will be open to-morrow and I will be a rich man.

Lundi, 20 Août. Paris.

Went down to the express office and cashed a large part of my order. Friends were with me, and they immediately relieved me of most of the burden. I was hungry for lunch, having had no breakfast. Meat was what I wanted, and meat was what I couldn't get. Which led me to inquire into the Rules de la vie of Paris.

1. Monday and Tuesday are meatless days.

2. All except Saturday and Sunday are heatless days. Hot baths are impossible on Mondays, Tuesdays, Wednesdays, Thursdays and Fridays.

3. Strong liquor is procurable between noon and two P. M. and seven-thirty and nine-thirty at night. At other times ye toper must be content with light wines.

4. All public places except the theaters must close and douse lights at nine-thirty in the evening.

5. There is no speed limit for taxis or privately owned cars. A pedestrian run over and killed is liable to imprisonment. The driver is not only innocent, but free to hurl as many French curses as he likes at his victims. If the pedestrian is not killed, he must explain why not to the judge.

6. It is not only permissible but compulsory to speak to any girl who speaks to you, and a girl who won't speak to you should be reported to the police.

7. No watch or clock is wrong. Whatever time you have is right and you may act accordingly.

8. Matches never ignite. A smoker must purchase a cigar or cigarette lighter and keep it filled with essence, the française term for gas. Sometimes the lighters work.

9. American cigarettes are not procurable. Bum ones may be bought at any tabac store or café for only five times what they are worth.

10. Water must never be used as a thirst quencher, and seldom for any other purpose. It's worse than bourgeois; it's unheard-of.

The lack of water, hot or cold, drove me to a barber shop this morning. The barber first made me put on a shroud, and I was afraid he was either going to cut me to pieces or talk me to death. But his operation was absolutely painless and his incessant conversation harmless, because I couldn't understand a word of it.

From the barber shop I went to the information department of American Army Headquarters. That's where you get permits to visit our camps. But of course, if you've run over here from America, you have lots of spare time on your hands, so they're doing you a favor if they hold you up a few days. What is a week or so when a man's here for a whole month?

They have queer ideas at the Maison de la Presse, which is the French equivalent for our publicity bureau. They receive you cordially there and treat you just as if you were not dregs.

I jumped thither after a futile visit to our own headquarters. I said I would like to go to the French front.

"Certainly," replied the man in charge. "Whenever is convenient for you, we'll see that you get a trip."

So I told him when it would be convenient and he's going to see me through. I hear that the British are similarly peculiar. They are polite even to newspaper men and magazine writers. They might even speak to a cartoonist.

Returning to our side of the Seine, I bumped into some Australians, here on leave. One had been in Germany before the war and could speak and understand the "schoenste language."

"They use me as an interpreter," he said. "When they bring in a bloody boche prisoner, I talk to him. First we give him a real meal, maybe bacon and eggs and coffee, something he hasn't seen for months. Then I ask him where he came from and how he got here. Most of them are glad to tell me the truth. Those that do, I mark them down as 'Very intelligent.' Those that volunteer information I record as 'Extremely intelligent.' Those that say 'Nicht verstehe' go down in the record as 'Not intelligent.' But the majority are so bloody well glad to be out of the war that they talk freely.

"I asked one Heinie if he was going to try to escape. 'Not me,' he said, 'I'm tickled to be here.' They're all fed up on the war. You'd be too with three years of it."

This young man admitted that he was one of the best football players in Australia. "Maybe I've forgotten how now," he said. "I've been over here three years. Just think of it—I traveled twelve thousand miles, or maybe it's kilos, to mix up in this."

Baseball, he told me, had taken a strong hold on Australia.

"I don't hit well," he said, "but I can catch what you call flies! I can catch the wildest flies that are knocked."

Which gift would probably be useless in America, where most of the flies knocked are bloody narrow.

Before I left him I learned also that Les Darcy was all right at heart, but that the professional "sports" spoiled him, and that he could have "knocked Jack Johnson, Stanley Ketchel, Billy Papke or Jess Willard clean out of the ring."

He is going back to the trenches to-night, and I hope there are plenty of extremely intelligent Heinies there to keep him busy interpreting till his next leave. Interpreting, I should think, would be much pleasanter than going over the top.

Tuesday, August 21.

This time it was an American of the French Ambulance Service.

"Say, listen," he said. "I can give you some mighty good stories. Real stuff, do you get me? Listen: One night there was a boche wounded out there and I brought him in. He had one leg all shot to pieces and we had to operate. I was going to give him the ether when he turned over and looked me in the face. 'Why, Dan,' he said, 'aren't you going to speak to me?' It was a chap I'd gone to school with in America. I could give you lots of stuff like that; do you get me? I used to be in New York, and Rube Goldberg used to call me up out of bed at six in the morning. 'Dan,' he'd say to me, 'I'm up against it for an idea. Will you give me an idea?' Do you get me? And there's a dramatic critic in New York—I won't tell you his name—but he used to tag around me after a first night and ask me what I thought of the show. Do you get me? I can give you a lot of good stuff."

I told him I was afraid that if he gave it to me all at once I wouldn't remember any of it. So he is coming to my hotel every day during his leave, to give me a little at a time—if he can find me.

Last night a good-hearted American officer took me to dinner at La Tour d'Argent, which is said to be the oldest restaurant in Paris and which, they say, is the place the Kaiser was going to have his banquet on a certain night three years ago if Gott hadn't gone back on him at the last moment.

We ordered duck, the restaurant's specialty. They cook it in your presence, slice off whatever is sliceable, and then put the bird in a press and give you the result as gravy. After the meal they hand you a post card on which is inscribed *le numéro de votre canard*. I looked up "canard" in my dictionary and found that it meant a drake, or false news, or a worthless newspaper. I have heard lots of false news, but I know no one took the trouble to count the items. Also I know that my newspaper is neither worthless nor numbered. So canard in this case must mean drake. The number of mine was 41654. If he had happened to disagree with me, I could have taken his number and traced him to the source. It's a very good idea and might be used in America on eggs or drinks.

I made another trip to the office which is supposed to be in charge of American correspondents and accommodations for them. I will go there again to-morrow and again the next day. I will bother them to death. Meantime I have applied to a person in London for permission to go to the British front, and have been assured a visit to the French lines late next week. I have wonderful vision and can see things twelve miles away.

P. S. It was revealed to me to-night that my detention and trial in Bordeaux was a frame-up conceived by loving friends aboard ship and carried out by that English-speaking cross-examiner, who, believe me, is a convincing actor.

Thanks, gents. It was good for about two thousand words.

I Try to Get to the American Camp—
but Meet Disaster

Wednesday, August 22. Paris.

THE gentlemen authorized to issue visitors' passes to the American camp and the various fronts don't seem to realize that a person may be in a hurry. They fail to appreciate the facts that hanging round Paris is financial ruin and that the world series, which one positively must attend, is drawing nearer every hour.

Permission to go to the British front was requested over a week ago. No reply. Daily calls at our own press bureau produce nothing but promises of a trip somewhere, some time. Monsieur Boss of the French Maison de la Presse says I may be taken through the devastated territory—in a week or so.

Meanwhile the Battle of Paris goes on, with Death always staring one in the face—Death from taxis, from starvation, from water thirst, from hand-to-hand encounters with the language.

Death from a taxi is the most likely form and the most distressing, for under the Parisian law the person run down and killed is the one at fault and the corpus delicti is liable to life imprisonment or worse. A pedestrian has no more rights here than the Kaiser, and it's almost impossible to cross the street unless you've gone through a course of intensive training in Detroit.

There would be little danger if all the crossings were on the upgrade, for the French cars—those which aren't in the military service—have a desperate time climbing. They have to shift speeds even to run up on the sidewalk, which is one of their favorite sports. But the Loop District of Paris is topographically on the level, and taxis can tear along like an eastbound Russian.

On occasions when you are run into and knocked down a gendarme appears on the scene with pencil and note-book. He takes

259

the name and address of the driver and escorts you to jail. If you die there, the driver is sent a medal for marksmanship.

Taxi fares are cheaper, probably, than anywhere else in the world. They amount to practically nothing if you have an accident—that is, a trip without a collision with something or somebody. But even if you enjoy an average tour and hit a building or another vehicle or a dog or a person, they soak you only about half as much as they would in New York or Chicago, where there are far fewer thrills per drive.

The tariff from the hotel where I put up (I haven't found out how much) to American General Headquarters, where I go every morning to be refused a pass to the camps, is one franc cinquante if you miss all targets. This forenoon it was two francs cinquante because we knocked the rear wheel off a young boy's bicycle.

The boy, after a hearty bawling out by the driver and two gendarmes, was carted to a police station. They'll hardly keep him in jail, though. Matteawan is the proper place for a boy who attempts bicycling on the streets of Paris.

Thursday, August 23. Paris.

One of several differences between an American and a Frenchman is that an American tries to understand a Frenchman's English and a Frenchman tries not to understand an American's French.

To-day I wanted to go from somewhere to the Hotel Continental.

"Hotel Con-tin-ent-al," I said to the driver.

He shook his head. I repeated. He shook his head again. This went on till I had pronounced the name five times and he had shaken his head that often. I said it the sixth time just as I had said it the other five.

"Oh-h-h!" shouted the driver, his face lighting up. "Hotel Con-tin-ent-al!"

And there wasn't a particle of difference between his version and mine.

There was excitement in our village last night. At twenty-three-thirty o'clock, as we Parisians say, began a chorus of screaming sirens, the warning signal of an air raid. Those of us living in upstairs rooms experienced a sudden craving for a home Somewhere in the Basement, and in gratifying it didn't stop to use the elevator. The majority taking part in the Great Descent wore pajamas or their female relatives, sometimes called chemises de nuit. A few, of which I was one, were still attired for the day, and we went outdoors and looked up.

A regular flock of planes was, you might say, planely visible, but there was no fight in the air and no dropping of bombs on our fair city. The birdmen soared round a while in a perfectly friendly manner and then retired to their nests. The sirens were stilled and we all went up-stairs, the majority, mentioned above, grateful for the war-time lack of lights.

It seems that a Frenchman, returning from his day's toil, forgot to flash his password, which is a red tail-light, or something. And the patrol took him for a boche and gave chase. Fortunately for himself, he glimpsed his pursuers in time and turned on the required signal.

To-day there has been a big demand for first-floor rooms.

Friday, August 24. Paris.

An American major—it is interdict by the censor to mention the names of any officers save General Sibert and General Pershing—asked a friend in London to buy him an automobile and ship it here for his use. The Londoner was able, after much difficulty, to purchase one of those things that grow so rapidly in Detroit. He packed it up and mailed it to Le Havre. From there it had to be driven to Paris.

The major had never learned to drive this particular brand. In fact, his proportions are such that not even a shoehorn could coax him into the helmsman's seat. He asked me to go up and get it for him. I declined on grounds of neutrality. That was a week ago.

Well, yesterday one Mr. Kiley, who has been over here some time in the ambulance service, came back to town with the car and four flat tires, which, evidently, were far past the draft age when the sale was made in London. Mr. Kiley helped himself to a stimulant and then told me about his trip.

He reached Le Havre last Saturday afternoon. He had in his pockets no papers except an order for the car. He had been in Le Havre about two minutes when a gentleman attacked him from behind with a tap on the shoulder. The gentleman pulled back his coat lapel and flashed a star bearing the insignia of the British Intelligence Department. He was curious as to Mr. Kiley's name and business. Mr. Kiley told him. Then he wanted to see Mr. Kiley's papers. Mr. Kiley showed him the order for the car.

"I'm afraid that won't do," said the officer. "I'd advise you to leave town."

"Give me just an hour," pleaded Mr. Kiley, "just time enough to get the car and get out."

"All right," said the officer, "and be sure it's only an hour."

Mr. Kiley hastened to where the car was reposing, displayed the order, and started joyously to wind her up. He cranked and he cranked and he cranked. Nothing doing. He gave her a push downhill and tried to throw her into speed. Nothing doing. It occurred to him that something must be the matter. A thorough examination resulted in a correct diagnosis. There was no gas.

Next to getting a drink of ice-water in Paris, the hardest job for a stranger is buying gasoline in any French town. Mr. Kiley was turned down five times before eighteen o'clock, when all the garages closed for the day.

He registered at a hotel and went into the café for dinner. He was just picking up the carte du jour when his friend, the officer, horned in.

"Mr. Kiley," said this guy, "you have been in town more than an hour."

"Yes, sir," said Mr. Kiley. "But I've had trouble. I found my car, but I can't run it because there's no essence."

"I think you'd better leave town," said the officer.

"If you don't mind," said Mr. Kiley, "I'll leave early in the morning."

"I wouldn't mind if you left right now," said he.

There followed a long discussion and a cross-examination even crosser than mine in Bordeaux. Mr. Kiley revealed his whole family history and won the right to stay overnight, provided he remained indoors and departed from town first thing in the morning.

But France is like America in that Saturday is usually succeeded by Sunday, and when Mr. Kiley arose from his hotel bed and resumed his search for gas he found every garage in town shut up tight. As I remember the United States, garages do not keep holy the Sabbath Day nor any other day. Over here, however, everything closes on Sunday except churches, theaters and saloons.

Mr. Kiley took in the situation and returned to his room to hide. Shortly before midi there was a knock at his door and a new officer appeared.

"You seem to like our town, Mr. Kiley," said he.

"I'll leave it as soon as I can get away," said Mr. Kiley.

"No doubt," replied the officer. "But I believe you will be here a long while."

Mr. Kiley tried to look calm.

"Bone," he said in perfectly good French.

"For the present," said the officer, "you must not leave the hotel. Later on we'll talk things over."

In the café on Sunday night Mr. Kiley met an American and told him his troubles. The American had a car of his own in Le Havre and plenty of gasoline. He would be glad to give Mr. Kiley enough to start him on his way.

"But I can't go," said Mr. Kiley, "till I've fixed it with the police. I'll have to look for them."

He didn't have far to look. No. 2 was in the lobby.

"Yes," said No. 2, "you can leave town if you leave quick. There must be no more foolishness. The only thing that saves you from arrest is your uniform."

Mr. Kiley left town and left quick, and, aside from his four blow-outs, had an uneventful trip to Paris.

But what if I had taken that assignment—I with no uniform except one willed me by the Chicago Cubs? O Boy!

Saturday, August 25. Paris.

On advice of counsel I went to Colonel Anonymous of the American General Staff and besought him to fix it so that I might get to one of our camps without further stalling. Colonel Anonymous said it was all right with him and telephoned to Major Noname, who seemed to have authority in affaires journalistic.

Major Noname, fortunately, is a baseball fan. I told him what I did know, and lots that I didn't know about our national pastime, and the reward was an American press pass to the infantry camp, S. in F.

I am going in a horseless carriage with Joe and Howard, fellow conspirators in the so-called journalistic game, and the start is to be made early Monday morning. Joe is going to drive his own car, and I hope he knows how.

Dimanche, 26 Août. Paris.

Yesterday was Saturday, and everybody had had a hot bath and felt like doing something. Three of us decided to take in the highly recommended show at Les Ambassadeurs.

A member of the Theatrical Geographic Society met us in the foyer and showed us a map of the playhouse. From it we were supposed to pick our seats. We chose three that, on paper, were in the sixth row in the center aisle. Our usher, female, led us to three which were in the tenth row, off to one side. Our usher stuck round as if she expected something. I was the party with the seat checks, and she got nothing. I was ignorant of the rules of the game. But not for long. Pretty soon in came three of the World's Greatest fighters, alias Canadian soldiers, and sat down behind us. Their usher was more persistent than mine.

"What do you want?" demanded one who seemed to be the financial leader. "I already gave you a franc."

"Un franc pour trois?" said the lady in horror.

"Yes, and that's enough," said the Canuck. "Aller!" he added in perfect Canadian.

"Je ne comprend pas," said the lady.

"Go to the devil then!" said the Canadian in perfect Portuguese.

The lady went somewhere, but whether to the proper destination I do not know.

"I wonder how much they charge to get out," wondered the Canadian.

Along about the middle of the show our own usher popped up before me and held out her right hand, at the same time exhibiting both teeth in an ingratiating smile. I shook the proffered hand. She withdrew her teeth.

"Non, non, non, non," she said.

I asked her what she voulez-voued. She was coy.

"Do you want a tip?" I inquired in plain Michigan.

Both teeth reappeared. A dental curiosity drove me to hand her three francs. I had not underestimated.

In the second act a very nice-looking lady sang *A Broken Doll* in plain Thirty-ninth Street. The stage chorus tried to help her out on the second refrain, but, with all due modesty, I must say that it was the Canadians and I who earned the vociferous encore.

Lundi, 27 Août. Paris.

The first batch of laundry was back when I returned from the theater Saturday night. Collars were done up in a neat package, tied with baby-blue ribbon. They looked just as when I had sent them out except that there was a high, shiny polish over the soiled spots. As for handkerchiefs, let us follow the British communiqué style:

"Eleven of our handkerchiefs went over the Blanchisserie lines. Two came back. Nine are missing."

Some practical joker suggested that I go out yesterday afternoon and watch a baseball game between a Canadian team and a club from the American Red Cross. St. Cloud was the battle ground. You pronounce St. Cloud exactly as it is not spelled.

A taxi man took us out there by way of Kansas City and El Paso, and during the forty minutes' trip he was in high speed at least one minute. We bumped into a ceremony of awards. French soldiers to the number of two hundred were being given the Croix de Guerre.

The ceremony over, we crossed the race track and got on to the baseball field. There was an hour of badly needed practise, and then the two belligerents went at each other in a so-called ball game. It was stopped at the end of the eighth inning on account of rain, eight innings too late.

The rain, I am told, was long overdue, and we may expect gobs of it between now and then.

I am writing this early Monday morning, and early Monday morning is when we were supposed to start for the American camp. But there seems to be a difference of opinion over the meaning of the French adverb "early."

Tuesday, August 28. Somewhere in France.

"Early" proved to be half past ten yesterday morning. Joe drove us to the city limits, and there we had to pause. According to this year's rules, ye automobilist pauses at the limits, has his gasoline measured, and then goes on. Returning to town, he has to pay a tax on the added amount of gasoline he brings, or something like that.

We were allowed to go out of town, and some thirty yards beyond the limits we found a garage. There we filled up with essence. Howard did the cranking, which is a necessity with all French cars, and away we went.

It was raining and it was cold. Joe and Howard were in the front seat, Joe driving and Howard studying the road map. I was in the back seat, catching cold.

"We'll go right ahead," said Joe, "to Such and Such a Place, and there we'll stop and have lunch."

Well, we stopped in Such and Such a Place, but it was not from a desire of lunch. It was because we were compelled to stop.

"Let's see your papers," said the stopper in French.

The stoppees, in English, displayed their passes to the American camp. The stopper didn't know whether they were good or not. He asked us to wait a moment and disappeared out of the rain. We waited several moments. Finally there appeared another stopper, who read carefully our passes and told us they were no good and that we would have to loom up at the City Hall.

We went there, with Joe and Howard in the front seat and an officer and I in the back, me still catching cold, especially in the feet.

In the City Hall were French officers attired in all colors of the French army, which made the colors of the rainbow look like Simon Pure White. Our crime, it seems, was in not having an automobile pass on a red card. Or maybe it was blue. One of the thirty gentlemen in charge said we would have to wait till he telephoned back to Paris. Knowing the French telephone system, we inquired whether we might go across the street and eat. We were told we might.

We went across the street and ate, and it was a good meal, with meat, on a day which was meatless in Paris. A subaltern interrupted the orgy and said we were wanted back in the City Hall. Back there the startling information was that no telephonic satisfaction had been obtained. We asked whether we might go back to the café. There was no objection. We played pitch. French soldiers by scores came up and looked on. Joe thought, sub rosa, that it would be a grand idea to startle 'em. So we played pitch for one hundred francs a hand, it being tacitly understood that the money didn't go. But we certainly had them excited.

Between pitch games in which thousands of francs were apparently lost and won, we visited, on summons, the City Hall five or six times. Every time there was the same heavy barrage of français.

Entered, finally, an English-speaking gent who said we might leave the city provided we went straight back to Paris.

"We'd much prefer," said Joe, "to go on to where we were going."

"You have the choice," was the reply, "of returning to Paris or remaining here, in jail."

Paris sounded the more attractive. They gave us back our car and away we went. It was after twenty o'clock, and it was pitch dark, and it was cold, and it was raining. And the man who had made the machine had forgotten to equip it with headlights.

A little before midnight, on the downhill main street of a village, we saw ahead of us a wagon. It was two feet ahead of us. There being nothing else to do we banged into it. Then we stopped. The driver of the wagon sat suddenly down in the middle of the street and apologized. We all got out to see whether any damage had been done to the car. The only wounds discernible in the darkness were a smashed radiator and a bent axle.

"It's lucky this happened in a town," said I. "We can probably find a hotel."

"We're not going to look for one," said Joe. "We're going to drive to Paris."

We got back in and, to our amazement, the darn thing started. There was plenty of headlight now, for the whole hood was ablaze. All lit up like a church, we went on our mad career until our conveyance dropped dead, overcome by the heat. This was four miles from a town that will be famous in the histories of this war.

"I guess we're through," said Joe. "One of us will have to stay with the car and see that nothing is stolen. The other two can go back to town and find a bed."

By a vote of two to one, Howard was elected to stay with the car. He was the youngest.

Joe and I hiked our four miles in silence. The town was as brilliantly lighted as a cemetery and apparently void of inmates. We groped for an hour in a vain search for a hostelry. At length we gave up and resolved to sleep on the huge cathedral's front porch. We were ascending the steps when a door opened and a human being stood before us.

"Arrested again," thought I.

But the human being turned out to be not a copper, but a priest.

"Bon soir, monsieur," said Joe. "Voulez-vous show us où we can find a hotel?"

He led us across the street to a place we had doped out as the high school. He rapped on the door with his foot. In a few moments an aged lady, dressed for the night, appeared. There was a rapid exchange of français, after which we thanked the priest and were taken through a courtyard and upstairs to our room. We said a prayer for Howard and went to sleep, and I had a nightmare. I dreamed of a porterhouse steak.

This morning we decided it wouldn't be clubby to have breakfast before we had rescued Howard and the car. We went to a garage which was equipped with a beautiful lady, but no automobiles nor tow-ropes. We found a livery stable that had everything but a horse. We commandeered a young man's delivery cart from in front of a grocery store and drove out to the scene of our car's demise. Howard and the corpse were still there. Howard thought it would be a good idea to go to the nearest farm-house and rent a horse and a rope from the proprietor. The proprietor was very ignorant. He couldn't understand our French. But in his employ was a German prisoner who could talk his own language and ours and the funny one that is prevalent round here. He explained our wants to the farmer and there ensued a few moments of haggling over price. We finally rented two horses and a rope for fifty francs and dragged the car back to town. From the looks of it, in daylight, I would say the economical course would have been to leave it out there in the road and keep the fifty francs.

The garage man says, in English, that he can make the necessary "reparations" in three weeks. So far as I'm concerned, he can devote three years to the job. Hereafter I'll do my cross-country flitting about on a train.

It's on one now, Paris bound, that I'm writing. There is nothing to do but write, for Howard is getting the sleep he missed last night and Joe is too angry to talk. He has spoken one sentence since we got up this morning.

"This is a queer war," he said.

Finally I Get to the American Camp; What I Find There

Thursday, August 30. At an American Camp.

ME and a regular American correspondent, Mr. Bazin, who has been here since before the war, but is still good-natured, took the train from Paris this morning and reached our destination shortly after lunch time. This is one of a string of villages in which the main body of the Expeditionary Forces are billeted.

We were met at the train by one of the correspondents' cars, a regular he-man of a car from home, with eight cylinders and everything. Each correspondent rents a seat in one of the machines at a cost of sixty dollars a week. For this trifling sum he may be driven anywhere he wants to go along the line.

The correspondents have a tough life. They are quartered in a good—judged by French standards—hotel, and are not what you could call overworked. There is nothing to write about, and if you wrote about it you probably couldn't get it through.

Mr. Corey, one of these slaves, invited me to accompany him to an infantry billet, some eighteen miles distant. We sailed along over the perfect roads at an average speed of about sixty, slowing up in the villages to dodge a harmless course among the cows, chickens and children, all of whom use the middle of Main Street for their playground.

We passed an occasional soldier, but it was a nice clear day, and the large majority were out in the fields and hills rehearsing. Our boys, I'm told, are getting quite a workout. Usually they leave their billets at seven in the morning, walk from six to twelve miles to a drill ground, and work till half past four in the afternoon. Then they take the long hike "home" and wonder how soon supper will be ready. Frequently, however, there is practise in night trench warfare, and then the grind continues till ten or eleven o'clock. The work is hard, but so, by this time, are the boys.

The captain on whom we called said he was glad to meet me, which is the first time that has happened in France. We asked him whether there was any news. He said yes, that the Salvation Army had established headquarters in the camp.

"I'm glad," he remarked, "that they've decided to go in on our side. It may influence the Kaiser's friend Gott."

The chief need of the soldiers, he went on, was amusement. The Salvation Army's and Y. M. C. A.'s efforts were appreciated, but continual rations of soup and meat palled at times, and a little salad and dessert, in the form of Charlie Chaplin or the Follies, would make life more bearable.

"Some American theatrical producer," said the captain, "could win our undying gratitude by shipping over a stock company with a small repertory of shows, with music, and *girls*. I believe he'd find it profitable too. When the boys get paid they don't know what to do with their money. There's nothing to spend it on in these parts."

The captain invited us to dinner, but we had a previous date with members of the Censorship Bureau. These entertained us with stories which I voluntarily delete. From their hotel we returned to our own, held a brief song service in the correspondents' mess, and called it a day.

Friday, August 31. At an American Camp.

"Would you like to meet General Sibert?" asked Mr. Corey.

General Sibert's name is one of the two that may be mentioned.

I said I would, and we left after breakfast for the next village, where headquarters is situate. In the outer office were some clerks and a colonel. The latter could never be accused of excessive cordiality.

"The general is busy," he said.

"How long will he be busy?" inquired Mr. Corey.

"I have no idea," said the colonel.

Mr. Corey and I felt we would be warmer outdoors, so we climbed back in our car and asked our sergeant-driver to take us to the nearest training grounds. Here an infantry regiment was going through simple drill, and calisthentics which were far from simple.

The nearest captain approached, smiled pleasantly and asked what he could do for us. We introduced ourselves.

"Correspondents, eh?" he said.

"Well, then, you can do something for us—make the newspapers and magazines quit calling us Sammies. We've never done anything to deserve a name like that."

"What's the matter with it?" we inquired.

"Everything!" said the captain. "It doesn't fit, it sounds childish, and we just naturally hate it."

We asked him whether there was an acceptable substitute.

"I don't know of any," he said. "In due time we'll wish one on ourselves that will have pep and sound real. Meanwhile call us Julias, Howards—anything you like, except Sammies."

We promised to do our best for him, and he was grateful enough to invite us to his mess for lunch.

This young man—he looks about twenty-nine—hasn't been to his home, somewhere out West, since he left West Point, six years ago. He hasn't seen a show in six years. Mexico and the Philippines have kept him busy. His promotion from lieutenant to captain is very recent, and he still wears only one stripe. "I suppose I'll be a major before I get the other," he said. "A man can hardly keep up with his rank these days."

He called our attention to the physical condition of his men.

"You've got to be in the pink to go through those exercises without yelling for help," he said. "These fellas couldn't have done it a month ago. Now they seldom get tired, though the hours are pretty stiff. To-day is a cinch. It's pay-day, and there's a muster soon after lunch. So most of us will get a half holiday and nobody'll object."

The captain blew his whistle to indicate that the game was over. His boys quit happily, and we left him after agreeing to show up at his billet in time for lunch.

"We have a fairly good cook," he promised. "But what is much more important, we have a beautiful young lady to wait on us."

Our next stop was at a trench school. Americans, under French tutelage, had constructed a perfect—so we were told—system of ditches and entanglements, and had shown aptitude in learning the offensive and defensive points of this pleasant method of warfare. They were now engaged in bomb-throwing drill. Some of them had tried the baseball throw, but had found the grenades too heavy. Several crooked-arm throws would do things to a person's elbow. But, according to the officers, the youngsters had done very well with the bowling motion and had surprised the French with their accuracy.

This officer, another captain, spoke in complimentary terms of the French assistance.

"They've been more than diligent with us," said he. "They've never shown impatience when we failed to grab their point, but have gone over it and over it till we've learned it to suit them. The difference in languages makes it hard sometimes to get what they're after, but they eventually manage to make themselves understood. The only fault I have to find with them," he confided, "is that they don't give us credit for knowing anything at all. They tell us this thing's a rifle, and the thing on the end of it is a bayonet, and so forth. And one of them showed me a barbed-wire entanglement one day, and told me what it was for. I'd always been under the mistaken impression that it was used for bed-clothes."

We had to turn down this captain's luncheon invitation, but we stopped at his house for light refreshment. His lieutenant, a young University of Michigan boy, had come over on the first transport, and related interesting details of that historic trip.

We went on to the other captain's, and lunched with him and his major and colonel. The beautiful young lady proved every bit as pretty as a pair of army shoes. But the food was good and the captain's French better. He kept hurling it at the beautiful young lady, who received it with derisive laughter. His accent, it appeared, was imposseeb.

"I like to make her laugh," he told me. "It takes me back home among the coyotes."

On the street of the village I held converse with a private, aged about twenty-three. I said I supposed he was glad it was pay-day.

"What's the difference!" he said. "I got more money now than Rockefella. I ain't spent more'n a buck since we been over, and then it was just to be spendin' it, not because they was anything to buy. I seen a fella the other day light a cigarette with one o' these here dirty twenty-franc notes. He was sick o' carrying it round. And they was another fella went up to one o' these here village belles and slipped her a hundred francs. He never seen her before, and he won't never see her again. He just says 'Souvenir' and let it go at that."

"Did she take it?"

"Oh, I guess not! She's to gay Paree by this time already."

"She won't burn up that town with a hundred francs."

"No, but all these girls don't think o' nothin' but gettin' there. From what I seen of it, I'd just as soon be in Akron."

"Oh, I'd hardly say that!"

"Talk about spendin' money! They was a poor fella here last week that got rid of a lot of it. He bought himself a bottle o' champagne wine. I don't think he'd tasted it before, but it's cheap over here. So he got a hold o' this bottle and poured it into him like it was excelsior water, and it acted on him like it was laughin' gas. He went up alongside the officers' billet and sang 'em a vocal solo. The captain heard him—you could of heard him in San Francisco—and the captain come out and invited him in. And when he got him in there he says: 'So-and-So, how much did this little bun cost you?' So the fella told him a buck and a half. So the captain says: 'You've underestimated the amount by about seventy bucks. You'll get your next pay the last day of October.'"

I asked my new friend how he liked his billet.

"Great!" he said. "I and a couple other fellas has a room next to a pig on one side and a flock o' chickens on the other. We never get lonesome, and it makes it nice and handy when we want some ham and eggs. I know one fella that rooms next to a settlement o' rats. Night times he sets his flashlight so's it throws a narrow path o' light acrost the floor, then he puts a little piece o' meat in the path and stands over it with a bayonet. When Mr. Rat gets there the fella comes down whang with the bayonet and fastens him to the floor. It's good target practise, and he'd ought to be sure fire by the time it's Huns instead o' rats."

"Maybe," said I, "the Huns would know better than to come out in the light."

"They'd go anywheres for a piece o' meat," said the private.

He had to depart and report for muster. We took another road home, a road frequented by sheep and railroad crossings, both of which slow you up considerably.

In France the gates—strong iron ones—at grade crossings are kept closed except when some one wants to cross the tracks. The some one makes known his desire by tooting his horn or shouting, and the gatekeeper—usually an old lady with the pipe-smoking habit—comes out of her shack and opens the gates, expending anywhere from ten minutes to half an hour on the task. The salary attached to the position is the same as that of a French private: ten centimes a day, which is two cents in regular money. I presume the gatekeepers have a hot time in the old town on pay night.

As for the sheep, when you come up behind them you might as well resign yourself to staying behind them till they reach the village for which they are headed. They won't get out of the way of their own accord, and neither the dog nor the aged shepherd will make any effort to sidetrack them.

Having led them into the village, the shepherd proceeds to deliver them to their respective owners. He stops in front of a house, plays a certain tune on his horn, and the sheep or sheeps belongings to that house step out of ranks and sheepishly retire for the night, or perhaps sit up a while in the parlor and talk war with the family.

There must be a lot of intermarrying among the sheeps of one village. A great many of those in the flock we saw looked enough alike to be cousins or something.

Somebody suggested a poker game for this evening's entertainment, but I got all I wanted of that great sport coming across the bounding blue.

It has rained only an hour in two days, and the boys say we'll get it good to-morrow.

Saturday, September 1. In an American Camp.

As exclusively predicted by everybody, it was pouring when we arose this morning, but rain doesn't keep you indoors in France. If it did, you would live indoors.

We splashed the thirty miles to the other end of the camp and inflicted ourselves on a major of marines. He seemed deliberately unfriendly at first, but it was only his manner. After five minutes of awkward monosyllabic dialogue he gave us the usual refreshments and took us out to see the town, the name of which should be Mud if it isn't.

"This is a grand climate," he said. "They must have had conscription to get people to live here."

He took us to the camp kitchen, of which he was evidently and justly proud. It was a model of convenience and cleanliness. He spoke to the cook.

"Are you very busy?" he asked.

"No, sir," was the reply.

"Then I'd shave if I were you," said the major.

"Daily shaving," he told us when we got outside, "ought to be compulsory in our army as it is in the British. When a man hasn't shaved he isn't at his best, physically, morally, or mentally. When he has he's got more confidence in himself; his morale is better. Shaving has a psychological effect, and I try to impress my men with the importance of it. They say it's a difficult operation here, but I guess if the Tommies can do it in the trenches, we can in these billets."

We remarked on the increasing popularity of mustaches among the men.

"I don't object to them," said the major. "Neither do I see any sense to them. To my mind they're in a class with monocles or an appendix. But so long as the men keep their cheeks and chins smooth, they're at liberty to wear as much of a misplaced eyebrow as they can coax out."

The major showed us his hospital and his dentist shop and marched us up a steep hill, where, in the rain, we saw a great many interesting things and promised not to write about them.

After lunch we decided it would be patriotic to go home and remove our wet clothes. In my case, this meant spending the rest of the day in my room, and that's where I am.

Sunday, September 2. Paris.

The driver assigned to take me to the train, which left from the next village this morning, lost his way, and we reached the station just as the engine was sounding the Galli-Curci note that means All Aboard. There was no time to buy a ticket, and you can't pay a cash fare on a train in France. But the conductor, or whatever you call him here, said I could get a ticket at the destination, Paris; in fact, I must get a ticket or spend the rest of my unnatural life wandering about the station.

I found a seat in a compartment in which were a young American officer, beginning his forty-eight hours' leave, and a young French lady who looked as if she had been in Paris before. The young officer and I broke into conversation at once. The young lady didn't join in till we had gone nearly twenty kilomet's.

Captain Jones, which isn't his name, called attention to the signs on the window warning MM. Les Voyageurs to keep their anatomies indoors. The signs were in three languages. "Ne pas Pencher au Dehors," said the French. The English was "Danger to Lean Outside." And the Wop: "Non Sporgere"—very brief. It was evident that a fourth variation of the warning had been torn off, and it didn't require a William Burns to figure out in what language it had been written.

"If there were a boche on this train," said Captain Jones, "he could lean his head off without hurting any one's feelings."

"Languages are funny," continued the captain sagely. "The French usually need more words than we do to express the same thought. I believe that explains why they talk so fast—they've got so much more to say."

I inquired whether he knew French.

"Oh, yes," he said. "I've been over here so long that I can even tell the money apart."

The dining-car conductor came in to ask whether we wanted the first or second "série" luncheon. You must reserve your seat at table on trains here or you can't eat. We decided on the second, and so did our charming compartment mate. Captain Jones, supposing she could not understand English, said: "Shall you take her to lunch or shall I?"

I was about to be magnanimous when she remarked, with a scornful glance at the captain: "I shall myself take me to lunch if monsieur has no objection."

The cap was temporarily groggy, but showed wonderful recuperative powers and in five minutes convinced her that he would toss himself into the Seine if she refused to eat with us. She accepted, after some stalling that convinced me she had been cordially inclined all the while.

General polite conversation ensued, and soon came the inevitable French question: How many American soldiers were there in France? I have heard it asked a million times, and I have heard a million different answers. The captain gave the truthful reply: "I don't know."

"This war," he said, "should be called the War of Rumors. The war will be over by Christmas. The war won't be over for ten years. The boche is starving. The Allies are getting fat. The boche has plenty to eat. The Allies are dying of hunger. Our last transport fleet sank five subs. Our last transport fleet was sunk by a whole flotilla of subs. Montenegro's going to make a separate peace with Bosnia. There is talk of peace negotiations between Hungary and Indiana. Ireland, Brazil and Oklahoma are going to challenge the world. They're going to move the entire war to the Balkans and charge admission. The Kaiser's dying of whooping cough. You can learn anything you want to or don't want to know. Why"—this to me—"don't you fellas print the truth?"

"And where," I asked him, "would you advise us to go and get it?"

"The same place I got it," said the captain.

"And what is it?"

"I don't know."

We adjourned to the diner. A sign there said: "Non Fumeurs." The captain pointed to it.

"That's brief enough," he said. "That's once when the French is concise. But you ought to see the Chinese for that. I was in a town near the British front recently where some Chinese laborers are en-camped. In the station waiting-room, it says: 'No Smoking' in French, English, Russian and Italian. The Russian is something like 'Do notski smokevitch,' and the Italian is 'Non Smokore.' Recently they have added a Chinese version, and it's longer than the Bible. A moderate smoker could disobey the rules forty times before he got through the first chapter and found out what they were driving at."

Be that as it may, I have observed that everybody in France smokes whenever and wherever he or she desires, regardless of signs. We did now, and so did our guest, while waiting for the first course, which was black bread baked in a brickyard.

"I would love to go to America," said mademoiselle.

"You wouldn't care for it," replied the captain promptly. "It's too wild."

"How is it wild?"

"Every way: manners, habits, morals. The majority of the people, of course, are Indians, and you just can't make them behave."

She asked whether either of us had ever been in New York. The captain said he'd passed through there once on the way to Coney Island. She wanted to know if New York was bigger than Paris. "It's bigger than France," said Captain Jones.

Monsieur was trying to make a game of her.

"Well, anyway," said the captain, "you could lose France in Texas."

What was Texas?

"Texas," said the captain, "is the place they send soldiers when they've been bad. It's way out west, near Chicago."

The lady had heard of Chicago.

"This gentleman works there," said the captain. "He's part Indian, but he was educated at Carlisle and is somewhat civilized. He gets wild only on occasions."

The lady regarded me rather scaredly.

"He lives on the plains outside the city," continued the captain, "and rides to his work and back on a zebra. Practically all the suburban savages have zebras, and the Chicago traffic police have a fierce time handling them during their owners' working hours. They run wild around the streets and in the department stores, and snap at women, especially brunettes."

We had attained the potato course. The French positively will not serve potatoes as other than a separate course. I was about to help myself to a generous portion when the captain cried: "Here! Better leave those things alone. You know what they do to you."

I told him I didn't believe two or three would hurt, and proceeded to take three.

"When a half Indian eats potatoes," said the captain, "he usually forgets himself and runs amuck."

Our guest probably didn't know what a muck was, but it had an unpleasant sound, and the look she gave me was neither friendly nor trusting.

"The greatest difference between France and America," continued Captain Jones, "is in the people. In America a man ordinarily takes the initiative in striking up an acquaintance with a woman. He has to speak to her before she'll speak to him. This would never do in France, where the men are too shy. Then there's a difference in the way men treat their wives and horses. Americans use whips instead of clubs. And Americans have funny ideas about their homes. Private bedrooms and playrooms are provided for their pets—zebras, lizards and wild cats—and the little fellows are given to understand that they must remain in them and not run all over the house, like one of your cows."

He paused to ask me how the potatoes were acting. I said it was too soon to tell, but I felt a little dizzy in the head. He suggested it were better to go back to our compartment, where there were less things to throw in the event of my reaching the throwing stage.

"On the other hand," I said, "if I am deprived of knives, forks and plates, I will pick on human beings, and I usually aim out the windows."

But he said he was sick of the atmosphere in the diner. We asked for l'addition and argued over who should pay it. I won, and when he had been given his change we returned to our own car, where mademoiselle demonstrated her fear of my expected outbreak by going to sleep.

We turned our attention to the scenery, the most striking feature of which was the abundance of boche prisoners at work in the fields.

"Lucky stiffs!" said the captain. "The war is over for them if they can just manage not to escape, and I guess there's no difficulty about that. Better food than the soldiers, a soft job, and a bed to sleep in. And wages besides. Every private in the Fritz army would surrender if the officers hadn't given them a lot of bunk about the way German prisoners are treated. They make them believe we cut off their feet and ears and give them one peanut and a glass of water every two weeks."

Paris hove into view, and we quarreled about the girl. The fair thing, we decided, would be to turn over her and her baggage to a porter and wish her many happy returns of the day. We were spared this painful duty, however, for when she awoke she treated both of us as strangers. And the gentleman who attended to her baggage was not a porter, but a French aviator, waiting on the station platform for that very purpose.

"She'll tell him," guessed the captain, "that an American soldier and half Indian tried to flirt with her on the train, but she froze them out."

Captain Jones stuck with me till my exit ticket was procured, a chore that ate up over an hour. Then we climbed into a dreadnought and came to this hotel, where I sat right down and versified as follows:

TO AN AMERICAN SOLDIER

If you don't like the nickname Sammy,
If it's not all a nickname should be,
You can pick out Pat or Mike,
Whatever name you like—
It won't make no difference to me.
Want a Thomas or Harry or Dick name?
Dost prefer to be called Joe or Lou?
You've a right to your choice of a nickname;
Oh, Mr. Yank, it's up to you.

My Adventures at the British Front

Monday, September 3. Paris.

IN this morning's mail was a letter from Somewhere in London, replying favorably to my request to go to the British front. I was directed to take the letter to the assistant provost marshal, who would slip me a pass and inform me as to the details of the trip.

At the A. P. M.'s I was given the pass and with it "an undertaking to be signed by all intending visitors to the front." There are ten rules in the undertaking, and some of them are going to be hard to obey. For example:

"I understand that it is impossible to arrange for me to see relatives serving with the fighting forces."

"I will not visit the enemy front during the present war."

But No. 6 is the tough one:

"In no circumstances will I deliver a political or electioneering speech to troops."

I must pray for strength to resist natural impulses along this line.

Wednesday morning, said the A. P. M., would be our starting time. And he told us when and where to take the train—"us" because I am to be accompanied by a regular correspondent, one who carries a cane and everything.

Mr. Gibbons, the regular correspondent, informs me I must wear a uniform, and to-morrow morning I am to try on his extra one, which he has kindly offered.

Another chore scheduled for to-morrow is the squaring of myself with the boss of the French Maison de la Presse, who invited me to visit the devastated territory Thursday and Friday. The invitation was accepted, but the British and French dates conflict, and I would rather see one real, live front than any number of broken-down barns and boched trees.

Tuesday, September 4. Paris.

I reported, after the French idea of breakfast, at the Maison de la Presse. This is situate on the fourth floor of a building equipped with an elevator that proves the fallacy of the proverb "What goes up must come down." You can dimly see it at the top of the shaft, and no amount of button pushing or rope pulling budges it.

During the long climb I rehearsed the speech of apology and condolence framed last night, and wondered whether monsieur would be game and try to smile or break down completely or fly into a rage. He was game, and he not only tried to smile, but succeeded. And his smile was in perfect simulation of relief. These French are wonderful actors.

I returned thence to Mr. Gibbons' room for my fitting. His extra uniform consisted of a British officer's coat and riding breeches, puttees and shoes. Cap and khaki shirt I had to go out and purchase. The store I first selected was a gyp joint and wanted twenty-seven francs for a cap. I went to another store and got exactly the same thing for twenty-six. A careful shopper can save a lot of money in Paris.

Provided with cap and shirt, the latter costing a franc less than the former, I went to a secluded spot and tried on the outfit, Mr. Gibbons assisting. We managed the puttees in thirty-five minutes. It is said that a man working alone can don them in an hour, provided he is experienced.

"You look," Mr. Gibbons remarked when I was fully dressed, "as if you had been poured into it."

But I felt as if I hadn't said "when" quite soon enough. Mr. Gibbons and I differ in two important particulars—knee joints— and though I tried to seem perfectly comfortable, my knees were fairly groaning to be free of the breeches and out in the open fields.

"Wear it the rest of the day and get used to it," advised Mr. Gibbons.

"No," I said. "I don't want to rumple it all up. I want to keep it neat for to-morrow." And against his protest I tore myself out and resumed my humble Chicago garb.

It's no wonder regular correspondents and British officers are obliged to wear canes. The wonder is that they don't use crutches.

We leave at nine to-morrow morning. This means that myself and puttees will have to get up at four.

Wednesday, September 5. With the British.

The major has a very good sense of the fitness of things. The room where I'm writing, by candlelight, is the best guest room in our château and was once occupied by the queen.

The rules of the household call for the dousing of down-stairs glims at eleven o'clock. After that you may either remain down there in total darkness or come up here and bask in the brilliant rays of a candle. You should, I presume, be sleepy enough to go right to bed, but you're afraid you might forget something if you put off the day's record till to-morrow.

I overslept myself, as they say, and had to get Mr. Gibbons to help with the puttees. The lower part of the breeches, I found, could be loosened just enough to make the knee area inhabitable.

We skipped breakfast and reached the station in a taxi without hitting anything. It was fifteen minutes before train time, but there wasn't a vacant seat in the train. A few of the seats were occupied by poilus, and the rest by poilus' parcels and newspapers. A Frenchman always gets to a nine o'clock train by seven-thirty. He picks one seat for himself and one or two on each side of him for his impediments. This usually insures him privacy and plenty of room, for it is considered an overt act even to pick up a magazine and sit in its place. Mr. Gibbons and I walked from one end of the train to the other and half-way back again without any one's taking a hint. We climbed into a carriage just as she started to move.

There were six seats and three occupants. We inquired whether all the seats were reserved, and were given to understand that they were, the owners of three having gone to a mythical dining-car.

We went into the aisle and found standing room among the Australians and Canadians returning from their leave. One of the former, a young, red-headed, scrappy-looking captain, smiled sympathetically and broke open a conversation. I was glad of it, for it give me an opportunity of further study of the language. I am a glutton for languages, and the whole day has been a feast. We have listened to six different kinds—Australian, Canadian, British, French, Chinese and Harvard. I have acquired an almost perfect understanding of British, Australian and Canadian, which are somewhat similar, and of Harvard, which I studied a little back home. French and Chinese I find more difficult, and I doubt that any one could master either inside of a month or so.

The red-headed captain remarked on the crowded condition of the trine. That is Australian as well as British for train. The Canadian is like our word, and the French is spelled the same, but is pronounced as if a goat were saying it. Lack of space prevents the publication of the Chinese term.

One of the captain's best pals, he told us, had just been severely wounded. He was a gime one, though even smaller than the captain. The captain recalled one night when he, the pal, took prisoner a boche lieutenant who stood over six feet. Fritz was asked whether he spoke English. He shook his head. He was asked whether he spoke French. He lost his temper and, in English, called the entire continent of Australia a bad name. The captain's little pal then marched him off to the proper authority, to be questioned in English. On the way the captain's little pal made him take off his helmet and give it to him. This was as punishment for what Fritz had said about Australia.

Before the proper authority Fritz was as sweet-tempered as a bloody bear. This puzzled the proper authority, for making a boche prisoner is doing him a big favor.

"What iles you?" asked the authority when Fritz had refused to reply to any of a dozen questions. "You ine't the first bloody boche officer we've tiken."

Then Fritz bared his grievance. He didn't mind, he said, being a prisoner. The size of his captor was the thing that galled him. "And for Gott's sake," he added, "make him give back my helmet."

The proper authority turned to the captain's little pal. "He's your prisoner," he said. "What do you want to do with the helmet?"

"Keep it, sir," said the captain's little pal.

And it will be used back in Australia some day to illustrate the story, which by that time will doubtless have more trimmings.

"But how about Fritz?" I asked. "When he gets home and tells the same story, he'll have nothing with which to prove it."

"He ine't agoin' to tell the sime story."

We were welcomed at our destination by a captain, another regular correspondent, and two good English cars. The captain said he was expecting another guest on this train, a Harvard professor on research work bent.

"I have no idea what he looks like," said the captain.

"I have," said Mr. Gibbons and I in concert, but it went over the top.

The professor appeared at length, and we were all whisked some thirty kilometers to a luncheon worth having. Afterward we were taken to the Chinese camp. Chinatown, we'll call it, is where the Chink laborers are mobilized when they first arrive and kept until their various specialties are discovered. Then each is assigned to the job he can do best. I was told I mustn't mention the number of Chinamen now in France, but I can say, in their own language, it's a biggee lottee.

They wear a uniform that consists of blue overalls, a blue coat, and no shirt whatever, which, I think, is bad advertising for their national trade. They brought shirts with them, it seems, but are more comfy without.

The minimum wage is three francs a day. Two-thirds of what they earn is paid them here, the other third given to their families in

China. The system of hiring is unique. No names are used, probably because most Chinks have Sam Lee as a monniker, and the paymaster would get all mixed up with an army of Sam Lees. They are numbered and their finger prints are taken by an agent in China. He sends these identification marks to the camp here, and when the Chinks arrive they are checked up by a finger-print expert from Scotland Yard. This gentlemen said there had been several cases where the Chinaman landing here was a ringer, some "friend" back home having signed up and then coaxed the ringer to come in his place, believing, apparently, that the plot would not be detected and that his profit would be the one-third share of the wage that is paid in China. The ringer's family would be done out of its pittance, but that, of course, would make no difference to the ringer's friend. The finger-print system serves not only to prevent the success of cute little schemes like that, but also to amuse the Chinks, who are as proud of their prints as if they had designed them.

We went into the general store, which is conducted by a Britisher. The Chinese had just had a pay-day and were wild to spend. One of them said he wanted a razor. The proprietor produced one in a case, and the Chink handed over his money without even looking at the tool. Another wanted a hat. The prop. gave him a straw with a band that was all colors of the rainbow. The Chinaman paid for it and took it away without troubling to see whether it fitted.

A block or so from the store we ran across two Chinks who had been naughty. Each was in a stock, a pasteboard affair on which was inscribed, in Chinese, the nature of his offense. One of them had been guilty of drinking water out of a fire bucket. The other had drunk something else out of a bottle—drunk too much of it, in fact. They looked utterly wretched, and our guide told us the punishment was the most severe that could be given: that a Chinaman's pride was his most vulnerable spot.

The gent who had quenched his thirst from the fire bucket was sentenced to wear his stock a whole day. He of the stew was on the last lap of a week's term.

We talked with one of the Lee family through an interpreter. We asked him if he knew that the United States was in the war against Germany. He replied, No, but he had heard that France was.

Just before we left the settlement a British plane flew over it. A Chink who was walking with us evidently mistook it for a Hun machine, for he looked up and said: "Bloody boche!"

From Chinatown we were driven to the American Visitors' Château, where gentlemen and correspondents from the United States are entertained. It's a real château, with a moat and everything. The major is our host. The major has seen most of his service in India and China.

He said he was glad to meet us, which I doubt. The new arrivals, Mr. Gibbons, the Harvard professor and myself, were shown our rooms and informed that dinner would occur at eight o'clock. Before dinner we were plied with cocktails made by our friend, the captain. The ingredients, I believe, were ether, arsenic and carbolic acid in quantities not quite sufficient to cause death.

Eleven of us gathered around the festal board. There were the major and his aids, three British captains, one with a monocle. There was the Harvard professor, and the head of a certain American philanthropical organization, and his secretary. And then there were us, me and Mr. Gibbons and Mr. O'Flaherty and Mr. Somner, upstarts in the so-called journalistic world.

The dinner was over the eighteen-course course, the majority of the courses being liquid. I wanted to smoke between the fish and the sherry, but Mr. O'Flaherty whispered to me that it wasn't done till the port had been served.

Mention was made of the Chinese camp, and there ensued a linguistic battle between the major and the Harvard professor. The latter explained the theory of the Chinese language. He made it as clear as mud. In the Chinese language, he said, every letter was a word, and the basis of every word was a picture. For example, if you wanted to say "my brother," you drew a picture of your brother in your mind and then expressed it in a word, such as woof or whang. If you wanted a cigar, you thought of smoke and said "puff" or "blow," but you said it in Chinese.

Mr. Gibbons broke up the battle of China by asking the major whether I might not be allowed to accompany him and Mr. O'Flaherty and one of the captains on their perilous venture to-morrow night. They are going to spend the night in a Canadian first-line trench.

"I'm sorry," said the major, "but the arrangement has been made for only three."

I choked back tears of disappointment.

The major has wished on me for to-morrow a trip through the reconquered territory. My companions are to be the captain with the monocle, the Harvard professor, the philanthropist, and the philanthropist's secretary. We are to start off at eight o'clock. Perhaps I can manage to oversleep.

Thursday, September 6. With the British.

I did manage it, and the car had left when I got down-stairs. Mr. Gibbons and Mr. O'Flaherty were still here, and the three of us made another effort to get me invited to the party to-night. The major wouldn't fall for it.

Mr. Gibbons and Mr. O'Flaherty motored to an artillery school, the understanding being that they were to be met at six this evening by one of our captains and taken to the trench. I was left here alone with the major.

We lunched together, and he called my attention to the mural decorations in the dining-room. It's a rural mural, and in the foreground a young lady is milking a cow. She is twice as big as the cow and is seated in the longitude of the cow's head. She reaches her objective with arms that would make Jess Willard jealous. In another area a lamb is conversing with its father and a couple of squirrels which are larger than either lamb or parent. In the lower right-hand corner is an ox with its tongue in a tin can, and the can is labeled Ox Tongue for fear some one wouldn't see the point. Other figures in the pictures are dogs, foxes and chickens of remarkable size and hue.

"We had a French painter here a few days ago," said the major. "I purposely seated him where he could look at this picture. He took one look, then asked me to change his seat."

The major inquired whether I had noticed the picture of the château which decorates the doors of our automobiles.

"When you go out to-morrow," he said, "you'll observe that none of the army cars is without its symbol. An artillery car has its picture of a gun. Then there are different symbols for the different divisions. I saw one the other day with three interrogation marks painted on it. I inquired what they meant and was told the car belonged to the Watts division. Do you see why?"

I admitted that I did.

"Well, I didn't," said the major, "not till it was explained. It's rather stupid, I think."

This afternoon an American captain, anonymous of course, called on us. He is stopping at G. H. Q., which is short for General Headquarters, his job being to study the British strategic methods. He and the major discussed the differences between Americans and Englishmen.

"The chief difference is temperature," said the captain. "You fellows are about as warm as a glacier. In America I go up to a man and say: 'My name is Captain So-an-So.' He replies: 'Mine is Colonel Such-and-Such.' Then we shake hands and talk. But if I go to an Englishman and say: 'My name is Captain So-and-So,' he says: 'Oh!' So I'm embarrassed to death and can't talk."

" 'Strawnary!' " said the major.

At tea time a courier brought us the tidings that there'd been an air raid last Sunday at a certain hospital base.

"The boche always does his dirty work on Sunday," remarked the American captain. "It's queer, too, because that's the day that's supposed to be kept holy, and I don't see how the Kaiser squares himself with his friend Gott."

I laughed, but the major managed to remain calm.

The American captain departed after tea, and the major and I sat and bored each other till the Harvard professor and his illustrious companions returned. They told me I missed a very interesting trip. That's the kind of trip one usually misses.

At dinner we resumed our enlightening discussion of Chinese, but it was interrupted when the major was called to the telephone. The message was from the captain who was supposed to meet Mr. Gibbons and Mr. O'Flaherty and take them to the trenches to spend the night. The captain reported that his machine had broken down with magneto trouble and he'd been unable to keep his appointment. He requested that the major have Mr. Gibbons and Mr. O'Flaherty located and brought home.

This was done. The disappointed correspondents blew in shortly before closing time and confided to me their suspicion that the trouble with the captain's machine had not been magneto, but (the censor cut out a good line here).

To-morrow we are to be shown the main British training school and the hospital bases.

Friday, September 7. With the British.

We left the château at nine and reached the training camp an hour later.

We saw a squad of ineligibles drilling, boys under military age who had run away from home to get into the Big Game. Their parents had informed the authorities of their ineligibility, and the authorities had refused to enroll them. The boys had refused to go back home, and the arrangement is that they are to remain here and drill till they are old enough to fight. Some of them are as much as three years shy of the limit.

The drill is made as entertaining as possible. The instructor uses a variation of our "Simon says: 'Thumbs up'." "O'Grady" sits in for Simon. For example, the instructor says: "O'Grady says: 'Right dress.' Left dress." The youth who "left dresses" without O'Grady's say-so is sent to the awkward squad in disgrace.

Out of a bunch of approximately two hundred only two went through the drill perfectly. The other one hundred and ninety-eight underestimated the importance of O'Grady and sheepishly stepped out of line. The two perfectos looked as pleased as peacocks.

We saw a bayonet drill with a tutor as vivacious and linguistically original as a football coach, and were then taken to the bomb-throwing school. The tutor here was as deserving of sympathy as a Belgian. A bomb explodes five seconds after you press the button. Many of the pupils press the button, then get scared, drop the bomb and run. The instructor has to pick up the bomb and throw it away before it explodes and messes up his anatomy. And there's no time to stop and figure in what direction you're going to throw.

The Maoris were our next entertainers. The Maoris are colored gemmen from New Zealand. They were being taught how to capture a trench. Before they left their own dugout they sang a battle hymn that would make an American dance and scare a German to death. They went through their maneuvers with an incredible amount of pep and acted as if they could hardly wait to get into real action against the boche. Personally, I would have conscientious objections to fighting a Maori.

Then we were shown a gas-mask dress rehearsal. A British gas mask has a sweet scent, like a hospital. You can live in one, they say, for twenty-four hours, no matter what sort of poison the lovely Huns are spraying at you. We all tried them on and remarked on their efficacy, though we knew nothing about it.

We had lunch and were told we might make a tour of inspection of the hospitals in which the wounded lay. I balked at this and, instead, called on a Neenah, Wisconsin, doctor from whose knee had been extracted a sizable piece of shrapnel, the gift of last Sunday's bomb dropper. This doctor has been over but three weeks, and the ship that brought him came within a yard of stopping a torpedo. Neither war nor Wisconsin has any terrors left for him.

To-morrow we are to be taken right up to the front, dressed in helmets, gas masks, and everything.

Saturday, September 8. With the British.

Two machine loads, containing us and our helmets, masks, and lunch baskets, got away to an early start and headed for the Back of the Front. In one car were the Captain with the Monocle, the Harvard prof., and the American philanthropist. The baggage, the philanthropist's secretary, and I occupied the other. The secretary talked incessantly and in reverent tones of his master, whom he called The Doctor. One would have almost believed he considered me violently opposed to The Doctor (which I wasn't, till later in the day) and was trying to win me over to his side with eulogistic oratory.

The first half of our journey was covered at the usual terrifying rate of speed. The last half was a snail's crawl which grew slower and slower as we neared our objective. Countless troops, afoot and in motors, hundreds of ammunition and supply trucks, and an incredible number of businesslike and apparently new guns, these took up a healthy three-quarters of the road and, despite our importance, didn't hunch to let us pass.

When we sounded our horns to warn of our approach, the subalterns, or whatever you call them, would look round, stand at attention and salute, first the Captain with the Monocle, and then, when our car came up, me. Me because I was the only one in the second machine who wore a British officer's cap. I returned about three salutes, blushing painfully, and then threw my cap on the floor of the car and rode exposed. Saluting is a wear and tear on the right arm, and being saluted makes you feel slackerish and camouflagy, when you don't deserve it.

We attained the foot of the observation hill round noon, left our machines, and ate our picnic lunch, consisting of one kind of sandwiches and three kinds of wine. Then we accomplished the long climb, stopping half-way up to don helmets and masks. Our guide told us that the boche, when not otherwise pleasantly employed, took a few shots at where we were standing to test his long-distance aim.

I wore the mask as long as I could, which was about half an hour. It was unpleasantly reminiscent of an operation I once had, the details of which I would set down here if I had time. Without it, I found, I could see things much more plainly. Through strong field glasses the British trenches were discernible. The German front line was behind a ridge, two hundred yards away—from the British, not us—and invisible. No drive was in progress, but there was the steady boom, boom of heavy guns, the scary siren, with a bang at the end, of grenades, and an occasional solo in a throaty barytone which our captain told us belonged to Mr. Trench Mortar.

The firing was all in one direction—toward the northeast. Fritz was not replying, probably because he had no breath to waste in casual repartee.

Convinced that our hill was a zone of safety, for this afternoon at least, I wanted to stay up there and look and listen till it was time to go home. But our captain had arranged a trip to a sniping school, and our captain would rather have broken his monocle than have made the slightest alteration in the program for the day.

To the sniping school we went, and saw the snipers sniping on their snipes. It was just like the sniping school I had visited at the American camp, and I got pretty mad at our captain for dragging us away from a sight far more interesting. But he redeemed himself by having the major in charge show us real, honest-to-goodness camouflage, staged by an expert.

We were taken to a point two hundred yards distant from a trench system.

"Standing up in front of one of those trenches," said the major, "there's a sergeant in costume. He's in plain sight. Now you find him."

Well, we couldn't find him, and we gave up.

"Move, Sergeant!" shouted the major.

The sergeant moved and, sure enough, there he was!

"I had him spotted all the time," said The Doctor.

The major directed the sergeant to change to a costume of a different hue. When the change had been made we were required to turn our backs till he had "hidden" himself again. Again he was "in plain sight," and again we had to give up. Again he was ordered to move, and we saw him, this time in colors diametrically opposed to those of his first garb.

"I had him spotted all the time," said The Doctor.

The sergeant went through his entire repertory of tricks, but the rest must not be reported.

It occurred to me on the way back to our machines that some football coach could make a fish out of the defensive team by camouflaging his back field.

Our captain and the Harvard prof. climbed into the front car, leaving The Doctor, his secretary, and me to bring up the rear. The sec. sat with the driver; The Doctor and I in the back seat.

"How long have you been over here?" inquired The Doctor at length.

I told him.

"How many American soldiers are there in France?"

I told him.

After an impressive pause, he said:

"As a matter of fact, there are really—" And he increased my estimate by four hundred per cent. "Of course," he continued, "I have the right figures. They were furnished me by the Defense League before I left home. They naturally wouldn't give them to a writer because they don't want them published."

"And naturally," says I, "whenever they tell a writer anything in strict confidence, he rushes to the nearest Local and Long Distance Telephone Booth and gets Wilhelmstrasse on the wire."

"Oh, no," said The Doctor. "But a writer might think it was his duty to send the correct information to his paper."

"Did you ever hear of the censorship?" I asked him.

"There are ways of eluding it."

"And do you think all writers are that kind?"

He shrugged a fat shoulder.

"Not all, possibly a very few. But one never can tell the right kind from the wrong."

His guard was down, and I took careful aim:

"Do you think the Defense League used good judgment in entrusting that secret to you, when you spill it to the first irresponsible reporter you happen to run across?"

If I hadn't won this argument, I wouldn't repeat it.

Not until we reached our château did I realize why I had been so catty. I'd gone without my tea.

Sunday, September 9. Paris.

Mr. Gibbons and I this morning bade good-by to our genial hosts and were driven to the station at which we arrived last Wednesday. On the Paris-bound train I wondered audibly why the servants had given me that queer look before we left.

"Did you tip them?" asked Mr. Gibbons.

"Certainly!" I snapped.

"I'll bet I know," said Mr. Gibbons. "You probably packed your own suit-case."

He was right.

How I Didn't Drive Major Blank's Car to Camp Such-and-Such

Monday, September 10. Paris.

THE American major who owns the car which Mr. Kiley drove down from Le Havre, whither it had been sent by the man who bought it in London for the American major—well, anyway, this American major, he's in the artillery camp at Such-and-Such, and he wants me to bring it down there for him. I've never handled, or, rather, footled one of the little birds, but it's something everybody should learn, like French and auction and how to swim. Besides, I want to see the artillery camp. So I'm accepting the commission and intend to get busy to-morrow morning.

Tuesday, September 11. Paris.

With an American pass and an order for the car, I taxied to the United States army garage, in the Quai Debilly.

"Avez-vous fixed voux with passes?" inquired a friendly inmate of the garage.

I showed him my American card.

"That isn't bien suffisant," he said. "You'll have to get a pink one to go through the French army zone."

I recalled then our troubles on a previous automobile trip and was glad he had spoken.

"Where do I go for that?" I inquired.

"Go," said he, "to the Préfet de Ligne du Communications." Or something like that.

"Où is il?"

"I think he's in the Rue François Premier."

"And is the car all right?"

"I guess so. Nos haven't looked at it yet."

I had let my taxi go, and twenty minutes were spent in getting another. It was another hour before we located the préfet.

A secretary examined my passport and American pass and took my dossier:

Name, nationality, birthplace, age, ancestry, real purpose in coming to France. Hair—black; forehead—high; eyes—brown; nose—prominent; mouth—medium; chin—round; complexion—dark; height—six one and three-quarters. Sign here.

"Now," said the sec., "monsieur will avez to come across avec a photophie."

"I'm just out," I said. "I'd no idea I'd be so popular."

"Nos can issue no passes sans a photophie" says he, so out I went in search of a rapid-fire studio.

The driver pulled up in front of a gallery on the Rue de la Paix, where the artist promised to have six copies of my map printed by midi.

To kill time I rode back to Billy's rue.

"The car's on the blink," said my friend in French. "The connecting rod is lâche and some bearings are burned out. Besides, vous would be a rummy to partir on these tires."

"Comme beaucoup new ones do je need?"

"Just plain quatre," says he.

"Well," says I, "put them on and get busy avec the reparations. I want to start away before dark."

"Ah, oui," says he, "but we have no tires and we have no tools to make the reparations avec."

"Can't you get them?"

"Vous devoir get them yourself."

"Où?"

"At the branch factory of the ———," and he said the name of the car right out loud.

"Où est le branch factory?"

"Il est in un suburb—Le Vallois-Perret. The address is 6163 Rue Corneille."

"What tools are required?"

"Une roue-tirer et un offset clef à vis."

Which means a wheel puller and an offset wrench.

"And can je aussi tires get there?"

"Ah, oui."

It was noon, and my trusting driver and I returned to the studio on the Rue de la Paix. The pictures weren't fini. They never are.

"Take me to Maxim's," says I, "and we'll call it a half day."

After lunch I walked back to the studio. The pictures were not fini, but would monsieur rester? Monsieur would. Monsieur rested till fourteen o'clock, got six photophies that had him looking more than ever like a German spy, and taxied back to the Rue François Premier. The préfet's joint was closed.

I asked the driver how far it was out to Le Vallois-Perret.

"Come on," he said, and I climbed in, but "come on," in French, means "I don't get you," so I had to repeat the directions four or five times.

"Ah, oui," he said at last. "Le Vallois-Perret. Quatorze kilomet's."

"What is that in American money?"

"Come on," said the driver.

"Hotel Con-tin-en-tal," I said.

I'll tackle 'em afresh to-morrow morning.

Wednesday, September 12. Paris.

The préfet's secretary approved my picture and gave me a beautiful salmon-colored pass. It is good for five days, which is plenty, as I will come back on the train.

At the city gates, en route to Le Vallois-Perret, my taxi and I were stopped and our essence measured. If we brought back more than we took out, we would have to pay taxes on the difference.

Quatorze kilomet's was a very conservative estimate of the distance, and it was nearly eleven when we reached Cornelia's rue and the branch factory.

An American heard my plea for four new tires, an offset wrench, and a wheel puller.

"It can't be done," he said. "All we do is own this place. But the French Government has taken it over and runs it."

"But this is a United States army car," I said, "and we're supposed to be allies of the French."

"Without special permission," said he, "you stand as much chance as if you were the Crown Prince."

"Where can I get special permission?"

"Your best bet is to see Captain Vandervelde. If anybody can fix it, he's the boy. You'll find him in the Passage de Haynau, Rue Croix Nivert."

"What number?"

"There is no number."

I thanked him, or perhaps I forgot to, and returned to my taxi.

"Passage de Haynau in Rue Croix Nivert," I said.

"Q'numéro?"

"There ain't none."

"Come on," demanded the driver.

"I told you there was no number. We'll just have to keep looking till we find it."

We convinced the guardian of the gate that we weren't trying to cheat on gasoline, and rolled into Rue Croix Nivert about thirteen o'clock. My chauffeur sat nonchalantly in his accustomed seat while I made a house-to-house canvass of Haynau's Passage. The last house was the right one. I knew it in an instant, for when I entered the corridor a French sentry popped up and placed the end of his bayonet within an inch of Nose-prominent.

"Captain Vandervelde," said I, making a short strategical retreat.

"Come on," said Frenchy without lowering his sticker.

A password was what he wanted, and Mr. Poincaré had forgotten to call me up and give me the correct one for the day. I produced a two-franc piece and held it out. The sentry withdrew his weapon, accepted the coin, and allowed me to pass.

"The word," I thought to myself, "must be Liberté, Egalité, Fraternité."

Captain Vandervelde was in and made me wait only half an heure, the while I thought more than once of yon taxi. Finally I was summoned to the inner office.

"What can je faire pour vous?" he inquired.

I told him I wanted an order on the———branch factory for some tools and four new tires.

"Rien fairing on the tires," he said.

"Pourquoi?" I asked him.

"Orders pour tires must come from the Maison de la Guerre."

"Can you fix me for the tools?"

"Ah, oui. What tools voulez-vous?"

"Une roue-tirer et un offset clef à vis."

"Votre papers, s'il vous plait."

I handed him passport, American pass, and salmon-pink card. He glanced them over, then began rummaging in a drawer. I knew what was coming—another dossier.

"Avez-vous une photophie?" he asked.

"Ah, oui," says I, and slipped him one of the remaining five.

He kept the dossier and photophie for the amusement of himself and progeny. He gave me only a mauve card which said I was entitled to one wheel puller and one left-handed offset monkey wrench.

I told my driver we had to hurry right back to Le Vallois-Perret. He looked crestfallen.

"Je have had no déjeûner," he said.

"Neither have je," I said, and climbed in.

Thursday, September 13. Paris.

Up early and to the garage. Delivered the tools. "Vous had better buy a tire pump," said my adviser.

"Je suppose," said I, "that I'll have to get an order for one from Papa Joffre."

"No," he said. "That's une chose vous can buy sans an order."

"Voulez-vous get to work on the car right away?"

"Ah, oui," says he.

I asked my chauffeur to take me to a maison du tire pumps. We found one on the Champs Elysées. Other things for sale in the store were watches and perfumery. I proceeded thence to French General Headquarters.

The gentleman authorized to sign orders for tires received me cordially and spoke English.

"Certainly," he said in an answer to my request, "if the car is for an American officer. And what is the license number?"

I had to confess I didn't know.

"Well," said he, "you go to the garage and find out. Then come back and I'll give you the order."

I went to the garage to find out. There was no license.

"Où can je get one?" I asked my friend.

He gave me the address of the license bureau, on Rue Oskaloosa or something. The driver knew where it was.

Monsieur du License surprised me by asking for a picture and taking my description, which I could almost have rhymed by this time—

Hair jet black, but a paucity of it;
  Forehead high as the Eiffel tower;
Prominent nose, but it's mine; I love it;
  Eyes the brown of the pansy flower;
Medium mouth, not the best for kisses;
  Chin as round as a billiard ball;
Dark complected—Oh, Mister, this is
  Me, and I'm better than six feet tall.

"What est the numéro of the engine?"

"Four hundred and fifty-six thousand three hundred and four," I replied sans batting an eyelash.

He took it down and disappeared into an adjoining room. In a little while he returned with a license plate—second-hand to match the car.

I carried it along to display to the man at G. H. Q., as it is technically known.

"Où can I get the tires?" I asked.

"Anywhere, with that order," he said.

So I told the driver to go anywhere, and he misunderstood and took me everywhere. The tire maison he chose was as far away as he could drive without crossing the Swiss border.

"Now back to the United States garage," said I, and we arrived just as they were closing.

My friend told me the car had been "taken down." When I saw it I was convinced that the "taking down" had been accomplished with shrapnel.

"How many months will it take to put it together again?" I asked.

"Très few minutes," said the mechanic. "It will be all finished to-morrow midi."

"It looks all finished now."

"Avez-vous votre license?" he inquired.

I displayed it triumphantly.

"Ah, oui," he said. "But that's just the license for the car. Vous must aussi have a driver's license."

"Bonne nuit!" I yelped. "And what for?"

"C'est la loi," said he. "Everybody who drives in France must have one."

"How do you get it?"

"You'll have to go to the Chef de Traffic Police and pass the examination."

"How long does it take?"

"Très brief. Not more than une heure."

"Well, will you guarantee to have the car all ready when I come for it at noon to-morrow?"

"Je promise," he said, and I drove back to the hotel.

Oh, Major, wait till you see that taxi bill!

Friday, September 14. Paris.

The traffic chief said that before he could examine me for a license I must show him my registration card from a regular police commissioner. I had been told I ought to have one of those darn things, but had passed it up. Now I was face to face with the necessity of acquiring the card and doing it quick. The nearest station was only a few blocks away. I found it jam-packed with people who looked as if they all worked in East St. Louis. I flagged an attendant.

"I want to register," I told him.

"You'll be called when it's your turn," he said, and gave me a number. It was 89,041.

"How long will I have to wait?"

He pondered.

"I think they're now in the twenty-thousands," he said.

Suddenly I bethought me of a document in my pocket, a letter from the boss of the Maison de la Presse. I flashed it on him.

"Ah-h-h!" he sighed, and led me through the mob to the inner shrine.

In ten minutes I had my card. The commissioner didn't even want a picture, or nothin'. I plunged through the gang again and was stared at enviously. Some of the poor blokes have undoubtedly been waiting there since the Kaiser was forced into the war.

Again I appeared before the traffic chief. "Of course," he said, "I will have to examine your papers. And avez-vous une photophie?"

I came through.

"Now," I said, "we're fifty-fifty. You have one and I have one."

But he wasn't listening. He was rummaging for the deadly dossier.

"This," he said, when he had found one, "will have to be filled out."

"Yes," I replied, "I think I recall filling one out last time I was in France."'

"This car belongs to an American army officer?"

"Ah, oui."

"What does he intend to do with the car?"

The temptation was strong to say he intended using it to tour the trenches. But it was no time to trifle.

"He expects to ride round the camp in it, sir. He is in one of the high commands and has to do a lot of inspecting."

"Do you know the traffic laws of Paris?"

"Ah, oui."

He didn't ask me what they were. But I could have told him. Any part of the street you like, with a minimum speed limit of forty miles on the straightaway and sixty-five miles round the corners.

"You are going to take the car right out of Paris?"

"Ah, oui."

"That's all," he said, and handed me a driver's license, horizon blue with saffron stripes.

I thanked him and bowed myself out of the place.

"From now on," I thought, "it's clear sailing."

The car was ready. I had in my mind's eye a near-by unfrequented street, where I was going to master the driving of it in ten minutes. Then I was going to shoot her up to the hotel, get my baggage and leave town.

"How about gas and oil?" I inquired.

"Oil, oui, but essence, no," said the mechanic.

"Well, thrown in ten gallons," said I.

"Ah, but has monsieur an essence ticket?"

Monsieur never heard of it.

"Ah, then, monsieur can get no essence."

"Well for—" and monsieur used harsh words.

"Monsieur can easily obtain a ticket," said the guy when things had quieted down. "Monsieur's military passes will be suffisant."

"Where at?"

"At the Maison du Contrôle de l'Essence."

"And that is—?"

"Vingt sept, Rue Yaki Hula Hickey Dula."

"Is that as far away as it sounds?"

"Monsieur can go there and be back in une heure."

Monsieur crawled wearily into a taxi and started for Honolulu. The military passes did prove suffisant, and there was no trouble getting a fifty-gallon book at two francs per gal.

"I'll save time now," I thought. "I'll pick up my baggage on the way back to the garage."

So I told my driver to stop at the hotel. A telegram was waiting there for me.

"Hold car in Paris," it said. "Camp may be moved any day."

This blow fell at fourteen o'clock this afternoon. By half-past fifteen I had called up every steamship office and learned that the next boat for America would leave from England next Wednesday night. I am going to be aboard.

And now I have for sale, at auction:

One pass through the French war zone.

One pass good in the American camp.

One driver's license.

One book of essence tickets.

One road map.

One registration card.

I think I will leave the four tires and the offset clef à vis and the wheel puller with the car. Also the car's license. The major is perfectly trustworthy. I only hope he doesn't get killed before my expense account reaches him.

I Start Home, with a
Stop-Over at London

Saturday, September 15. Paris.

THE gentleman at the American Embassy, which I visited late yesterday afternoon, spake truth when he said it was some job to get away from this place.

"If you want to leave on Sunday," quoth he, "you'll have to rise early Saturday and keep going all day. See our consul first thing in the morning, and he'll tell you all you have to do."

So I saw our consul first thing this morning. In fact, I beat him to his office. When he came in he was cordial and unsuspicious, rare qualities in a consul. He stamped my passport "Bon pour se rendre en Amérique par Grande Bretagne" and a great deal more.

"Now," he said, "you'll have to be viséed by the préfet de police and approved by the British Military Control. I don't know in what order. They change it every two or three days to keep you guessing."

I chose the British Control first and, of course, was wrong. But it took an hour to find this out.

There was a big crowd of us, and we were all given numbers, as in a barber shop of a Saturday night. But the resemblance to the barber shop ceased with the giving, for they called us regardless of number. A guinea sitting next to me was 42 and I was 18. He preceded me into the sanctum. And I got there ahead of No. 12, a British matron.

My session was brief.

"The police visé must come first," said the officer in charge.

Monsieur le Préfet has his office conveniently located about eight miles away from the Control, over the river. And he's on the fourth floor of a building constructed before the invention of the elevator. From behind an untrimmed hedge of black whiskers he

questioned me as to my forebears, musical tastes and baseball pref-
erences. Then he retired into his chambers and presently issued
forth with my passport, on which his stamp had been added to the
beautiful collection already there. It says I'm Bon for a trip to
Amérique par Angleterre, so I don't know whether I'm to go that
way or through Grande Bretagne.

Thence back to Rue Napoléon Lajoie, and another long wait.

"Yes," said the officer when my turn came again, "the visé is all
right, but where is your steamship ticket? You'll have to show that
before we can pass you."

In order to show it I had to go and buy it, and in order to buy it I
had to scare up some money, which is no mere child's play in Gay
Paree these days. I called on four people before I found one who was
touchable. With what he grudgingly forked over I hastened to the
booking office and felt at home there, it being on Rue Scribe. There
was a customer ahead of me—our president's youngest son-in-law.

"Do you know who that was?" said the agent excitedly when
the young man had departed.

"Yes," I replied, "but we don't speak to each other."

"Now," said the agent, "I'm afraid I'll have to ask you a few
questions. It's annoying, I know, but it's the war-time rule."

"Shoot," I told him. "I'm thoroughly used to being annoyed."

He ran through the familiar list and saved a new one for the
wind-up.

"Why are you going to America?"

I could have spent an entire week replying to that, but even
minutes were precious.

"Because it's where I live," proved satisfactory.

He apologized again for having to propound the queries, which
shows he must be new on the job. The rest of them don't care
whether you like it or not. I signed six or seven pledges, gave over
the bulk of my borrowed fortune, and set out again with my ticket
for the Rue Jacques Johnson. I got there just in time, for they close
early on Saturday. Other days the poor devils have to work right
through from ten to four.

The officer also wanted to know why I was going to America. And he asked me at what hotel I would stop in London. I told him I'd never been there and knew nothing about the hotels.

"You must make a choice," he said. "We have to know your address."

"Is there one called the Savoy?"

"Yes."

"Well, let's say the Savoy."

"All right. You're to stay there, then, while you're in London, and you're to leave England on this ship Wednesday night. Otherwise you may have trouble."

I'll be surprised if I don't anyhow.

He decorated my passport with a heliotrope inscription, naming the port from which I'm to depart from France, the hotel in London, and my good ship, and sent me into the next room, where a vice-consul confirmed the military visé and relieved me of two francs.

The train leaves at seven to-morrow morning, and between now and then I have only to pack and to settle with the hotel. The former chore will be easy, for I possess just half as much personal property as when I came. Parisian laundries have commandeered the rest.

Monday, September 17. London.

With tear-dimmed eyes, I said farewell to Paris yesterday morning at the unearthly hour of seven. There was not even a gendarme on hand to see me off.

The trip from Paris to England is arranged with the customary French passion for convenience. They get you out of bed at five to catch the train, which arrives in the port at noon. The Channel boat leaves port at ten o'clock at night, giving you ten solid hours in which to think. Not ten either, for the last two are consumed in waiting for your turn to be examined by the customs and viséed by the Authorities du Exit.

Customs examination in this case is a pure waste of time. The gentleman only wants to know whether you are trying to smuggle any gold money out of France. I'd like to see the departing guest who has any kind of money left to smuggle.

The Authorities du Exit are seven in number. They sit round a table, and you pass from one to the other until something has been done to you by each. One feels your pulse, another looks at your tongue, a third reads your passport right side up, a fourth reads it upside down, a fifth compares you with your photograph, a sixth inspects your visés for physical defects, and the seventh tries to throw a scare into you.

I got by the first six easily. No. 7 read both sides of the passport and then asked by whom I was employed. I told him.

"Where are your credentials?" he demanded.

"What do you mean, credentials?"

"You must have a letter from the magazine, showing that it employs you."

"You're mistaken. I have no such letter."

He looked very cross. But there were others left to scare, so he couldn't waste much time on me.

"I'll pass you," he said, "but if you come back to France again, you can't leave."

He and I should both worry.

But it does seem pathetic that the written and stamped approval, in all colors of the rainbow, of the Paris chief of police, the American consul, the British Military Control, the British consul, the French consul in New York, and nearly everybody else in the world, including our own Secretary of State, sufficeth not to convince a minor-league official that an innocent native of Niles, Michigan, isn't related by marriage to the Hohenzollerns.

On the dark deck of our Channel boat I had a 'strawnary experience. A British colonel to whom I had not been introduced spoke to me. He wanted a light from my cigarette. And when I had given it to him he didn't move away, but stayed right there and kept on talking.

"This is my first leave," he said (but in his own tongue), "since last March. Last year we were let off ten days every three months. Now we get twenty days a year."

"In 1918," said I, for something to say, "you'll probably have no vacation at all."

"In 1918," he replied confidently, "I believe we'll get three hundred and sixty-five days."

We settled the war in about half an hour. Then he asked me to join him in a Scotch and soda. I was too gentlemanly to refuse. The bar, we ascertained, was closed. But we might find something in the dining-room. We did, but to make it legal we had to order biscuits, alias crackers, with the beverage. We didn't have to eat them, though. They looked to be in their dotage, like the permanent sandwiches which serve a similar purpose in certain blue-law cities of Les Etats Unis.

We settled the war all over again, and retired, the colonel politely expressing the hope that we would meet for breakfast.

The hope was not realized. I was through and out on deck by the time we docked at the British port, which was about six o'clock this morning.

No one was permitted to leave the ship till the customs officials and alien officers reported for duty, two hours later. Then we were unloaded and herded into a waiting-room, where an usher seated us. Another usher picked us out, four at a time, for examination, using a system of arbitrary selective draft. Mine was a mixed quartet, three gents and a female.

An officer looked at our passports and recorded details of them in a large book. Another officer ran the gamut of queries. And here I got into a little mess by telling the truth. When he asked me what countries I had visited, I told him France and added "Oh, yes, and for one day Belgium." He marked this fact on a slip of paper and sent me to the next room. The slip of paper was there ahead of me and I was once more a suspect.

The young lady of our quartet, a French girl, was getting hers, and there was nothing for me to do but listen. She had a letter from her mother to a friend in England. The mother, it seems, had expected to come along, but had decided to wait three weeks, "till the submarine warfare is over." The officers were very curious to know where the mother had picked up that interesting dope. The young lady couldn't tell them. Well, she would not be permitted to leave town till an investigation had been made. She was led back into the waiting-room and may be there yet for all I can say.

It was my turn.

"Are you an American?"

"Yes, sir."

"How long ago were you in Belgium?"

"About ten days ago."

"You told our officer outside that you had been in Paris five weeks."

"I told him Paris had been my headquarters and I'd made frequent trips in and out."

"How did you get to Belgium?"

"In an automobile."

"An automobile!"

"Yes, sir."

"What were you doing?"

"I was being the guest of your army."

A great light dawned upon them.

"Oh!" said one, smiling. "He means he was behind our lines, not theirs."

"I should hope so," said I.

"We're sorry to have misunderstood, sir," said the other, and I was escorted into the baggage-room. There my sordid belongings were perfunctorily examined, the official not even troubling to open my typewriter case nor a large ungainly package containing a toy for certain parties back home.

It was eleven o'clock when the examinations were all over and we entrained for this town. I got off at Waterloo and asked a taxi to take me to the Savoy. It did and it drove on the left side of all the streets en route. I'm still quaking.

Tuesday, September 18. London.

This morning I had my first experience with an English tele-phone. I asked the hotel's operator to get me the office of Mr. O'Flaherty, the American correspondent I had met at the British front. In a few moments she rang back.

"Are you there?" she said, that being London for "Hello."

"Here's your number, then. Carry on," she said.

But carrying on was not so easy. There is a steel spring on the combination transmitter-receiver which you must hold down while you talk. I kept forgetting it. Also I kept being electrically shocked. But in the course of half an hour, with the operator's assistance, I managed to convey to the gentleman an invitation to call.

He came, and we started for the Bow Street police station, where every visitor has to register within twenty-four hours of his arrival. On the way we met Lew Payne, the actor, and Gene Corri, racing man and box-fight referee. Gene has friends among the bob-bies, and I was put through in record time. They told me I'd have to go to the American consul for a visé and then come back for a sec-ond registration with the police. Mr. O'Flaherty opined that these jobs should be attended to at once, as my boat train was supposed to leave at nine to-morrow morning. Mr. Payne had a better idea.

"Let's telephone the steamship office," he said, "and find out whether your ship is really going to sail on schedule. They usually don't these days."

Mr. O'Flaherty did the telephoning and, sure enough, the blamed thing's been postponed till Saturday night.

They asked me what I wanted to do next, and I said I'd like to pay my respects to George and Mary. But I hadn't let them know I was coming and they're both out of town.

We went to Murray's (pronounced Mowrey's) Club for lunch, though no one in the party was a member and you have to sign checks to get anything. Unlike most clubs, however, you pay cash simultaneously with signing the check, so we weren't cheating. I signed "Charles Chaplin" to one check and it went unchallenged.

Gene's two sons are in the British army, and the conversation was confined to them. I was told they were the best two sons a man ever had, but I knew better.

Murray's Club's orchestra is jazz and it gave Mr. O'Flaherty and me an acute attack of homesickness.

From there we rode to the National Sporting Club, of which Mr. Corri is king. He asked me to put on the gloves with him, but I'm not one of the kind that picks on people five or six times my age.

On Mr. Payne's advice, Mr. O'Flaherty and I purchased seats for a show called *Seven Day's Leave*, and that's where we've been to-night, we and another scribe, Mr. Miller of Dowagiac, Michigan, which, as every one knows, is a suburb of Niles.

The show is a melodrama with so many plots that the author forgot to unravel two or three hundred of them. Of the fifteen characters, one is the hero and the rest are German spies, male and female. The hero is a British officer. Everybody wanted to kill him, and so far as I could see there was nothing to prevent. But he was still alive when the final curtain fell. The actors made all their speeches directly to the audience, and many of them (the speeches) were in the soliloquy form ruled off the American stage several years ago.

In the last act the hero pretends to be blotto (British for spiflicated), so that, while he is apparently dead to the world, he can eavesdrop on a dialogue between two of the boche plotters and obtain information invaluable to England. The boches were completely deceived, which is more than can be said of the audience.

Wednesday, September 19. London.

Took a walk past Westminster Abbey and Buckingham Palace and found they looked just like their post-card pictures.

It's almost as bad crossing streets here as in Paris. The taxis don't go as fast, but their habit of sticking to the left side keeps an American on what are known as tenterhooks.

Mr. O'Flaherty loomed up at noon and guided me to the office of a friend with money. This rara avis honored a check on an American bank, and now I think there's enough cash on hand to see me through. The only trouble is that my education in English money has been neglected and I don't know when I'm being short-changed. Constantly, I presume.

Living conditions here have it on those in Paris. There are no meatless days, and a hot bath is always available. The town is dark at night, but it's said to be not for the purpose of saving fuel, but as a measure of protection against air raids.

One of those things was staged last week and a bomb fell uncomfortably close to ye hotel. The dent it made in Mother Earth is clearly visible to the naked eye. I trust the bombers take every other week off. At dinner we met two American naval officers—a captain from Baltimore and a lieutenant from Rockford, which is in Illinois. What they told us was the most interesting stuff I've heard yet. But, like all interesting stuff, it's forbidden to write it.

Thursday, September 20. London.

The American naval officers took me to luncheon. After luncheon I went to the American consul's where I was viséed. Thence to the Bow Street station for final registration.

This evening to *The Boy,* a musical play which could use some of the plot so prodigally expended in *Seven Days' Leave.* But the music isn't bad.

Friday, September 21. London.

The naval officers and three of us holdup men had a bitter argument over the respective merits of Baltimore, Dowagiac, Rockford, Niles, and What Cheer, Iowa, of which Mr. O'Flaherty is a native, and, so far as I know, the only one. It was finally voted to award What Cheer first prize for beauty of name, Dowagiac for handsome young men, Niles for scenic grandeur, Rockford for so-cial gaieties, and Baltimore for tunnels.

I wanted to do some work, but the rest of the crowd seemed to think my room was open house for the balance of the day, and here they stuck despite all efforts to oust them.

To-night it was *Chu Chin Chow* at His Majesty's Theater. You have to keep going to theaters in London. They're the only places that are lit up.

Chu Chin Chow is a musical comedy based on *The Forty Thieves*, and the music, according to our unanimous opinion, is the best since *The Merry Widow*. I seem to have resigned as war correspon-dent to accept a position as dramatic critic. But, as Mr. O'Flaherty says, there's nothing to write about the war, and what you do write the censors massacre.

Our ship still thinks it's going to sail to-morrow night, and the train leaves at nine-thirty in the morning. I am to be convoyed to port by the captain and the lieutenant, whose holiday is over.

Saturday, September 22. In Bond.

We're anchored in the middle of the river and have no apparent intention of moving to-night. And everybody's out of cigarettes, and it's illegal to sell them while we're in bond, whatever that may mean. But I guess I'd rather be in it than in a spy's cell, which seemed to be my destination at one time to-day.

The United States naval gentlemen were down at the train early and commandeered the best compartment on it. They had saved a seat for me and an extra one on general principles. This was awarded to Mr. Hanson, one of the active members of the French Line conspiracy which caused my arrest in Bordeaux. I hope he's seasick all the way home.

On the trip up from London we scored a decisive verbal victory over the submarines and formulated the terms of peace. Captain Baltimore and Lieutenant Rockford said farewell at the Liverpool dock and started for wherever they were going. We found seats in the inspection room and waited. Mr. Hanson grew impatient at length. He flashed his passport, a diplomatic one, on the usher and was sent through in a hurry. Not so with this well-known suspect. I was among the last to be called. My passport, strangely enough, was approved, but the baggage examination was yet to come.

I found my four pieces—two containers of clothes and such, a typewriter, and the ungainly toy—and had them hoisted on to the inspection counter. The most curious man I ever knew went at them.

The typewriter came first.

"What is this?" he asked when he had opened the case.

"A typewriter."

"Where did you buy it?"

"In Chicago."

"What do you use it for?"

"For typewriting."

"Typewriting what?"

"Stuff for newspapers and magazines."

"Pretty handy, isn't it?"

"Very."

"Have you written any articles over here?"

"Yes."

"Where are they?"

"Some are in America by this time; others are in the censors' hands."

He wanted to know what publications I was connected with, and I told him. He allowed me to close up the typewriter case, and next launched an offensive against a young trunk. He examined my collars one by one and found them all the same size. He came upon a package containing five or six hundred sheets of blank copy paper. He inspected every sheet, holding many of them up to the light. He gave individual attention to each of the few bits of lingerie the Parisians had not considered worth keeping. He exhibited an amazing interest in my other suit. He fondled a beautiful gray sweater for fully five minutes. He went through a copy of the *Chu Chin Chow* score, page by page. I wondered he didn't sing it. Holding out only the blank paper, he repacked, and tackled the suit-case.

He counted the bristles in the tooth-brush. He found two French dictionaries and a French grammar and studied them for approximately one semester. He opened a nest of shirts and hand-kerchiefs and spread them out for a thorough review. I should hate to be a clerk in a gents' furnishing store and have him wished on me as a customer.

In the lower southeast corner he discovered an unopened box of shaving cream. As every one knows, this commodity comes in a tube, which is wrapped in transparent paper, and the tube, thus wrapped, is contained in a pasteboard box for protection or some-thing. Old Curiosity opened the box and extracted the tube. He gazed at it through the wrapper, then removed the wrapper and stared at the nude tube.

"Where is this made?" he asked.

"In America. It comes out like a ribbon and lies flat on the brush."

Without comment, he reclothed the tube as well as he could in its mutilated wrapper, put it back in its box, and repacked the suit-case and shut it.

"Is that all you have?" he inquired.

"No," I said. "There's that big square package containing a toy."

Now about this toy. It's a complete but ridiculously impractical system of trenches. French soldiers of leaden composition are re-sisting a boche attack. Some are supposed to be throwing bombs. Others are fighting with bayonets. A few are busy with the trench guns. There are threads to represent barbed-wire entanglements and a few Huns enmeshed in them. Other Huns are prone, the vic-tims of the sturdy poilu defense.

The package had been opened for private exhibition purposes in London, and as I am an awful washout (British slang) at doing up bundles, I had left the job to a chambermaid, who had discarded the Parisian wrapping paper and used some on which no firm name appeared.

Well, Mr. Question Mark now laboriously untied the cord, took off the paper and the cover of the box, and exposed the toy to the public and official view. Instantly two British officers, whom we shall call General Bone and Major Thick, flitted up to the counter and peered at the damning evidence.

"What is this gentleman's name?" asked the general.

He was told.

"When did you make this thing?" he demanded.

"I didn't," said I. "It was bought in a shop in Paris."

"What shop?"

"You can't expect a person to remember the name of a Parisian shop."

"Where is the firm's name on the paper?"

I explained that the original wrapper had been left in London.

"What is your business?" demanded the major.

"He's a correspondent," replied the inspector.

There ensued the old familiar cross-examination and the request for credentials I didn't have. The major asked the inspector whether I was carrying any papers.

"These," said the latter, and showed him the pile of blank copy sheets.

The major dived for it.

"It's all blank paper," said the inspector, and the major registered keen disappointment.

Next to my suit-case lay a bag belonging to a gentleman named Trotter, and on it was a Japanese hotel label. The general glimpsed it and turned on me. "When were you in Japan?" he asked.

I told him never.

"That piece isn't his," said the inspector. "It belongs to a Mr. Trotter."

"His first name is Globe," said I, but it was a wild pitch.

The major and the general had a whispered consultation. Then the former said: "Well, I guess he's all right. Let him go."

Some devil within me suggested that I say good-by to them in German, which I learned in our high school. I cast him out, and here I am, aboard ship, sitting still in the middle of the river. But I don't like being indefinitely bottled in bond and I appeal to you, Mr. Captain—

Take me somewhere west of Ireland where they know I'm not a spy,
Where nobody gazes at me with a cold, suspicious eye—
To the good old U. S. A.,
Where a gent can go his way
With no fear of being picked on forty thousand times a day.

Back in Old "O Say"; I Start Answering Questions

Sunday, September 23. At Sea.

A CARD on the wall of my stateroom says: "Name of Steward—Ring Once. Name of Stewardess—Ring Twice." If they'll give us deck space, we can put on a three Ring circus.

The ship was still in bond when we awoke this morning, and the cheerful rumor floated round that she sometimes remained in harbor a week before securing the Admiralty's permission to sail. But life-boat drill was ordered right after breakfast, and Ring Once told me this indicated a speedy departure. My boat is No. 9. It's a male boat except for one Japanese lady, Mrs. Kajiro Come-here-o, whose husband is also of our select crew.

Our drillmaster advised us to wear plenty of heavy clothes till we were out of the danger zone, advice which it is impossible for me to follow. He said five blasts of the whistle would mean we were attacked. I think, however, that if I hear as many as three I'll start sauntering toward No. 9.

At noon we felt the throb of the engines, and forty minutes later we were out of bond and able to buy cigarettes.

Before luncheon we were assigned to our permanent seats. Naturally, I am at the captain's table, with a member of the House of Commons, a member of the House of Lords, a plain English gentleman, a retiring attaché of our embassy in London, his journalistic wife, and M. de M. Hanson of Washington and Peoria, his first name being Mal de Mer.

The talk to-day has been of nothing but submarines. The superstitious call attention to the fact that with us is a lady who was on the *Lusitania* when they torpedoed it. To offset that, however, we carry the president's youngest son-in-law, and surely there must be a limit to boche ruthlessness.

323

Monday, September 24. At Sea.

Our ship's cargo consists principally of titles, rumors and celebrities. Most of the titles belong to members of the British Commission which is coming over to talk food to Mr. Hoover. But there is also a regular baroness, round whom the young bloods swarm like bees.

The rumors deal with the course of the ship. Some folks say we are going up Ireland way; others that we are headed straight south; a few that we are taking the Kansas City route, and so on. The sun refuses to come out and tell us the truth, but there's a shore line in sight on our starboard, and Ring Once tells me it's the east coast of Ireland. That ought to indicate something about our general direction, but I don't know what. Of the celebrities, most of them are American journalists and other spies.

Tuesday, September 25. At Sea.

Between eight and nine every morning the bath steward, one Peter James, raps on the door and says: "Your bath is ready, sir." And you have to get up and go and take it for fear of what he'd think of you if you didn't. But it's pretty tough on a man who's just spent a month in France and formed new habits.

I stayed up all night playing bridge. I wanted to be sleepy today because I needed a hair cut and the best way to take 'em is unconsciously. The scheme was effective, and I didn't hear a word the barber said.

The three others in the bridge game were members of the British Food Commission. Britishers, I notice, are much slower at bridge than we are. They think a long while before they make a play; then they make the wrong play. I do the same thing with only half the expenditure of thought and time.

Wednesday, September 26. At Sea.

Captain Finch appeared at breakfast this morning. It was the first time he had honored us. His presence at table, I'm told, indicates that we are out of the danger zone.

On board we have a doctor, a D. D., who intends to lecture in America on the war. He happened to be at our table in the lounge this afternoon. Some one asked him if he had visited the front.

"Indeed, yes," he said. "I was there less than a month ago. The British entertained me and showed me everything. Why, one day they were taking me through the front-line trenches and I asked how far we were from the German front line. 'Hush, Doctor,' said one of the officers. 'The Germans can hear you talking now. They're only twenty yards away.' "

I asked him what part of the front he'd been on. He told me. It was exactly the same front I'd seen. But when I was there—and it was also less than a month ago—the depth of No Man's Land was two hundred yards, and there weren't any noncombatants batting round within sixty feet of a boche trench. No, nor a British trench either. I said as much right out loud, and I'm afraid I've spoiled his trip.

But honest, Doc, somebody was kidding you or else your last name is Cook.

Thursday, September 27. At Sea.

The sea was calm, the day was fair.
E'en Mal de Mer came up for air.

The voyage is getting sort of tiresome to us Americans. For the British it's not so bad. Their five meals per day break the monotony. They breakfast from nine to ten, lunch from one to two, tea from four to five, dine from seven to eight, and sup from eleven on. But we can't stand that pace, and have to waste a lot of time reading.

There is a ship library full of fairly good stuff, but by far the most interesting matter is to be found in a paper published on board every day. Its title is *The Ocean Times and the Atlantic Daily News*. It contains two pages of news, two pages of editorial causerie, one of them in French, and four pages of real hot stuff, such as "Softness and Grandeur. A Brief Appreciation of a Delightful Excursion in Norway"; "Chance Meetings. The Long Arm of Coincidence and the Charm of Surprise"; "The Introduction of Electric Tramways into Cape Town." These essays and articles are boiler plate, as we journalists say, and we find them an excellent sedative.

The news is received by wireless from both sides of the ocean. To-day's dispatches from Washington fairly made our hair stand on end. One of them said: "The decision of the milk dealers here that they would not pay more than thirty-two cents per gallon for milk after October one was met by a counter-proposal on the part of the Maryland and Virginia Milk Producers' Association last night with an offer to fix the price at thirty-three and one-half cents per gallon instead of at thirty-five cents as originally planned." Another informed us that Brigadier-General Somebody, for three years assistant to the Major-General Commandant at the Marine Corps Headquarters, had been ordered to command the Marine Cantonment at Somewhere, Virginia. A person who fails to get a thrill out of that must be a cold fish. But I can't help wishing they'd let us know when and where the world series is to start.

It is announced that Doc Cook will preach at the ship's service Sunday morning. His text, no doubt, will be "Twenty Yards from the German Trenches."

Saturday, September 29. At Sea.

Captain Finch says we will reach New York Tuesday. But if they don't quit turning the clock back half an hour a day we'll never get there.

Sunday, September 30. At Sea.

The doctor preached, but disappointed a large congregation with a regular sermon.

After we had sung *God Save the King* and *America*, I came to my stateroom to work and immediately broke the carriage cord on my typewriter. I said one or two of the words I had just heard in church; then borrowed a screw driver from Ring Once and proceeded to dilacerate the machine. It took over an hour to get it all apart and about two hours to decide that I couldn't begin to put it together again.

I went on deck and told my troubles to Mr. Hollister of Chicago. Mr. Hollister was sympathetic and a life-saver. He introduced me to a young man, named after the beer that made Fort Wayne famous, who is a master mechanic in the employ of the Duke of Detroit. The young man said he had had no experience with typewriters, but it was one of his greatest delights to tinker. I gave him leave to gratify his perverted taste and, believe it or not, in forty minutes he had the thing running, with a piece of common binding twine pinch-hitting for the cord. Then I went entirely off my head and bought him wine.

Monday, October 1. Nearly There.

It's midnight. An hour ago we went on deck and saw the prettiest sight in the world—an American lighthouse. First we felt like choking; then like joking. Three of us—Mr. and Mrs. P. Williams and I—became extremely facetious.

"Well," said Mrs. Williams, "there's ''Tis of Thee.' "

"Yes," said her husband, "that certainly is old 'O Say.' "

I've forgotten what I said, but it was just as good.

The light—standing, they told me, on Fire Island—winked at us repeatedly, unaware, perhaps, that we were all married. I'll confess we didn't mind at all and would have winked back if we could have winked hard enough to carry nineteen nautical miles.

Ring Once was waiting at the stateroom door to tell me to have all baggage packed and outside first thing in the morning.

"I'll see that it's taken off the ship," he said. "You'll find it under your initial on the dock."

"What do you mean, under my initial?"

He explained and then noticed that my junk was unlabeled. I'd worried over this a long while. My French Line stickers had not stuck. And how would New Yorkers and Chicagoans know I'd been abroad? I couldn't stop each one and tell him.

The trusty steward disappeared and soon returned with four beautiful labels, square, with a red border, a white star in the middle, and a dark blue L, meaning me, in the middle of the star.

"Put those on so they'll stay," I instructed him. "There's no sense in crossing the ocean and then keeping it a secret."

Tuesday, October 2. A Regular Hotel.

M. de M. Hanson, looking as if he'd had just as much sleep as I, was in his, or somebody else's deck chair, reading a yesterday's New York paper, when I emerged to greet the dawn.

"I don't know where this came from," he said, "but it's got what you want to know. The series opens in Chicago next Saturday. They play there Saturday and Sunday, jump back to New York Monday and play here Tuesday and Wednesday."

"And," said I, "may the better team win—in four games."

We were anchored in the harbor, waiting for a pilot, that was, as usual, late. I was impatient but M. de M. didn't seem to care. He's wild about ocean travel so long as it's stationary.

Presently the youngest of the food commissioners, one Mr. Bowron, joined us. He asked the name of every piece of land in sight. We answered all his questions, perhaps correctly.

"That one," said M. de M., pointing, "is Staten Island. Of course you've heard of it."

"I'm afraid not," said Mr. Bowron.

"What!" cried Mr. Hanson. "Never heard of Staten Island!"

"The home of Matty McIntyre," I put in. "One of the greatest outside lefts in the history of soccer. He played with the Detroit and Chicago elevens in the American League."

Mr. Bowron looked apologetic.

"And in that direction," said Mr. Hanson, pointing again, "is Coney Island, where fashionable New York spends its summers."

"Except," said I, "the aristocratic old families who can't be weaned away from Palisades Park."

Mr. Bowron interviewed us on the subject of hotels.

"There are only two or three first-class ones," said Mr. Hanson. "The Biltmore's fair. It's got elevators and running hot water."

"But no electric lights," I objected.

"Oh, yes," said Mr. Hanson. "They put in electricity and set the meter the week we left."

Breakfast was ready, and for the first time on the trip Mr. Hanson ate with a confidence of the future. For the first time he ordered food that was good for him. Previously it hadn't mattered.

When we went back on deck, the world's largest open-face clock was on our left, and on our right the business district of Pelham's biggest suburb. And immediately surrounding us were Peter James and Ring Once and the lounge steward and the deck steward and the dining-room stewards—in fact, all the stewards we'd seen and a great many we hadn't.

"We're trapped," said Mr. Hanson. "Our only chance for escape is to give them all we've got. Be ready with your one-pounders and you're silver pieces."

At the end of this unequal conflict—the Battle of the Baltic—Rear-Admiral Lardner's fleet was all shot to pieces, most of them the size of a dime, and when Mr. Brennan of Yonkers announced that his car would meet the ship and that he would gladly give me a ride to my hotel I could have kissed him on both cheeks. It took my customs inspector about a minute to decide that I was poor and honest. The baroness, though, when we left the dock, was engaged in argument with half a dozen officials, who must have been either heartless or blind.

Mr. Brennan's chauffeur drove queerly. He insisted on sticking to the right side of the street, and slowed up at busy intersections, and he even paid heed to the traffic signals. In Paris or London he'd have been as much at home as a Mexican at The Hague.

The hotel gave me a room without making me tell my age or my occupation or my parents' birthplace. The room has a bath, and the bath has two water faucets, one marked hot and one marked cold, and when you turn the one marked hot, out comes hot water. And there's no Peter James around to make you bathe when you don't feel the need.

The room has a practical telephone too, and pretty soon I'm going to start calling up acquaintances with kind hearts and good cooks. The first who invites me to dinner is in tough luck.

Friday, October 5. Chicago.

"Miner" Brown, the great three-fingered pitcher, used to be asked the same questions by every one to whom he was introduced. As a breath-saving device he finally had some special cards printed. On one side was his name. On the other the correct replies:

1. Because I used to work in a mine.
2. It was cut off in a factory when I was a kid.
3. At Terre Haute, Ind.
4. Rosedale, right near Terre Haute.
5. Not a bit.

When he left home in the morning he was always supplied with fifty of these cards, and sometimes he got rid of the whole supply before bedtime.

I departed from New York Wednesday night. Our train picked up the New York Baseball Club at Philadelphia. I was acquainted with about fifteen of the twenty (odd) athletes. Every one of the fifteen, from Mr. Zimmerman down, shot the same queries at me. Every person I've encountered here at home too, and usually in the same order:

1. How'd you like it over there?
2. Did you see any subs?
3. Did you see any fighting?
4. Could you hear the guns?
5. How close did you get to the front?
6. Did you see any American soldiers?
7. How many men have we got over there?
8. How are things in Paris?
9. Were you in England?
10. How are things in London?
11. Were you in any air raids?
12. How long is it going to last?

Now truth may be stranger than fiction, but it's also a whole lot duller. Most of my answers have very evidently bored my audiences to the point of extinction. Yet I hesitate to start weaving the well-known tangled web. I'd be bound to trip in it sooner or later. Last night, in desperation, I drafted a card along the line of Mr. Brown's. But it lacked wallop, as you can see for yourself.

1. Oh, pretty well.
2. No.
3. A little.

4. Oh, yes.

5. A mile and a half, on the observation hill.

6. Oh, yes.

7. That's supposed to be a secret.

8. Pretty gay.

9. Yes.

10. All right, so far as I could see.

11. No.

12. I don't know.